Hermeneutics and Honor

HARVARD MIDDLE EASTERN MONOGRAPHS

XXXII

Hermeneutics and Honor

Negotiating Female "Public" Space in Islamic/ate Societies

EDITED BY

Asma Afsaruddin

FOREWORD BY

Mary-Jo DelVecchio Good

WITH CONTRIBUTIONS BY

Anan Ameri, Margot Badran,
Virginia Danielson, Shahla Haeri, Leslie Peirce,
Julie Peteet, and Nayereh Tohidi

DISTRIBUTED FOR THE
CENTER FOR MIDDLE EASTERN STUDIES
OF HARVARD UNIVERSITY BY
HARVARD UNIVERSITY PRESS
CAMBRIDGE, MASSACHUSETTS
LONDON, ENGLAND

Contents

Foreword

The culmination of five years (1991 to 1996) of the seminar series on Women and Gender in the Middle East and Islamic Societies in this fine collection of essays brings to realization the seminar's original goal—to further studies of gender in the Middle East. In late spring and summer of 1991, a group of scholars affiliated with Harvard University's Center for Middle Eastern Studies met to consider ways to bring the increasingly excellent research on gender to our students and colleagues. Together and with the support of the then director of CMES, William Graham, and assistant director, Susan Miller, they launched a Committee for the Study of Women and Gender in the Middle East and Islamic Societies in the fall of 1991. Given the Committee members' contacts and diverse disciplinary and regional foci, we were able to establish a thriving and intellectually stimulating seminar series that has continued into the present. The Committee's originally stated goals were "to encourage comparative and cross-cultural studies of women and gender in diverse Middle Eastern, North African, South Asian, and Central Asian societies" and to serve as an umbrella for scholars who wished to develop seminars and research initiatives. This volume of essays represents the comparative and interdisciplinary focus that characterized the diverse and marvelous presentations that were made over the course of the seminar. As a member of the Committee and as chair for its first four years, I found it not only intellectually stimulating to be steeped in the multidisciplinary discourses and studies on gender in the Middle East but also gratifying to find that gender studies at large have benefitted theoretically as well as substantively from the work of many scholars who presented and participated in this seminar.

I salute the scholars who are included here and thank them once again for their contributions. Dr. Asma Afsaruddin, co-chair of the Committee from 1994 to 1995 and chair from 1995 to 1996, is to be especially commended for bringing the seminar project into published form and realizing the Committee's goals.

Mary-Jo DelVecchio Good

Acknowledgments

It gives me great pleasure to acknowledge the help of the following individuals who contributed to the success of the Speakers Series of the Committee for the Study of Gender and Women in the Middle East and Islamic Societies at Harvard University and to the production of this monograph. First of all, I must mention, of course, Mary-Jo DelVecchio Good, professor of medical anthropology at Harvard University, who conceived of the plan to form this committee in 1991 under the umbrella of the Center for Middle East Studies (CMES) Forum. The growth and enduring success of this committee, reflected in its ability to draw outstanding scholars who specialize in gender studies to take part in its activities, is in large measure due to her commitment and dedication to this project. Tom Mullins, associate director of CMES, provided the committee with critical funds from the Program for Contemporary Arab Studies, part of which has gone into defraying the costs of producing this monograph. Roger Owen, currently the director of CMES and A. J. Meyer professor of history and at that time chair of the CMES forum, supported and actively participated in many of our proceedings. William Graham, professor of religion and director of CMES at that time, also visibly demonstrated his support for the committee's activities. Thanks also go out to Barbara Henson, in charge of accounting and finances at CMES, who astutely managed the budget for the committee. I must not forget my graduate student assistants, who, during my sojourn as chair, volunteered their time and energy generously in helping to set up our schedules and publicize our activities: Lalita Bolden, Diana AbouAli, and Nilufer Shaikh. A great measure of debt is owed to Habib Ladjevardi, who encouraged the idea of this monograph and patiently shepherded it through from inception to conception. I also owe thanks to the members of the Editorial Board at CMES, who accepted this volume for publication in the Middle East Studies monograph series. I would like to express my gratitude as well to our anonymous reader for her careful and trenchant comments on the manuscript. Heart-felt thanks also go out to Margot Badran for her comments on Chapter 1 and to my husband, Steve Vinson, for similar feedback and encouragement for the project.

A comment on the transcription of words in non-Western scripts adopted in this monograph seems appropriate here. We have not indicated diacritics for most foreign words; for Arabic words, we have maintained a distinction only between the pharyngeal *'ayn* represented by ' and the glottal stop *hamza* represented by '. The definite article in Arabic *al-*, also rendered as *el-* or *el*, are ignored for purposes of alphabetization. The name *El Guindi*, therefore, would be listed under *G* and not *E*. When the definite article is assimilated with the following consonant, as in *an-Na'im*, it would be listed, as in this case, under *N*. Variants of foreign proper names inevitably occur in a few cases; for example, *al-Sha'rawi* (which is the closest rendering of the Arabic) as occurs in the text appears as *Shaarawi* in bibliographic citations because this is how commercial publishers have chosen to loosely transcribe her name. Only the first occurrence of a foreign word is italicized within each chapter.

Finally, I must thank the speakers themselves, who have shared their research, rich insights, and valuable time to contribute to the resounding success of the Speakers series, which now finds reflection in this published monograph. Many of them have become dear colleagues and friends over the course of time. I feel particularly fortunate in continuing to enjoy their friendship and in being able to make their presentations available to a broader audience. I must also thank all those—students, faculty, staff, and members of the larger community—who, as part of the Harvard audience, facilitated spirited discussion and collegial exchange. This volume, I hope, will in some measure convey to our readers that infectious spirit of scholarly camaraderie and exchange.

Asma Afsaruddin

Hermeneutics and Honor

· ONE ·

Introduction: The Hermeneutics of Gendered Space and Discourse

Asma Afsaruddin

The study of gender as an academic discipline is a fairly recent development in the humanities and social sciences. Pioneering works that have focused on gender have considerably affected academic discourse on how we interpret the paradigms of social, economic, and ultimately power relations between men and women, in both modern and pre-modern societies. The study of the roles of women and related issues of gender in Islamic/ate societies is an even more recent phenomenon and one that spans several disciplines. Its growing importance and relevance to our times are reflected in the current explosion of publications on this theme and the spirited debate that often accompanies this topic.

The Committee for the Study of Women and Gender in the Middle East and Islamic Societies at Harvard University has been particularly fortunate in contributing to this scholarly discourse by providing a forum for distinguished scholars for the dissemination and discussion of their works. This monograph is a collection of some of the papers that were presented under the auspices of this committee between 1993 and 1996 (with the one exception of a specially invited paper) and that address the broad topic of women's participation in the public sphere and their

1

efforts to connect what has traditionally been connoted by the term *private* (construed as the feminine realm) to the *public* (construed as the masculine realm). The predominant academic discourse in the West about these binarily contrasted spheres, especially in the Middle Eastern and Islamic/ate context, has been somewhat skewed, rooted as it has been in Western self-referential understanding of these terms and ahistorical scholarship (Nelson 1974; Rohrlich-Leavitt 1975). Social and feminist historians have recently begun to emphasize that the notions of private and public must be historicized by linking them to the hierarchies of power and social relations in which they are embedded (Rosaldo 1980; Landes 1998). They argue that the public-private dichotomy is meaningless unless it is studied in reference to "the specificities of gender, culture, class, race, ethnicity, sexuality, and historical time" (Helly and Reverby 1992, 6). In Middle Eastern history, Peirce (1992, 1993) has shown that the inner sanctum of the imperial harem, in the Ottoman milieu of the sixteenth century, was in fact the real locus of both male and female political power. Public inaccessibility of the individual, whether male or female, was an indicator of personal high social status, demonstrating that "conventional notions of public and private are not congruent with gender" (Peirce 1993, 45). Judith Tucker (1985, 102–31) in her study of women in nineteenth-century Egypt points out that lower-class urban and rural peasant women were involved to a considerable extent in the social and economic institutions basic to their society in that century. In Margot Badran's translation of the memoirs of the Egyptian feminist Huda al-Sha'rawi (d. 1947), we find women of the elite class in the first quarter of the twentieth century, while the harem system still prevailed, occupied with philanthropic activities, attending lectures in (segregated) public space, and participating in the male-led nationalist movement (Shaarawi 1987). Mary Ann Fay (1996, 1997), in her recent research into the lives of elite women in eighteenth-century Cairo, found them actively engaged in administering their households and property that they held independently of their husbands. Such studies subvert the private-public binary and popular perceptions of the harem, especially as lodged in the Western consciousness (Tapper 1979; Ahmed 1982; Alloula 1986; Kabbani 1986) and fostered in certain quarters of academe by a peculiar anthropology of the Orient, especially of the Muslim Orient (Carrier 1992; Asad 1986)[1]—spawned by that dialectal process termed *Orientalism* by Edward Said (1978). A majority of the papers in this collection challenge the notion of rigidly demarcated and mutually impenetrable territories of male versus female inhabitancy. Rather, they serve to show that the private and public spheres have often been anything but bipolar and that, indeed, the two may be plotted along a continuum yielding far more points of contact with the other in varying historical and social circumstances.[2] Such an insight impels us to reexamine the notion of one grand paradigm of gender relations and gender exclusivity in cultures dominated by what are generally perceived to be Islamic/ate values.

A word or two about the use of the various terms *Muslim, Islamic, Islamicate,* and *Islamist* in this introduction seems appropriate here. *Muslim* and *Islamic* are used interchangeably for societies that have a large Muslim population and whose value systems are derived from a commonly shared Islamic tradition (whether Sunni or Shi'i) before the period of European colonization or of the influence of Western political ideologies (whether Western capitalism or Marxism). I am using *Islamicate,* to resuscitate Marshall Hodgson's term (1974, 1:58–59), for the subsequent pre-modern and modern periods (roughly from the nineteenth century on) to describe societies and nation-states that maintain and/or have consciously adopted at least the public symbols of adherence to traditional Islamic beliefs and practices. Such societies or considerable segments within such societies may regard Islam as a civilizational-ideological construct on a par with and complementary to the constructs of Western secular culture and feel themselves free to borrow haphazardly from both systems. They do not, however, found the greater part of their legal system on an Islamic basis nor attribute their state formation to the realization of religious objectives (with very few notable exceptions). Islam in such countries is more a shared "idiom" (Mardin 1989, 3–7) and a cluster of "signals," such as collective celebrations and festivals, individual and communal rituals (Arkoun 1994, 62), that are assumed to be characteristic of Islamic societies. Most countries of the world today that have a majority of Muslim inhabitants would be considered examples of modern Islamicate societies. The imperative for maintaining this distinction between *Islamic* and *Islamicate* arises from the fact that there is no counterpart on the *Islamic* side to the epithet *Western* as used to describe societies of modern Europe and North America today. *Western* in reference to these regions evokes *inter alia* their shared Judeo-Christian heritage, whose primacy, however, has become greatly attenuated and superseded by politico-cultural values that are essentially areligious. A parallel use of *Eastern* for countries traditionally regarded as Islamic is, of course, not possible since the term *Eastern* encompasses broadly divergent social, cultural, and religious systems, the Islamic one being only one of them. Although not a term that has gained wide currency, *Islamicate,* for all the insightful reasons Hodgson enumerated, seems currently to be the appropriate available term to designate such countries where allegiance to Islam is cast in emotive, broadly cultural, and experiential terms rather than in legal and theological terms.

Islamist is reserved for certain political activist groups within Islamicate societies (for our purposes; such groups can, of course, exist in societies with minority Muslim populations) whose primary wish is to govern and be governed only by Islamic principles as they define them. On this account, these groups are described as subscribing to "political Islam" (see, for example, Beinin and Stork 1997). Some of these activists advocate total adherence to the *Sharī`ā* (religious or canon law) as formulated in the medieval period and see in Islam a monolithic religio-political construct to countervail competing Western ideologies. As a consequence, they have been labeled *Muslim* or *Islamic fundamentalists* by some (see, for example, Esposito

1997), a nomenclature that is not without its problems (Beinin and Stork 1997; Ghadbian 1997). Such activists may be of the view that the Islamic East and the secular West are irreversibly set on a collision course, evoking the specter of Samuel Huntington's "clash of civilizations" (Huntington 1993, 1996).[3] Others maintain that there is a distinction between *Muslim fundamentalists* as described above and *Islamists,* the latter term being reserved for political activists who are also engaged in "modernist" interpretations of Islamic scripture and the Shari'a (Zubaida 1997; Krämer 1997). *Modernist* in our usage may be understood to refer to a "tendency to emphasize the flexibility of Islam in the public sphere and to use this flexibility to interpret Islam in terms congruent with, or at least in very positive dialogue with, one or more Western ideologies" (Shepard 1987, 311). The lines of distinction between *fundamentalist* and *Islamist* remain somewhat blurred; certainly, in present usage, the two terms are used quite interchangeably without reflection.[4] I should point out that the contributors to this monograph do not necessarily use my terminology or may use similar terminology but in a different sense, with which I have not tampered since these terms are still evolving and being used with considerable imprecision.[5]

The unifying theme of the papers contained in this volume is women's traversal of public space and the process of negotiation of their gendered identities that this entails. Many of the chapters detail women's exploration of avenues that enable self-empowerment. *Empowerment* here for our purpose connotes the carving out of public space by women for themselves, sometimes paradoxically by not even leaving the home, through which space they are able to derive benefits for themselves and impose their presence on society at large. Identity empowerment theory in feminist scholarship emphasizes "that all women can make some constructive changes to enhance and improve their situations, however restricted those situations" (Hall 1992, 2), particularly by consciously linking the private and public aspects of their lives (Bernard 1981). Too often, the *power* in empowerment has been equated with physical visibility and prowess, which automatically privileges the traditionally masculine realm of the outside world as the real locus of meaningful activity (Smith 1990; Harding 1991). In the traditional Islamic milieu, the general occultation of women from public view (more so for upper- and middle-class rather than for working-class women) has not necessarily nullified effective participation in public venues and the extraction of benefits from public institutions. Rather, a lack of knowledge of the avenues that exist for exacting social redress and an inability to exploit these avenues on the part of women have often led to their disenfranchisement. In her recent study of Yemeni society, Sheila Carapico has observed that women's roles and rights were contingent more on "specific features of status, class, and the politics and economics of development" (1996, 96) than on immutable religious and social values. Such observations have been replicated in the study of women's lives in other parts of the Middle East in both the pre-modern and modern periods—for example, in Iran (Friedl 1991), in Turkey (Marcus 1992a, 1992b), and in Iraq (Rizk Khouri 1996, 1997). Empowerment theory suggests "that women's behavior and quality of life can be changed by increasing their awareness of the strength of social influences and of the interplay between intended and unintended consequences of women's decisions and actions" (Hall 1992, 2). Women everywhere, after all, possess some degree of influence or informal power. How and to what extent this power is exercised is as much a result of a woman's internal development as it is of the external factors that impinge on her life (Leacock 1986). For women of means and education in Islamic/ate societies, the exercise of power, formal or informal, and negotiation of public space have frequently been less of an ordeal than for women who do not enjoy the same advantages. The papers in our collection show time and again that social class, economic status, and educational attainment are variables that profoundly dilute the traditional dichotomy between the public and private spheres.

The public-private discourse in the Islamic setting inevitably raises the issues of veiling and feminine modesty and the consequences they create for the definition of both individual and collective honor. Interestingly, both the phenomena of veiling (and its attendant practice of seclusion) and unveiling in Islamic/ate societies have, by social historians and Muslim modernists, been attributed to alien influence—Byzantine and Persian for the former and modern Western European for the latter. This attribution pits Muslim modernists against Islamist activists in a distinctive "discourse of the veil," in which the former inveighs against the veil's foreign provenance on the basis of the first attribution, while the latter upholds its essentially Islamic character on the basis of the second attribution. The Arabic word *hijab* is generally understood to refer to the practice of veiling or to the veil itself (which in itself can assume various forms). In a recent study of the word itself, Stowasser (1997) has shown it to be a complex term that has implied different usages in different stages of its evolution and application. The term taken exclusively to refer to concealing attire today (divorced from the notion of seclusion) represents the last stage of its semantic development. From the non-Muslim and especially modern Western viewpoint, female coveredness has often impressionistically served as a barometer for gauging female subjugation; a casual exposure to Western print and broadcast media coverage of the Middle East tends to confirm this impression. Veiling as a consequence becomes equated with powerlessness and dependency, while its absence is associated with independent feminine agency (Ahmed 1992, 142–68). Some Muslim modernists and feminists, especially of the late nineteenth century and early twentieth century, have accepted this equation as well. Muslim reformists like Muhammad 'Abduh (d. 1905), who served as the rector of al-Azhar University in Cairo, and Qasim Amin (d. 1908), a prominent Egyptian lawyer, blamed the practice of veiling for having contributed to the "backwardness" of Muslim women and their general disenfranchisement (Ahmed 1992; Badran 1991, 204–5). This rough and ready correlation between veiling and powerlessness has been challenged by the attempts of social historians to restore women to the historical mainstream. Recent and not-so-recent scholarly studies make it difficult to reconcile the above equation with the life of, for example, 'A'isha bint Abi Bakr, the wife of the Prophet, (a commonly evoked symbol of early Muslim feminism), who we may assume was always veiled but who displayed an aggressive public persona in seventh-century Madina (Abbot 1942a; Spellberg 1994). How, we may ask, would this pat formula apply to women who, especially in the formative and early medieval periods of Islamic history, have gone into battle, imparted religious knowledge to men and women, endowed charitable institutions, offered political advice to rulers and ruled themselves, and presided over literary salons, among other activities (for example, Abbott 1942b, 1942c, 1946; Ahmed 1992; Siddiqi 1993, 117–23; Berkey 1992, 161–81; Mernissi 1993; Walther 1993, 103–53; Hambly 1998)? How would we then explain the power of certain dynastic women in sixteenth-century Ottoman Turkey who, despite their residence in the harem, exercised considerable influence in the court politics of their time (Peirce 1993)? What are we to make of twentieth-century educated Muslim women who charge into public professions, clothed from head to toe (Makhlouf 1979; Macleod 1990; Zuhur 1992; Hessini 1994)? Clearly, the variegated nature of Muslim societies over time and place and the complexities of the lives of Muslim women do not allow for such a meretricious equation.

In modernist Islamist circles, the adoption of veiling by women acquires a distinctive semiotic connotation whereby it is equated with moral, cultural, and political authenticity and superiority for both the woman and her family, especially her male relatives, in the face of Western encroachment (El Guindi 1981; Rugh 1984, 1986; Bennigsen 1985; Badran 1994b, 203).[6] In the Islamicate milieu of the late twentieth century, the conscious adoption of the veil by Islamist women as a marker of their professed ideology is sometimes coupled with greater political activism on their part and ironically, therefore, with greater public visibility. Nilüfer Göle, in her recent study of Muslim women activists in Turkey, has recently underscored this seeming paradox when she states, "The new social visibility of Islamist women, who are outspoken, militant, and educated, brings about a shift in the semiotics of veiling, which has long evoked the traditional, subservient domestic roles of Muslim women" (1996, 21). As Juan Cole has remarked, veiling by educated women today in the urban centers of the Middle East and other parts of the Islamicate world, may be "the farthest thing from 'traditional'" (1994, 27).

The writings of recent feminists thus rightly warn of the dangers of engaging in a reductive, gender-based essentialism that portrays gender—and its concomitants—as a globally constant phenomenon. McNay (1992, 64) has remarked that due to a "failure to carry through a differentiated analysis of different cultural and historical contexts, areas of women's experience are either not understood in their full complexity, are devalued or remain obscured altogether" (see also Showstack Sassoon 1987, 19). Responsible scholarship that offers us a dispassionate, nuanced look at the various ways in which women (regardless of their attire) appropriate public space and assert their presence through the social and political channels, not always formal, that are available to them in widely varying political and historical contexts opens up whole new vistas for understanding—and valorizing—women's ad hoc attempts at self-empowerment.[7]

Honor, which figures prominently in the title to this collection, is another concept that is laden with culturally specific semantic connotations. To an overwhelming extent, honor in Islamic societies, for both men and women, is rooted in the sexual behavior of women in common with other traditional, especially Mediterranean, societies. Sexual impropriety may imply not only illicit sexual relations but violation of an elaborate code that prescribes circumspect and decorous social relations between the sexes. The term *honor* is the most common English word used in translation of the corresponding terms *sharaf, 'ird, 'izzat,* and *namus* (originally Arabic terms borrowed into other Islamic languages as well) current in various Islamic/ate societies. Anthropologists have attempted to study the multifaceted implications of honor (and, its concomitant, shame) in relation to Mediterranean, including Arab, societies (for example, Peristiany 1966; Schneider 1971; Wikan 1984; Abu-Lughod 1986; Gilmore 1987; Peristiany and Pitt-Rivers 1991; Stewart 1994). The interpretations they offer of this slippery yet powerful notion often overlap with the meanings, pregnant with the immediacy of women's personal experiences, that become apparent in the essays presented here. Abu-Lughod (1990, 47) has commented in her study of Bedouin society in this century that "most people's ordinary public responses are framed in terms of the code of honor and modesty" and that "violations of the code must be understood as ways of resisting the system and challenging the authority of those who represent and benefit from it." These essays, more than any abstract theorization, convey eloquently the diverse inflections of this ubiquitous code in its various cultural contexts and women's attempts to accommodate, challenge, and negotiate with it in their quest for self-empowerment.

The first essay in this collection, by Anan Ameri (Chapter 2), discusses efforts by contemporary Palestinian women to gain more effective political representation under the recently formed Palestinian National Authority (PNA) headed by Yasir Arafat. She gives us a detailed look at the history of the grassroots movement that grew up among Palestinian women in conjunction with more conventional women's groups in the formative period of the Palestinian resistance movement against the Israeli occupation. In the post-Oslo environment, the conventional women's groups have been subsumed under the more powerful and better organized men's groups, including both Fatah and Hamas, which often had their own agendas for women. Ameri's article highlights in particular the difficulties faced by women who seek to articulate their needs in the postcolonial phase of state formation in the Third World where "the State is potentially a mechanism either for social change or social control in women's lives" (Alvarez 1990, 273; see also Chhachhi 1991; Rai

1996). Although the Palestinian National Authority is not a state in the usual sense of the word, it has assumed a similar regulatory function in its capacity to define the public role of women. State formation in the Third World, however, is markedly different from the Western experience. These differences in the formation of the state and of civil society are evoked in Gunnar Myrdal's (1968, 1970) classic formulation of the "strong" state and the "weak" state. In general, strong states tend to be characterized by a healthy infrastructural system that permits state policies to be effectively implemented and allows for the central coordination of civil activities. The weak state is bedeviled by an ineffectual, often corrupt, bureaucracy unable to implement its policies effectively because of a disjunction of interests between the state and the civil polity (Mann 1984; Myrdal 1970). According to this paradigm, most Third World states are to be characterized as weak. Endowed with a weak infrastructural power, as Rai (1996, 33) points out, "the implementation of [state-sponsored] directives can become hostage to random factors outside the control of the state," which impedes its ability to effect social and economic transformation. The role of the global economy is also an important consideration that affects women and development (Moghadam 1996, 1998). Some (for example, Rosa 1987; Saadawi 1980; Marsot 1996) regard global capitalism and modernization as adversely affecting state formation in the Third World, leading to the exacerbation of social crises within weak states, including a further degradation of women's positions in such societies. Many of these factors appear to be all too painfully applicable in the current Palestinian situation. Sara Roy (1994, 1995a, 1995b) has documented the serious social and economic malaise that has afflicted Gazan society in the aftermath of the September 1993 Oslo accord between the Palestine Liberation Organization (PLO) and Israel, a phenomenon she has termed "de-development." Roy (1995a, 13) particularly points to the weakening of critical support structures such as schools, the extended family, and political institutions under limited self-rule leading to a "decline in collective

and participatory behavior [as] are seen in the lack of community consensus and withering away of community action."

In her survey, Ameri shows the impact of many of the above
factors on the current process of creating a Palestinian civil
society and on the women's movement in particular. She documents the changing nature of women's organizations, particularly the General Union of Palestinian Women, which in their
formative period were more concerned with rallying political
support for the PLO under Israeli occupation than with explicitly feminist objectives. By 1978, the Women's Work Committees
had been formed with leftist support, which represented a
broader spectrum of women and had a more consciously feminist agenda. During the Intifada of the late 1980s, these women's
groups gained heightened local prestige and international visibility because of their active role in combating Israeli repression,
which gave them added confidence in themselves (see also Holt
1996). In the post-Oslo context, the situation has changed dramatically; the marginalization of the left, the indifference of the
Palestinian National Authority toward women's issues, and the
growth of Islamist movements that looked askance at, particularly, secular feminism, have fractured and demoralized these
women's committees. The general trend has been away from
grassroots activities and toward institutionalization. As Ameri
describes it, the women's movement as a consequence "seems to
have boiled down to a few internationally funded, city-based,
well-furnished, and well-equipped offices." Women at the grassroots level feel betrayed by the leadership of the Palestinian
National Authority and by the women's groups coopted by the
PNA who drafted the Women's Charter without consultation
with them. As a consequence, these women feel that the Charter
does not adequately address their concerns and interests. This
has allowed religious fundamentalists to gain ground at the
grassroots level by providing basic social services, which the
institutionalized groups cannot or will not do, consequently
earning the loyalty of marginalized groups, including certain
women. While secular women have regarded this development

with dismay (remembering Hamas's efforts in the past to impose veiling on women), even they concede the appeal of Islamist groups who do provide essential services—in lieu of rhetoric—to women. The move toward institutionalization has been perceived by some as being dictated by the interests of the international donor community, which seeks to depoliticize women and integrate Palestinian society within the global economy. These foreign donors mandate "gender training," among other things, as part of the agenda of nongovernmental organizations (NGOs), to the mystification of some grassroots activists who view such activities as unrelated to the actual empowerment of women. Caught between the proverbial rock and a hard place, the future of women's grassroots organizations remain at best tenuous since they lack the paraphernalia and financial support of more conventional organizations. The attempts of women to arrogate to themselves the right to articulate their own concerns in a public forum unmediated by establishment (and, therefore, largely masculine) sanction have evoked not sympathy but local and international suspicion.

Shahla Haeri's article (Chapter 3) on the connection between the physical rape of individual women in Pakistan and the political rape of a prominent female political personality, Benazir Bhutto, who also served as that country's prime minister, is both provocative and illuminating. It is disturbing to note that a country that can elect a woman to its highest office, when such a phenomenon is hardly a common occurrence elsewhere in the world, can also witness incidents of rape that are acts of political and/or tribal vendetta. Rape in this instance earmarks the violated woman as a medium for getting back at politically active male relatives—what Haeri describes as "a modern improvisation on the theme of 'feudal honor rape.'" Under Benazir Bhutto, this scenario acquired an additional gruesome twist. Haeri suggests that because the political leader in this case was a woman who was otherwise unassailable, male politicians from rival political camps got "even" with her by terrorizing less powerful female proxies who directly stood in for their more powerful equivalent. A woman raped is a woman totally debased and shamed by her male assailant. When the assaulted woman stands in for a woman more powerful and that powerful woman herself may represent a whole nation, then it is the rape of a whole nation, Haeri avers. This is so because the honor of *both* men and women hermeneutically inhere in the woman; she is regarded even as the very personification of honor. Her loss of honor leads to the accrual of collective shame that cuts across gender lines. These gruesome events demonstrate that, unlike the male politician, the female politician who is considered to have stepped out of line invites reprisals constructed in gendered, sexual terms. In spite of having acquired the trappings of public, and therefore masculine power, she is still perceived as being trapped in her private and therefore feminine persona; the politically wayward woman is the equivalent of a morally wayward woman who must be punished in a sexually atavistic manner.

Haeri further depicts how women who do choose (rarely) to step forward to point an accusing finger at their rapists are usually ostracized by Pakistani society and by their own families and tribes. To make matters worse, the Hudood Ordinances of Pakistan that deal with rape and its penalty place the onus of proof on the raped woman, making her susceptible to charges of fornication/adultery (*zina*) should she categorically fail to establish the guilt of the man.[8] Such a "fallen" woman may then be subject to punitive measures, including honor killing, levied by the men in her family and tribe in order to recover their lost collective honor. As a result, very few women who have been raped choose to speak up and visit its drastic consequences on themselves or their families. In recent times, women's and human rights groups have increasingly begun to speak out against the plight of raped women and have offered moral and emotional support to such women who have sought legal retribution in limited cases. One may cautiously see in this a glimmer of hope for the foreseeable future.

Julie Peteet's paper (Chapter 4) offers us another look at

Palestinian women, whose identity as political actors is still inextricably bound to their biological functions and sexual roles, creating what she calls a "discourse of somatization." This discourse is concerned with gender and sexuality at one end and with class and nationalism on the other. The uneasy alliance between nationalism and feminism, already brought into relief by Ameri, is similarly underscored by Peteet. Nationalism, at best, has an ambivalent relationship to feminism; as an oppositional movement, nationalism tends to be supportive of feminist objectives. When nationalist movements come to power, more frequently than not they prove to be the *bête noire* of feminism, adopting an adversarial stance toward feminist movements and viewing them as subversive of nationalist aims. The latter situation, as shown by both Ameri and Peteet, now prevails in PNA-controlled areas. With men effectively in control of the discourse of somatization, women's identities as citizens and political actors, in both the pre- and post-Oslo phases, have been subsumed by familial and social roles that emanate from their biological functions and their relationships to men. This is clearly illustrated by the fact that Palestinian citizenship is strictly defined in patrilineal terms; a Palestinian woman cannot transmit Palestinian nationality to her children in the event of her marriage to a non-Palestinian man.

The situation is further complicated by the Islamist coloring that Palestinian nationalism has acquired. This development has had a strong impact on the lives of women and particularly on the issue of veiling. The semiotics of veiling prevalent in Islamist circles is a development that has occurred in the aftermath of European colonialism and with the construction of modern Western society as the "other" in the Islamist consciousness (Tavakoli-Targhi 1994). The adoption (or nonadoption) of veiling has acquired such political (and moral) valency that the entire ideological confrontation between the Muslim East and the (post-)Christian West, appears, at least impressionistically, to become reduced to this one practice.[9] Foucault has commented on how the body can serve as the site of a "micro-physics of power" (1979, 28) through which the larger social struggles over power are refracted. Islamist ideologues have been fully prepared to exploit this strategy.[10] As Peteet points out, as Hamas Islamized Palestinian nationalism, it called on women to veil themselves so that they could contribute to the Palestinian resistance movement in the most morally effective manner. The private comportment of women was thus reformulated as an act of public resistance that symbolized the seizure of the higher moral ground against the Israelis. Here we find the private merging with the public in a spectacular fashion where veiling forefronts not feminine modesty but defiance (traditionally prized in men only) of a repressive authority. Women who resisted the efforts of Islamist men to appropriate their bodies as the loci of nationalist resistance could then legitimately be seen as betraying the national cause. Framing nationalism within an Islamist discourse of morality allowed Hamas activists to gain unprecedented leverage over women's private and public conduct and to rescript their own suppression of women's civil rights as a justified part of a program of moral resistance to a greater political repression by an occupying force.[11]

The failure of nationalists to intervene in this situation on behalf of women has led to women's disillusionment with nationalism. Peteet ends by pointing out that in the post-Oslo phase of nation-building, Palestinian women are increasingly appealing to democratic and human rights, rather than specifically feminist rights, to challenge Islamist and nationalist gender-based, patriarchal notions of women's private conduct and public agency. By reappropriating the discourse of somatization and reformulating it within the framework of secular and democratic values, they are seeking to break down the bifurcation of private and public spheres. The private is public after all, they insist; in a democratic, pluralistic society, the woman in her role as an independent public citizen should gain control of her private life as well—through state intervention if necessary.

The similarity of women's experiences in Islamicate societies seeking to assert their identities during the process of formation of civil society and modernization becomes apparent in the article by Nayereh Tohidi (Chapter 5), who treats of many of the same social phenomena described by Peteet and Ameri but does so in relation to the former Soviet Republic of Azerbaijan. Tohidi makes the telling point that no one paradigm—whether that of Islamic determinism current among Western Orientalists or that of economic reductionism popular among Marxist-Leninist ideologues—captures or adequately explains the diversity of women's experiences and gender issues in post-independence Azeri society. Women's organizations under Soviet sponsorship suffered from the same disjunction described elsewhere between state-imposed policies and the actual needs of women in the real world. Although these state-sponsored organizations were high on rhetoric and short on deliverance, Tohidi points out that a small number of educated, politically active women were able to wrest some benefits for themselves and for the women's movement in general from these organizations. Tohidi's analysis shows that women's ad hoc clubs established by Azeri women themselves, outside of state-sponsored circles, were the most successful in representing women, for they were "consonant with their own demands and aspirations, an extension of the Jadid goals, rather than a set of alien or imported colonial ideas." These ad hoc clubs were often just the local sewing circles and even women's bath houses, proving once again the fluidity with which the private can become transmuted into the public. The issue of veiling versus unveiling remained a minor one at this stage, although potentially charged with political implications.

The resurgence of traditional Islamic and nationalist values in pre- and post-Soviet Azerbaijan has complicated the issues of gender relations and women's presence in the public sphere. On the one hand, Tohidi points out, conservative Muslim clerics opposed secular modernization, including the women's movement, while on the other, Azeri Muslim modernists, who launched the Jadid movement in the nineteenth century, adopted women's issues as part of their reformist and modernizing movement. The Jadidists promoted female education among other measures to improve the position of women. Like-minded intellectuals founded journals like *Ishiq* that advocated women's rights and quoted Qur'anic verses and *hadiths* (statements attributed to the Prophet Muhammad) in support of their position. Here we find a typical hermeneutic tension between religious conservatives and modernists: the former claims to find in Islam a mandate for women's subjugation to men, while the latter postulates that Islam has provided a blueprint for women's liberation. Tohidi points out that ambivalence toward women's rights lingers today because in some quarters the issue of women's emancipation is further complicated by its association with Soviet cultural imperialism.

Post-independence Azerbaijan is today characterized by political fragility and economic uncertainty. As has occurred repeatedly throughout history in different times and places, a nation that is seeking to find its way and is unsure of its identity generally holds women's desires for professional and public fulfillment hostage to its own quest for security.[12] That this mind-set is replicated in today's Azerbaijan is, therefore, not surprising. The stress on family cohesiveness bolsters its sagging morale; the pervasive code of honor (*namus*) maintains social order. Women, as the culture bearers and moral exemplars of the nation, represent the last defense against corrosion of its family and ethno-cultural values from within and encroachment on them from without. Tohidi, however, finds in the versatility of Azeri society, with its fluid interpretation of Islamic norms and of national, cultural, and gender issues, the potential for future amelioration in the status of women.

Virginia Danielson's article (Chapter 6) takes us away to the somewhat different realm of music and cultural activity. One important point to emerge from her presentation is that this realm was a kind of gender-neutral zone where the private and the public could interface with almost casual ease. One reason for this, as Danielson points out, appears to be that this realm, in the early stages of its evolution, was often peopled by the female performer's family, friends, and neighbors, who as extensions of her private world, mediated and facilitated her public role. This transitional "cultural zone," if I may call it that, facilitated the acceptance of such performance on the part of women and the extension of such activity beyond its original sphere. Danielson charts the development of commercial entertainment establishments in Egypt in the nineteenth century under the patronage of the Khedives, reflecting European influence. The commercialization of "the cultural zone" had significant repercussions on public perceptions of the female entertainer. The entertainment industry was now seen as alien, inherently iniquitous, and therefore threatening to the moral fabric of society. Women performers were not required to retreat altogether from public entertainment but rather had to prove that in spite of their heightened public presence, they still subscribed to traditional norms of moral behavior and respectability. Danielson indicates the creative ways in which the performers responded to the situation without sacrificing professionalism. One principal and very public manner of indicating conformity with society's expectations was to adopt modest attire. In Islamic/ate societies, modest garb on professional women helps blur the lines of demarcation between the private and public, allowing them to inhabit both spaces simultaneously (for example, Hessini 1994). In lieu of supportive family members who "buffered" the female performer from the intrusiveness of the public zone, modest clothing allows the woman to retain the privateness of her identity in the realm of public performance, investing her activity with a legitimacy that it would otherwise lack in the collective perception. The photographs that accompany this article graphically convey the artful, imaginative ways in which these professional women engaged with public expectations of honorable behavior and respectable attire while negotiating their inroads into public space.

Leslie Peirce's article (Chapter 7) transports us back in time to the sixteenth-century courts of Ottoman Turkey to engage us in legal discourse concerning the status of women. In this period, two broad categories of women were identified in Ottoman society—*muhaddere* (respectable) women and by default non-muhaddere women. As Peirce emphasizes, these were also terms that connoted class affiliation, the former term referring to "elite" women, the latter to "common" women; as primarily status terms, they were thus also applied to non-Muslim women. In the original Arabic from which the term is borrowed, *muhaddar* refers to what is sedentary and, therefore, civilized, reflecting an early cultural bias that was to develop in the Islamic world in favor of the urban, organized mode of existence over the itinerant lifestyle of the Bedouin, often regarded as beyond the reach of civilization. This world-view, in the urban context, would also come to recognize differences in social status based primarily on lineage and occupation. That such a world-view found eventual codification in law is not surprising; law is, after all, not merely "abstracted discourse" about social realities but is in itself shaped by those very realities (Hallaq 1997, 162). Ottoman court records thus tend to reveal elitist interpretations of the law by the imperial muftis, even in the shari'a courts, reflecting an amalgam of *'urfi* (customary) law and normative law. In one instance, Ibn Kemal (d. 1534) the famed jurist, is recorded as saying that he would exempt a *seyyid* (a descendant of the Prophet) from incurring punishment if he were to curse an ordinary person; if the latter, however, were to respond in kind, he would have to suffer the consequences of his deed. This kind of legal reasoning is based on the recognition of what anthropologists call a system of "vertical" honor or "positive" honor, which has been defined by Stewart (1994, 59) as "the right to special respect enjoyed by those who are superior, whether by virtue of their abilities, their rank, their services to the community, their sex, their kin relationship, their office, or anything." Curiously, this notion of vertical or positive honor breaks down in sexual matters. Peirce points out how the elite class, and, especially elite women, could incur a higher penalty than the lower classes in matters of sexual indiscretion, for the ensuing social fallout would be greater in a case involving a muhaddere woman, both for the woman herself and her closest male relatives.

In his study of an Islamic law court in modern Morocco, Lawrence Rosen (1989, 44) remarked "how cultural assumption, legal approach, and substantive law are all deeply entwined." His observations led him to conclude that he was dealing with a legal system "whose constant emphasis is not on a series of antecedent concepts but on evaluating the consequences of people's actions" (1989, 45), a remark that seems equally apposite in relation to the sixteenth-century Ottoman court. Classical Islamic legal theory evidences a strong concern for promoting the public good or interest (in Arabic *maslaha*) that manifests itself on the ground as showing more of a regard for the spirit of the law rather than its text (Hallaq 1997, 89). The punishment should fit the crime as perceived in terms of public utility; the sexual impropriety of a high-born woman is far more disruptive of social harmony that that of a woman from the lower echelons of a society and thus must be punished accordingly. The rationale behind the Ottoman mufti's pronouncements in our specific case is, therefore, best discerned through a cultural analysis of the intricate nexus of class and gender relationships that defined Ottoman society and maintained social equilibrium. The calculus of consequence evoked by the mufti is found to be eminently sensible when viewed against the backdrop of cultural assumptions of honor and the complex, myriad ways in which these assumptions, referenced by class and gender, impacted on people. As Peirce herself had remarked earlier (1993, 8), Ottoman society of the sixteenth and seventeenth centuries tended to resolve itself more along the lines of privileged versus the common and the sacred versus the profane rather than public versus private—with all their attendant connotations. When law is understood as largely embedded in culture, even to *be* culture itself, it is not surprising that these cultural delineations of social reality find ample legal articulation.

Our final paper (Chapter 8) is by Margot Badran, who discusses "Islamic feminism(s)" and the multiplicity of identities and discourses such a term currently implies. Badran provides an extensive review of what feminism has meant in the nineteenth and twentieth centuries in Islamicate countries as they engaged with modernity and as women, primarily from the upper-and middle-classes, sought to challenge masculinist constructions of modernity. Whereas masculine attempts to negotiate with modernity were regularly (but not always) seen as politically legitimate, women's attempts to gender the discourse of modernity were more commonly viewed as subversively linked to an imperialist West that sought to undermine essential Islamic values, especially concerning the family and the private sphere. Egypt, as Badran points out, was in the vanguard of such feminist movements at the turn of the century in which women insisted on claiming agency for themselves in defining their rights and did so *within* the larger Islamic framework (also Tucker 1985; Badran 1989b, 1993). Badran stresses that Islam has provided the subtext for much of the feminist discourse generated in the last and present centuries in the Middle East, much more than is currently acknowledged; the notable exception would be "state-sponsored" femininism in Kemalist Turkey, which consciously strove to divest republican Turkish feminism of Islamic content. Lack of sufficient historicization and of critical deconstruction of concepts having to do with gender, she says, has led to mislabeling and erroneous depictions of feminist movements in the Islamicate context, both by indigenous and Western commentators.

Badran heavily underscores the role that women's "revisioning of Islam," as she terms it, through the hermeneutic of *ijtihad*— that is, through critical rereading of Scripture and canon law— has played and continues to play in the shaping of a distinctive Islamic feminism. There is at present a growing body of literature that illustrates how Muslim feminists have sought and continue to seek support for self-empowerment in Islamic prescriptions, deliberately challenging those who maintain that Islam and human rights for women are conceptually at odds with one another. These feminists have tended to affirm that androcentric interpretations of various Qur'anic verses by male exegetes and the propagation of certain spurious hadiths with misogynist content have mandated the formation of patriarchal societies and an inferior role for women in such societies (Ahmed 1992; Mernissi 1991a, 1991b). They tend to emphasize interpretive readings of the Qur'an premised on the notions of equality and justice that they insist it upholds for both men and women, thus allowing for an understanding of male and female social roles as complementary and egalitarian rather than hierarchical and unequal (Muslim Women's League n.d.; Sisters in Islam 1991; Badawi 1995; Muslim Women's Georgetown Project 1995; al-Hibri 1997, 1998; Najmabadi 1998, 65–72). They point out that the Qur'an uses gender-inclusive language that addresses believing men and women equally (Wadud-Muhsin 1992; Ahmed 1992) and that it relates accounts of virtuous women as exempla for all humankind (Wadud-Muhsin 1992, 29–42; Stowasser 1994, 67–81). Muslim feminists and modernists tend to stress that the position of Muslim women was much more egalitarian in the early years of Islam before the final codification of the Shari'a by the tenth century by male legists who sought to circumscribe women's public activities in the interests of maintaining patriarchal social order (Esposito 1982; Ahmed 1992; Afshar 1996; al-Hibri 1997). A new term—*womanist Islamic thought*—has recently been used to refer to this school of thinking engendered by this type of hermeneutic initiative on the part of Muslim feminists and modernists (al-Hibri 1998, 542).

Badran astutely shows us how Muslim women activists, both in the world of Islam and in diaspora, are progressively and successfully gendering Islamist discourse by appealing, therefore to the scriptural basis for gender egalitarianism.[13] In many ways, the feminist movement in the Middle East has come full circle. Whereas the earliest feminist movement in Egypt formulated its discourse in Islamic terms, subsequent feminist movements

sometimes consciously strove to remain secular in tandem with
the men's secular nationalist movements with which they were
allied. Secular, however, did not necessarily imply the wholesale
rejection of religious values but rather the recognition of religious difference while upholding equal political citizenship for all.
Thus the feminist movement sought to broaden its platform and
its constituency to include non-Muslim women as well, such as
the Coptic Christians in Egypt. Such a development paralleled
the men's secular nationalist movement, which, in its quest of
similar objectives, sought to divest the public, political realm of
overt religious content and relegate religion to the private, domestic sphere. But whereas men could compartmentalize their
lives easily into distinctive private and public zones, women
could not. Their lives were still heavily circumscribed by patri-
archically interpreted religious laws operative in the private
sphere that restricted their access to the public sphere. This
awareness has created a widespread recognition among both
secular and Muslim feminists that religious reform must be part
of their agendas.

In the late twentieth century, Badran continues, the predominant feminist discourse is once again inevitably being
constructed within an Islamic paradigm, with women insisting
on the right to reinterpret and recast this paradigm. Although
such an enterprise is associated primarily with Islamist women,
secular feminists are also engaging with religion in their political
activities. A dramatic indicator of this newly coalescing alliance
is the new support of secular feminists in Turkey for the
right of Islamist women to openly sport head scarves as crucial
signifiers of their Islamist identity. According to Badran, Islamic
feminism, in Turkey as in Iran, Egypt, and elsewhere, is steadily
blurring "the borders between [secular] feminisms and gender-
progressive Islamisms." This has enabled Muslim feminists
to win a new legitimacy for themselves and consequently greater
political and ideological credibility for Islamic feminism.
A gendered Islamist discourse of this nature is helping to

bridge the gap between secular and religious feminists on the one hand and male and female Islamists on the other, creating a "middle space," an "independent site between secular feminism and masculinist Islamism" where these groups can meaningfully come together. Such an undertaking is full of danger, Badran remarks, but also full of enormous opportunity; the new alliance that such groups are capable of forging in this middle space could rewrite history, as she predicts, in the twenty-first century.

Even in this relatively small collection of essays, we discover the multiplicity of voices that lend tenor and timbre to the discourse about gender and space in Islamic/ate societies.[14] These voices harbinger genuine transformation of gendered social and national identities in such societies. One of the most prominent Muslim feminist voices (some would argue *the* most prominent Muslim feminist voice) of this century belongs to Huda Shaarawi, founder of the Egyptian Feminist Union in the 1920s. In the epilogue to her memoirs (Shaarawi 1987), there is one telling episode that nicely encapsulates the process of challenging and redefining gendered discourses and boundaries and its potential for social transformation. In the early stages of her feminist activity, Huda at one point agonized over what to name the women's organization she had helped found; she, like others, recoiled from the use of the word *nadi* (club) with its dangerous associations with men's very public activities in a realm physically off limits to the harem dweller. In 1925, Huda not only named her association the Club of the Women's Union, but by the early 1930s she had also moved the headquarters of the Egyptian Feminist Union right into the heart of Cairo (Shaarawi 1987, 132–33). It was a dramatic gesture of proud self-assurance, signaling the coming of age of the women's movement in Egypt, its arrival at the center from the margins. The trajectory of this movement demonstrates persuasively that the private cannot be neatly delimited from the public in the dialectics of gender role configuration and transformation. Although their means may differ, women everywhere are increasingly intent on conjoining the two spheres.

NOTES

1. Asad is particularly critical of the approaches of Western anthropologists like Ernest Gellner and Clifford Geertz, who, in their respective works *Muslim Society* (1981) and *Islam Observed* (1968), resort to a "certain schematization of Islam" that "as a drama or religiosity expressing power is obtained by omitting indigenous discourses, and by turning all Islamic behavior into *readable gesture*" (emphasis in text; Asad 1986, 9). He suggests that we may arrive at a more authentic anthropology of Islam by seeking "to understand the historical conditions that enable the production and maintenance of specific discursive traditions, or their transformation—and the efforts of practitioners to achieve coherence" (17).

2. One of the best studies to make this point persuasively is by Mary Elaine Hegland. In her study (Hegland 1991) of the lives of Iranian village women in Aliabad from the feudal period through the post-Revolution period, the author shows that the traditionally erected dichotomy between the public and private realms breaks down to a considerable degree.

3. For a trenchant critique of this thesis by a historian of the Middle East, see Mottahedeh (1995).

4. Ghadbian (1997, 7) suggests that "'Islamist' ('Islamiyyun') is what people belonging to Islamic movements call themselves, while 'fundamentalist' is what their opponents derisively call them in a foreign tongue."

5. See Shepard (1987) for an excellent discussion of this problem of nomenclature, particularly p. 327 n. 2, which also provides a useful review of the literature on this issue up to 1987.

6. The flip side of this argument is that Muslim feminism is then attributed to Western and, therefore, imperialist provenance (see, for example, Ahmed 1984; Badran 1991).

7. For a study of ad hoc women's groups, see March and Taqqu (1986). See also Tucker (1983), in which she shows that women's informal political and economic activities have tended to be undervalued by mainstream society, and Rizk Khouri (1996) for her

discussion of women's attempts to circumvent and recreate gendered boundaries and spaces.

8. For a detailed look at rape laws in Pakistan, see Quraishi (1997). I am grateful to Professor Azizah al-Hibri of the University of Richmond School of Law for bringing this reference to my attention.

9. This is a view that is endemic in both Islamist and Western polemical discourse. For a discussion of how this ideological war has been waged centered around Muslim family mores and especially the status of the Muslim woman, see, for example, Mernissi (1984), Boudhiba (1985), Ahmed (1992, 144–68), and Göle (1996). Yvonne Haddad has referred to the veil as "the Silk Curtain" that demarcates the Muslim East from the West in a talk sponsored by the Committee for the Study of Women and Gender in the Middle East and Islamic Societies, Center for Middle East Studies, Harvard University in March 1996.

10. A recent *New York Times* article by Elaine Sciolino (1998) highlights this battle of civilizations as encoded in female attire. According to this article, a Christian female missionary during a visit to Iran resolutely refused to trade in her hat, which to her symbolized her Christianness and her Western heritage, for an Islamic head scarf. In turn, the Iranian authorities insisted that she discard her otherwise modest hat for a head scarf, the only appropriate non-Western and authentically Muslim head covering acceptable to them.

11. In other parts of the Islamicate world, Islamist activism has been associated with mandatory veiling for women and curbing of their public activities, as, for example, occurred in Iran after the Islamic Revolution of 1978 and more recently in Algeria and Afghanistan. However, this situation cannot be generalized to all parts of the Islamicate world; the relationship between subscription to political Islam and suppression of women's civil rights is not an absolute, linear one. Tessler and Jesse (1996) in their recent study of Islamist activities in Egypt, Kuwait, and Palestine found that in Kuwait and Egypt, in particular, men who supported Islamist movements did not display more conservative attitudes regarding women's status than men who did not support Islamist movements. Thus, they conclude, "There is no inevitability about the connection between attitudes toward political Islam and attitudes toward women,

meaning that support for Islamist organizations does not necessarily come from those who hold conservative views about the status of women" (215).

12. For this phenomenon, see Jayawardena (1988) and Hélie-Lucas (1994).

13. A stunning example of recent feminist hermeneutic initiative is offered by Najmabadi (1998, 66). The Iranian journal *Zanan* in an article has challenged the conventional interpretation of a specific Qur'anic verse in the chapter called "Women" (Surat al-Nisa' 4:34), the first part of which is commonly translated as "Men are in charge of (*qawwamun 'ala*) women because God has preferred the one over the other (or some of them over others) and on account of what they spend of their wealth." Instead of understanding the Arabic verb *qawwama* as being derived from the root *qym*, which would yield the meaning of guardianship, the authors of the article argue that the verb is instead derived from the root *qwm*, which would imply standing up in support of someone, a radically different exegesis that undermines the very basis of a patriarchally constituted family. For other traditional and modernist interpretations of this verse, see Stowasser (1998) and al-Hibri (1997). For *Zanan*'s activities, see also Mir-Hosseini (1996a, 1996b). For discussions of how modern feminist discourse relies on scripturalist interpretation to legitimize women's access to higher education, see, for example, Omid (1994) and Barazangi (1997).

14. Recently, Lila Abu-Lughod has referred to this multifaceted discourse about gender and modernity as "feminist stories," which "include not just education, unveiling, political rights, and domesticity but also reveiling and reinterpreting Islamic law" (Abu-Lughod 1998, 25). Such "stories" about many of the same issues find reflection in our own collection.

· TWO ·

Conflict in Peace:
Challenges Confronting the Palestinian
Women's Movement

Anan Ameri

INTRODUCTION

In the aftermath of the signing of the historic Declaration of Principles on September 1993 between the Palestine Liberation Organization (PLO) and Israel, the Palestinian leadership and people in the West Bank and Gaza find themselves confronted with a difficult challenge: building a democratic, egalitarian society in which all citizens, including women will have equitable access to social, economic, and political resources. The potential for achieving women's equality in the new era of Palestinian self-rule is shaped by the following two factors: first, the past and present efforts of women's organizations to stimulate feminist consciousness and, second, their successes and failures in building participatory structures and traditions capable of realizing women's sociopolitical rights. These factors are important to keep in mind against the backdrop of the experiences of many Third World countries, which suggest that once national liberation is achieved, women (as well as other traditionally disenfranchised sectors of society like the urban poor, refugees, labor, and peasants) who have actively worked for statehood are often prevented from fully enjoying the fruits of "liberation." While their efforts are usually acknowledged and praised, they are rarely translated into concrete gains. The question the Palestinian people, men and women alike now face is whether they will be able to avoid repeating the negative outcome of other national liberation movements.

I intend to examine issues confronting Palestinian women in ensuring the realization of their gender-specific interests. This project has two components. First, I examine the role of women's organizations in the national liberation struggle. Second, I look at their present efforts to set the conditions for the social, economic, and political emancipation of women.

Women's emancipation is a complicated process. It is often influenced by a number of conflicting and contradictory variables. Around the globe, change in women's status has been influenced by macro-level variables such as urbanization, industrialization, and transformation into market economy. It has also been influenced by micro-level activism and grassroot organizing (Moghadam 1993, 69). In this study, we examine how Palestinian women's organizations were shaped by the Israeli occupation, the resistance of Palestinians to that occupation, the revival of the Palestinian national movement in the diaspora, the rise of Muslim fundamentalism, and the present formation of a Palestinian entity and its integration into the world system.

The focus of this study is the Palestinian women's movement in the West Bank and Gaza Strip since the Israeli occupation in 1967. It looks into how women's organizations adjust their agendas, structures, and goals as the political situation changes and how these changes affect women's lives. This study aims to answer the following questions:

- To what extent will the participation of different groups in the national struggle for liberation grant women their rights after independence? What is the relationship, if any, between national liberation and women's emancipation?

- How do organizations adjust their structures, goals, agendas, and activities as the political situation changes? In this case, we consider the adjustment from occupation to self-rule.
- Who determines the direction of the change? Who dictates the agenda? And who benefits from it?

THE IMPACT OF THE ISRAELI OCCUPATION

The Israeli occupation in 1967 has resulted in the total subordination and integration of the Palestinian economy to the Israeli economy. Israel's relationship to the occupied Palestinian territories was typical of a colonizer to the colonized—the relationship of the core to the periphery—and has resulted in the destruction of the Palestinian economy, suppression of its national identity, and denial of its civil rights (Roy 1995b, 122). As Sara Roy (1995b, 6) has commented, "Through its policy, the government of Israel has structurally and institutionally dismantled the Palestinian economy as well as undermined the fabric of the Palestinian society and the expression of cultural and political identity. The economy is but one (critical) reflection of this phenomenon."

In the agricultural sector, land confiscation, water expropriation, restrictions on movement of people and their produce, constant curfews and road blocks, and restrictions on exports have made it impossible for Palestinians farmers to compete with the heavily subsidized Israeli agriculture. The same has been true of the infant industrial sector. This has resulted in the transformation of Palestinian peasants, along with other workers, into cheap daily wage laborers in Israel: 38 percent of the Gaza Strip labor force, 25 percent of the West Bank, and 20 percent of Arab Jerusalem residents work in Israel (Heiberg, Ovenson, Brungorg, et al. 1993, 224). The territories also have been transformed into a market for Israeli products.

This period had witnessed the deterioration of the territories' infrastructure (roads, sewerage, electricity, and so on) and other public and private human services such as health, education, and social services. For example, in 1993, the percentage of Palestinians living in the West Bank and Gaza who could read and write was less than that of Jordanians or Kuwaitis (Heiberg, Ovensor, Brungorg, et al. 1993, 24). This Israeli policy of "de-development," as Sara Roy describes it, has resulted also in the reduction of the size of the urban and rural middle class and in large-scale migration of professionals and skilled labor. Migration (and imprisonment) was higher among males, causing women to be left behind to take care of families and the land in rural areas.

In the Middle East, as in most Third World countries, socioeconomic changes such as modernization, urbanization, and a growing middle class are the most important factors in advancing women's causes (Moghadam 1993, 69). Governments—through public education, improvement of health and other social services, enactment of laws, and provision of jobs—are instrumental in promoting women's emancipation and equality. Furthermore, as in all Third World countries, urban middle-class women play an important role as vanguards or agents of change (Moghadam 1993, 26).

In the case of the Palestinian occupied territories, the absence of a local government to provide these services was partially compensated for by the development of an extensive network of grassroots and professional organizations, including women's organizations. This network had basically two functions: one was to provide badly needed services such as health, education, child care, and community social services; the other was to organize the various sectors of Palestinian society such as labor, women, students, and youth, to resist the Israeli occupation.

The emergence of such an elaborate network of grassroots and, at a later stage, professional nongovernmental organizations (NGOs) was greatly influenced by the then exiled PLO. In 1974 the PLO decided to focus its organizational efforts and to redirect its resources from the diaspora to the occupied territories (Hiltermann 1991, 12). Later political developments in the region (such as the Camp David agreement between Egypt and Israel and the 1982 Israeli invasion of Lebanon) reinforced and accelerated the execution of that decision. This PLO decision proved to be critical in enhancing Palestinian resistance to the Israeli occupation. As Hiltermann (1991, 14) remarks, "A division of labor has developed whereby the inside leadership directs the masses on a day-to-day basis, while the PLO provides the strategic framework for the movement and presents itself as the official Palestinian side in peace negotiation."

The main characteristics of this network of Palestinian grass-roots organizations and NGOs can be summarized as follows:

1. Most of these organizations drew their legitimacy from the surrogate power afforded by the PLO and from national and community struggles (Usher 1995, 46). They gained popularity through providing badly needed services and from defending the political and human rights of the Palestinians. For example, in 1993, NGOs were in charge of no less than 60 percent of primary health-care services and 49 percent of secondary care; they also managed 100 percent of preschool programs (Barghouthi 1994, 6). These organizations therefore became a symbol of Palestinian nationalism and composed a counterhegemonic nationalist block against the occupation, an infrastructure of resistance. This infrastructure not only developed in the absence of the state structure but was defined by that very absence.

2. Most organizations, including those on the left, were led mostly by the educated and professional urban middle class. Class struggle or class conflict was not an issue because of the "indiscriminatory" oppressive character of the Israeli occupation. According to Hiltermann (1991, 208), "The economic and political violence perpetuated by the occupier affected all sectors of the population regardless of their class base, which facilitated the

forging of a broad base of alliances of classes against the occupation." In this arrangement, the petit-bourgeoisie provided leadership, while the grassroots workers, urban poor, and refugees helped cement the mass base of the movement through their own organizations (Hiltermann 1991, 9).

3. Although the alliance between classes was cemented by the national struggle, a fierce competition among various political parties was a distinctive feature of the movement. All the grassroots organizations—including those that were established according to sectors such as women, labor, merchants, writers, and so on—were divided along factional lines. The mainstream group was the nationalist Fatah, while on the left were the Democratic Front for the Liberation of Palestine (DFLF), the Popular Front for the Liberation of Palestine (PFLP), the Palestinian Communist Party (PCP), and later Hamas. Thus there were four women's organizations, all known as women's committees.

THE WOMEN'S MOVEMENT

The Palestinian women's movement, like most women's movements in the Third World and the Middle East, has been strongly intertwined with the political history of the Palestinian people. Thus it is almost impossible to talk about a Palestinian women's movement as an independent or a feminist movement separate from that of the Palestinian national movement. The earliest recorded women's activity was an anti-British demonstration in 1917 protesting the Balfour declaration (according to which Britain promised to help create a Jewish state in Palestine). In 1920, women were included in a Palestinian delegation that met with the British High Commissioner. The year 1921 witnessed the foundation of the first women's organization, the Palestinian Women's Union, which held its first national conference in Jerusalem in October 1929. Between 1921 and 1948, the union organized a number of conferences and demonstrations and participated in a number of political activities against the British mandate and Jewish immigration to Palestine (Kuttab 1993, 69–85). As Kuttab states (1993, 71),

> The nature of the activities of the women's union indicates that the national struggle was adopted as a priority. . . . Moreover, the women's activities during that phase were closely coordinated with the national movement. It should be obvious that Palestinian women who lived in a traditional environment governed by patriarchal structure and ideologies would not have been able to enter the public male sphere if it were not for the national struggle.

Although their actions challenged the male dominion of national politics, unlike Egyptian women at the time Palestinian women did not openly link their national activism and their subordination as women (Berger 1995, 5–15). After 1948, the Palestinian women's organizations activities were mostly limited to providing relief and social services to Palestinian refugees. This was the case in the diaspora in Jordan, Syria, Lebanon, and the West Bank and Gaza strip. With the emergence of the PLO in the mid-1960s, the General Union of Palestinian Women (GUPW) was established in the diaspora, with branches in the West Bank and Gaza. As was the case with other General Unions (students, labor, writers, and so on), its main objective was to rally political support for the PLO.

From the first day of the 1967 Israeli occupation, Palestinian women joined in nationalist and political activities aimed at confronting the occupation. Their activities varied from armed resistance to demonstrations and sit-ins. In the first year of the occupation, over 100 women were jailed by the Israelis. By 1979, over 3,000 had been jailed (Jad 1995, 6–7). Again nationalism provided women with a platform to participate in the public political sphere. Women were also active in the growing number of charitable organizations that provided a variety of social, health, educational, and training services. However, for the first decade of the Israeli occupation, the women's move-

ment, including the GUPW, was confined to charitable services
and to antioccupation activities such as demonstrations protesting land confiscation, home demolitions, and deportations and
support committees for prisoners and deportees. They did not
address the needs of women as such—that is, they lacked an
explicit feminist consciousness and a feminist agenda. These
organizations were highly centralized, had headquarters in the
cities or towns, and were controlled by elected boards of educated urban middle-class women. Giaccaman (n.d., 18) comments thus on the makeup and function of these organizations:

> Activities and programs are based on the perception of the con-
> trolling body of the needs of the recipient population, whether
> rural or urban. In other words, the organizational and structural
> framework of the movement does not really allow for the repre-
> sentations of the needs and aspirations of women from all sectors
> of the society, thus reducing most of those involved into the role
> of the beneficiaries.

The year 1978 witnessed the birth of a more progressive and
"feminist" women's movement—namely, the women's committees. Although funded by women from the same background as
their predecessors (from the well-educated, urban middle class),
these women were younger, politically affiliated, and ideologically committed. Kuttab (1993, 73) says that "they were drawn
from different academic, professional, and vocational backgrounds and were interested in targeting national liberation and
social emancipation simultaneously."

The Women's Work Committees were initiated by women
associated with the Democratic Front for the Liberation of Palestine. In their early stage, the committees included women from
all the political parties, especially on the left, as well as independent women. However, they were unable to maintain their
unity and soon split along factional lines. By 1982 four women's
groups existed, each allied with different political parties. Despite the division, they were able to maintain a relatively decent

level of cooperation and coordination (Hiltermann 1991, 149). The various women's committees had similar agendas and structures, especially those associated with the left—that is, the Union of Palestinian Women's Committees (UPWC), the Union of Palestinian Working Women's Committees (UPWWC), and the Women's Work Committees (WWC), later renamed the Palestinian Federation of Women's Action Committees (PFWAC), due to their common understanding of the relationship between national and social struggles.[1] Jad (1995, 11) has observed that "emancipation of Palestinian women was an item on the agenda of all the committees, especially those on the left."

Many of the programs of the women's committees were similar to those offered by the charitable organizations. They included nurseries, traditional training programs in sewing, knitting, and embroidery, literacy centers, workshops, and small-scale cooperatives. The major difference was that programs offered by the women's committees were designed to empower women economically, socially, and politically over the long term rather than simply to meet their immediate needs. The political consciousness of the women who supervised the programs evoked a similar consciousness in participants. The structure of the program gave participants experience in democratic decision making, holding elections, and negotiating common agendas. It also gave women great visibility and enhanced their self-confidence and self-esteem. Issues related to women's inferior status in society and improving that by creating a feminist consciousness were often discussed in committee meetings (Jad 1995, 11–12).

The women's committees organized women in cities and towns, as well as in villages and refugee camps. To ensure the participation of women from different backgrounds, local committees were established in neighborhoods, camps, villages, and factories. Each committee elected one member to represent it in a regional committee. The same principle was followed in the regional, provincial, and higher committees (Giaccaman n.d.,

21). This decentralized model proved to be powerful in dealing with the Israeli authorities and was duplicated by other grassroots organizations (Hiltermann 1991).

The main characteristics of the women's committees can be summarized as follows:

- The committee leadership, which came from the educated urban middle class, was ideologically motivated and politically experienced.
- The committees concentrated on organizing women in villages and refugee camps.
- The committees had decentralized structures and focused on creating leadership at the grassroots level.
- The committees addressed both national and women's liberation at the same time.
- The committees provided women with training, jobs, literacy training, cooperatives, loans, kindergartens, nurseries, and health services.

On the eve of the uprising of 1987, an extensive network of organizations existed to provide basic services in the communities and to mobilize the masses to confront the occupation. By producing leadership and heightening feminist awareness among women, the women's work committees became one of the most important parts of this grassroots movement. The image of Palestinian women leading the Intifada and boldly confronting the Israeli soldiers generated international interest in what was a totally neglected issue—that of the Palestinian women (Schiff and Ya'ari 1989, 126):

> The old rules were changing . . . as the image of Palestinian women underwent considerable revision. While few women had joined demonstrations in the past, and then only in quiet protest actions, masses of them now sought violent contact with the soldiers without fear of compromising their "feminine modesty." The fact is that one fifth of the wounded during the first three months of the Intifada were women and girls.

The Intifada also brought Palestinian women in contact with the international feminist movement. Many international delegations visited the occupied territories at that time, and Palestinian women were invited to participate in women's conferences in various countries. The Intifada induced some Palestinian and Israeli women's activists to work together as well. During the Intifada, more PLO and international funds became available to grassroot organizations and other NGOs, which allowed women to increase their projects such as cooperatives, day-care centers, and kindergartens. A number of women's research centers were established. This period also witnessed the beginning of the institutionalization of the women's movement (Hammami 1995, 51–64).

On the other hand, the Intifada brought many difficulties as the number of deaths, injuries, imprisonments, home demolitions, and deportations increased. The economic situation deteriorated even further, as Israel closed its borders to Palestinian labor. Domestic violence was also on the increase. Closures of schools and restrictions on movements resulted in increased numbers of teenage girls dropping out of school, earlier marriages, and earlier child bearing. During the early stage of the Intifada, Israeli authorities outlawed all neighborhood committees in which women were most active. The Intifada also witnessed the emergence of Hamas and its confrontation with the secular women's movement, which was mostly felt through attempts by Hamas to enforce the hijab (veiling). The lack of any reaction from the secular national movement, especially the left, marked the beginning of a rift between women and their male-dominated political parties.

THE CHALLENGES OF PEACE

As the possibility of a political resolution to the Palestinian Israeli conflict appeared on the horizon (by the second year of the Intifada), conflict within the Palestinian national movement started to emerge. The conflict became more acute after the Oslo agreement and the subsequent arrival of the Palestinian National Authority (PNA) in the occupied territories.

For the last three decades, Palestinian nationalism, like any other nationalism, united Palestinians in their struggle against Israeli occupation. But nationalism tends to blur ideological, class, and gender differences and tends to use and sometimes abuse the weaker segments of society, such as women, peasants, refugees, laborers, and the urban poor. In the first half of this century, nationalism was viewed as a force that would benefit all segments of societies including women, but the experience of many Third World countries called for the reevaluation of many of these assumptions. In her classic study *Feminism and Nationalism in Third World Countries*, Kumari Jayawardena (1986, 3) describes how early twentieth-century nationalism provided women with a platform that allowed them to participate in political and public life and thereby fostered women's awareness of and demands for equality and emancipation. Some feminists believe that this continues to be the case (Kandiyoti 1995, 5–16), while others believe that today feminism and nationalism view each other with antagonism and suspicion (Moghadam 1994, 3). The relationship between nationalism and feminism, as I discuss shortly, continues to be a crucial component of the debate as the Palestinian women's movement faces the challenges of a new era.

THE PALESTINIAN WOMEN'S MOVEMENT: WHAT FUTURE? WHICH DIRECTION?

Palestinian women at one time were confident that their contribution to the national struggle would realize concrete gains once "liberation" was accomplished. "What happened to Algerian women will never happen to us!" was a slogan that was repeated by both the leadership and women at the grassroots level. The lack of enthusiasm by the male-dominated PNA, the marginalization of the left, which had been instrumental in building the Palestinian women's movement, and the emergence of Muslim fundamentalism are all discouraging developments. The once proud and self-assured women's movement finds itself today disempowered, fragmented, and apprehensive about the future. "We have worked so hard for so long, but we do not see the fruits of our work," remarked a woman human rights activist.[2] The conflict between the women's movement and the PNA (regardless of their political support or opposition to Oslo accords) has two components: (1) a general conflict between the NGOs and the PNA, as the latter tries to control the resources and the activities of the NGOs, of which the women's organizations are a part, and (2) a specific conflict over the PNA position toward feminist issues.

The conflict between the PNA and the women's movement started to surface in 1993 over the draft of the Palestinian constitution in which the only reference to women is, "All citizens are equal before the law regardless of their religion, sex, or race." Women were also discouraged when Arafat appointed the technical committees to deal with different aspects of negotiation with Israel and the construction of the Palestinian civil administration. Out of 340 members, only four were women. The low number of women appointed to high-ranking positions is not limited to the technical committees but tends to be the case throughout the Palestinian administration.[4] Thus, many women feel that the PNA did not reward the women according to their contribution to the national struggle. One woman in Gaza from Fatah told me:

> In all revolutions the need for secrecy and underground demands the participation of women. But when gains are made, the women get nothing. Take for example our party, Fatah—the ruling party. Arafat rewarded the male members, including the political prisoners, with jobs or money. We, the women members, got nothing.[3]

After unsuccessful attempts to persuade Anis al-Qasim (who drafted the constitution) to change the draft, the women formed their own twenty-three-member committee, inclusive of all political groups, and drafted the "Documents on Principles of

Women's Rights," which became known as the Women's Charter. Also the quasi-governmental Women's Affairs Committee was established by women from Fatah and Fida, the two political parties in the PNA, to promote women's participation in the government, through appointments and elections. Islah Jad, a member of the Women's Affairs Committee, said to me:

> When we met with Arafat to demand representation as women under the new authority, he asked us about the power we have in the streets. How can we pay him back? Our interest in the election goes beyond our interest in being elected or represented in the PNA; we have to prove to Arafat that we have influence over women and that we are a power to deal with.[5]

Many women believe that in his dealing with the fundamentalists, Arafat would be willing to compromise on issues of concern to women, the weaker segment of society. In articulating this concern, Amal Khreisheh suggested that women should aim at creating a movement that will be in a position to put pressure on the Authority or on any group that opposes women's rights (Women's Studies Center, Bir Zeit University 1995a, 5).

THE FUNDAMENTALIST CHALLENGE

The Palestinian occupied territories have witnessed the emergence and the growth of Muslim fundamentalists over the past decade. The Islamist Resistance Movement, known as Hamas—the best known fundamentalist group—was established in 1988, the first year of the Intifada. In a relatively short time, it gained considerable following and influence, especially in the Gaza Strip. Unlike the secular parties, Hamas does not have a separate women's organization, but it does have a following among women. The Saraya al-Jihad (Legions of the Struggle), a much smaller and less conservative fundamentalist movement, recently established its own women's organization.

The first confrontation between the women's movement and Hamas came during the Intifada when Hamas tried to impose the head cover (hijab). In the name of national unity, the secular leftist parties decided not to confront Hamas and failed to support women in their defiance of Hamas's demand, while Fatah asked their women to adhere. As a result, Hamas was able to impose the hijab in Gaza and in the two West Bank cities of Nablus and Hebron. Women, including Christian women, who refused to wear the hijab were harassed. After the arrival of the PNA, many women stopped wearing the hijab, and Hamas did not challenge them.

Of course, the question of Muslim fundamentalism goes beyond a dress code. It touches people's daily lives through its impact on institutions such as schools and the law. For example, many secular women are lobbying for the adoption of secular family law instead of Islamist law. Kuttab (1994b, 8–10) quotes one woman as asking, "Are we going to adopt civil laws of a secular nature, or are we going to surrender to the religious and traditional powers to govern the future of women's status?"

At the same time there are fundamentalist women activists who see Islam as a force that supports women, advances their position in society, and protects them, as well as the larger society, from the ills of modern life. One woman activist with Saraya al-Jihad told me that only through Islam can women fight against reactionary traditions that discriminate against women in education, health, and the workplace.[6] A relevant study on Moroccan women found that many professional and educated women in Morocco are choosing to wear the hijab. Furthermore, the study found that those who wore the hijab among university women were the most outspoken and articulate. This contradicts the widespread Western belief that equates the veil with female subservience (Hessini 1994, 40–56). The emergence and spread of Islam and its impact on women has raised many questions regarding modernization, Eurocentricism, universalist values, and cultural specificity (Moghadam 1994, 7).

Although secular women feel that their civil rights are threatened by the power gained by fundamentalism and by the Palestinian National Authority's willingness to accommodate them, they seem to respect the choices made by Islamist women (as long as it is their choice and not imposed). Many secular women also realize that fundamentalists are gaining ground at the grassroots level where they provide essential services to women, at a time when the secular women's movement is reducing its services and losing its ties to the grassroots.

Fundamentalist and secular women do not necessarily have an antagonistic relationship at all times. There is actually a dialogue and sometimes coordination between them. Many secular women feel that people who become disenchanted with nationalism, communism, and Western democracy often turn to religion as their only secure and safe refuge.[7] Sara Roy (1995, 22) makes the following prognostication:

> Their strength undoubtedly will grow in the 1990s, a pattern that can be found in other parts of the Arab world for many of the same reasons. The strength of Islamism is rooted in the territory's extreme poverty, isolation, and traditional social structure, and its growth has been nourished by a profound sense of popular despair over the steady disintegration of daily life and the consistent failure of the nationalist movement to achieve any political resolution to the Palestinian-Israeli conflict and to end the occupation.

DIVISION WITHIN THE SECULAR WOMEN'S MOVEMENT

During the years of Israeli occupation, women were divided along factional lines, but in practical terms the four secular committees agreed on the need to free women from their household chores and to involve them in political, social, and economic activities outside their homes and family spheres (Hiltermann 1991, 134). Palestinian women were united in their commitment to address the needs of women at the grassroots level and to provide them with basic services. They were also united around the national objective of mobilizing women to confront the Israeli occupation. This unity made women capable of playing such a significant role in the national struggle, especially during the Intifada. Today, Palestinian women find themselves divided by political, ideological, and class differences. Suha Barghouti (Women's Studies Center, Bir Zeit University 1995a, 3–6) addresses this issue:

> In the past there was a lot of factionalism, but there were also many common denominators because we all had a clear relationship to the struggle against the occupation. Now the common denominators on the political and national levels have decreased tremendously, and there is a situation of contradiction and stagnation.

The first sign of division in the women's movement surfaced as early as 1990 when there was a split within the ranks of the Palestinian Federation of Women's Action Committees (PFWAC). Although it is difficult to assess the exact number of each faction, the division was to a great extent horizontal. Most of the leadership went with Fida, the faction supporting the PLO peace proposal, while the grassroots stood in opposition. This division had a lasting effect on the whole movement, especially since the PFWAC was the largest and most innovative of the women's organizations and produced the largest number of Palestinian female leaders. The division within the women's movement manifests itself on the ground as differences over the priorities of the women's movement in this new era of Palestinian self-rule.

INSTITUTIONALIZATION VERSUS GRASSROOTS MOBILIZATION

The most striking changes that have taken place over the last few years is the institutionalization of the Palestinian women's grassroots movement and the transformation of its leaders into "professional" feminists. The movement's previous emphasis on popular organization and flexible structures is being replaced by more stable bureaucracies situated in offices. The once vibrant movement that included women from cities, towns, villages, and refugee camps seems to have been reduced to a few internationally funded, city-based, well-furnished, and well-equipped offices. These offices employ a limited number of urban educated women and are often headed by the leadership of the movement—who, through the course of struggle, established contacts with international women's movement and donors.

The move toward institutionalization started during the Intifada (Hammami 1995, 55). Some women's organizations are becoming institutionalized out of fear that the PNA intends to limit the scope of mass organizational activities. However, it is clear that the move toward institutionalization dominates the movement at the expense of grassroots activism. Women who support the move toward institutionalization argue that at this stage of self-rule, women need new skills that are different from those needed in the previous era. Islah Jad affirms,

> We are training women in the NGOs and in the PNA; our training includes workshops in negotiation skills, human and women's rights, administration and civil service skills. In the previous era, women's organizations mobilized women to go on strikes, demonstrations, sit-ins, etc. These activities required certain skills such as agitation and mobilization; these skills are not needed in this era.[8]

But there is ample evidence that these programs are training the same women who were trained in the previous era and improving the skills of already skilled women: their impact is hardly felt in the villages and refugee camps. And while women's institutions are being established in urban areas, many of the kindergartens and women's centers have been closed. This was also the fate of most of the cooperatives. Few cooperatives have been privatized, and one in Kufr Nea'meh became a sweat shop for an Israeli garment factory.[9]

There is strong resentment among the women in the villages and refugee camps that they have been used and even betrayed by their women leaders. Today there is a growing wedge and almost a total separation between the leadership and the grassroots. The leadership retreated to the cities, where many found employment with the PNA or the women's institutions.

There is also a feeling among some women that institutionalizing the movement and moving away from grassroots activities will actually weaken the women in face of the PNA and the fundamentalists who are taking over at the grassroots level. A number of women expressed their frustration over the way the Women's Charter was written without consultation with the grassroots membership. They further question whether the document addresses the need of the few women who drafted it. Women at the grassroots were never asked if the document met their demands and addressed their concerns, and the plan to discuss it with them had not taken place at the time of this research (July 1995), almost a year after it was drafted.[10] While women in general feel betrayed by the PNA, political women feel betrayed by the male leadership of their political parties, and women at the grassroots level feel betrayed by their women leaders.

FEMINISM VERSUS NATIONALISM

For the first time, Palestinian women are engaged in developing strategies to advance women's and feminist issues rather than subsuming these issues as part of a social and political national liberation movement. Among the issues they are addressing are legal and social discrimination against women in education, health, and the workplace, domestic violence against women, and women in the government. This change in the agenda stems partially from the rise of Muslim fundamentalism and the arrival of the PNA. Many women believe that at this stage of "state" formation, women have an opportunity to influence legislation, the practices of the PNA, and the emerging institutions to be gender sensitive and to address the needs of women.[11] Others believe that this shift in the women's movement agenda is also donor imposed, which is discussed later.

Irrespective of their political affiliation or perspective, all women agree that during the previous period women's issues were subordinated to national issues. They also agree that men, who lead the political parties, including the left, were not sensitive to women's issues and favored the interest of the party at the expense of women's interests and needs. However, there is no agreement on how to evaluate the past or plan for the future.

Some women believe that the women's movement needs to address the needs of women by shifting from a nationalist agenda to a feminist agenda. Their assessment of the accomplishments of the women's movement during the years of the occupation is rather bleak and negative, for they note that the heroism of women during the Intifada was not matched by concrete improvement in the status of women (Jad 1995, 18). Thus they believe that they should focus their energy at this stage on women's issues, which include elections, lobbying, women and violence, women in the PNA, and gender training. In the words of Siham Barghouti (Women's Studies Center, Birzeit University 1995a, 4), "Just as the women's movement was able to build a wide popular base around the national agenda, we can do the same around women's issues today."

On the other hand, some women do not believe that the 1993 agreement will end the political control or economic domination of Palestinian territory by Israel. They also consider the historical prevalence of the political agenda over the feminist agenda within the women's movement as legitimate, understandable, and natural rather than a defect. They do not believe in what they call the arbitrary separation between national and feminist issues or national liberation and women's liberation. At a roundtable organization in 1995 held at Birzeit University, Suha Barghouti commented that it was the responsibility of women to work to build a better society that is free from occupation and not to work to improve the status of women alone (Women's Studies Center, Birzeit University 1995a, 5). Another woman has remarked,

Take, for example, the state security courts, the death penalty. Shall we as women say that it is not our business, that we should only deal with the feminist agenda, or are we using this as an excuse, as a justification because we either support the PNA or because we are terrified by it?[12]

These women's assessments of their accomplishments during the Israeli occupation are positive, and they acknowledge that the national struggle has an important impact on the women's movement, gender relations, and feminist consciousness. Giaccaman (1995, 53–59) underscores this when she says,

> The main tenets of this consciousness rest on an embryonic analysis of power relations in politics and in society, and in particular a growing refusal to accept gender hierarchies as natural and given. This refusal has been deeply influenced by political activism.

DONORS AND INTERNATIONAL AGENCIES

In the aftermath of Oslo, there has been an international effort to rally financial support for the new Palestinian authority. Only a few weeks after Oslo, an International donors conference was held in Washington, D.C. Participants pledged $2 billion to be given in five years. The World Bank prepared its seven-volume document called *Developing the Occupied Territories: An Investment in Peace*. While there is no doubt that the Palestinians need the assistance to rebuild their society, the aid has not been unconditional. Most donors have their own agendas.

For example, governments, especially the American government, want to ensure the success of Oslo and the end of any Palestinian resistance to Israel. Thus, security is given priority, which in practice means that most of the aid given to the PNA will be used to build the police and security forces and to buy popular consent by providing employment—either in the police and security or in government bureaucracy. Since the resources available are limited, such spending will be at the expense of social services, including health and education. Furthermore, violations of human rights by the PNA are overlooked and sometimes encouraged by Western governments.

The World Bank and the International Monetary Fund (IMF) also have their own agendas and priorities. They believe that the role of the PNA (as is the case with other Third World governments) is to build an infrastructure to encourage, attract, and facilitate the work of the private sector, a policy that in all Third World countries has helped the rich at the expense of the poor. For example, the women's cooperatives are viewed as economically unsound. Instead of seeing women's empowerment as a value in itself, these agencies assess only the economic feasibility of a project. Eileen Kuttab (1995, 47–52) comments on this situation:

> Economic projects for Palestinian women were utilized as tools for political and social mobilization. So although these projects were economic in nature, raising political, social, and gender consciousness were the main objectives. . . . For instance, women who participated in cooperatives have acquired new skills in administration, new understanding in concepts like democracy, division of labor, ownership as related to work, and development versus welfare. In this context the cooperative movement succeeded in transforming attitudes, in addition to deepening the participants' understanding of their situation and ways to challenge it.

In contrast, international donors appear not interested in the political mobilization of women; if anything, demobilization seems to be their objective. Women's past roles and contributions have come under severe attack. Drastic changes in the orientation of the entire women's movement are reflected in the new language and vocabulary that are being used: terms like *business incubators, economic feasibility, private loans,* and *enterprise* have come to replace terms like *women's empowerment, community projects,* and *cooperatives.* Many argue that the institutionalization of the women's movement and the shift in its agenda is donor driven and that the donors' policies include the depoliticization of women and the integration of Palestinian society in the global economy (Giaccaman 1995, 55). A report published by the Women's Studies Center at Birzeit University states, "It is an implicit condition imposed by international funders to divert mass organizations from grass roots work, to specialized efforts within the confines of an institution" (Women's Studies Center, Birzeit University 1995b, 20).

While the donors set the priorities and the agenda, many women's organizations are modifying their agendas to meet the donors' conditions in order to receive funds. Topics such as "Women and the Law," "Violence against Women," and "Gender Training" are items on the agendas of almost all women's organizations. The funds that are made available to them are for women's training in the areas of civil administration, elections, and lobbying activities. These issues, which are replacing the goals and programs previously promoted by women's organizations, are the ones that donors will fund. As one woman remarked in exasperation,

> Training fits nicely with NGO's trends and what donors like to give money for! Because it is cheap. Training, training, training, but where is this training leading to? No one knows.[13]

This training often targets a small number of women—usually urban, well-educated, employed women who have already attended a number of training seminars and workshops. Very few efforts are being made to reach the urban poor or women in the refugee camps or rural areas. This change in the agenda of women's organizations has alienated women and has had the effect of bypassing their concerns completely. Unlike the previous orientation of the women's movement, which aimed at empowering the weaker segment of women, the new trend tends to ignore even those who spent many years in the struggle should they lack the needed skills to be employed by the women's institutions, other NGOs, or the government bureaucracy. As a long-time activist told me,

Every one is talking about gender training. I do not know what that means, nor do I speak English. After fifteen years of working with women, all of a sudden I feel ignorant and useless.[14]

CONCLUSION

Among the most significant contributions of the Palestinian women's movement was its ability to organize women from all sectors of society and to empower them politically, socially, and economically. However, as soon as a political resolution to the Palestinian-Israeli conflict appeared on the horizon, divisions within the Palestinian women's movement started to emerge. This division—along with the retreat from grassroots organizing to the confines of the "professional" urban-based women's institutions, the increased influence of Muslim fundamentalists, and the lack of interest on the part of the PNA to address women's concerns—has altered the nature of the Palestinian women's movement.

The history of the Palestinian women's movement was and continues to be intertwined with and shaped by the socioeconomic and political history of the Palestinian people. The recent victory of the Israeli right-wing Likud party headed by Benjamin Netanyahu, the increased repression by the PNA, and the continuous deterioration of the economic situation in occupied territories are all discouraging developments. Unless these trends are reversed, the fruits of almost a century of women's contributions to the Palestinian national struggle would at best be limited to a few already privileged women. At present, such reversals do not seem imminent. The tenuous position of the PNA, besieged as it is by opposition from within and from without, makes the implementation of a consistent policy of national and social development next to impossible. Furthermore, in the absence of international guarantees for the political and territorial rights of Palestinians, the outlook for the foreseeable future remains grim. In such a precarious situation, women's issues are of extremely low priority and one fears, with considerable justification, that the derailed women's movement may not get back on track for some time yet.

NOTES

1. The Union of Palestinian Women's Committees (UPWC) is affiliated with the Popular Front for the Liberation of Palestine. The Union of Palestinian Women's Work Committees (UPWWC) is affiliated with the Communist Party. The Palestinian Union of Women's Work Committees (PUWWC), later named Palestinian Federation of Women's Action Committees (PFWAC), is affiliated with the Democratic Front for the Liberation of Palestine. The Women's Committee for Social Work (WCSW) is affiliated with Fatah (Hiltermann 1991, 134).
2. Interview with Ruqaya Alami, Palestine Human Rights Information Center, Jerusalem, June 1994.
3. Interview with Sabah Ahmad, Gaza Women's Affairs Center, July 1995.
4. Interview with Suha Hindiyyeh, Women's Resource Center, Beit Hanina, July 1995.
5. Interview with Islah Jad, Women's Affairs Committee, Ramallah, June 1995.
6. Interview with 'Iffat al-Jabari, Hebron, June 1995.
7. Interview with Asia Habash, Early Childhood Resource Center, Jerusalem, 1995, by the Women's Resource Center.
8. Interview with Islah Jad, Women's Affairs Committees, Ramallah, June 1995.
9. Interview with Nahla Qura, Fatah Women's Organization, Ramallah, June 1995.
10. Interviews with Jamila Abu Dahu, Bisan Institution, Ramallah; Sama Liftawi, Women's Resource Center, Beit Hanina; Ruqayya Alami, Palestine Human Rights Information Center, Jerusalem; Asia Habash, Early Childhood Resource Center, Jerusalem, May–July 1995.
11. Interview with Siham Barghouti, Women's Affairs Committee, Ramallah, May 1995.

12. Interview with Eileen Kuttab, Birzeit University, Women's Studies Program, June 1995.
13. Interview with Rema Hammami, Women's Affairs Center, Gaza, July 1955.
14. Interview with 'Aida 'Issawi, Palestinian Federation of Women's Action Committees, Beit Hanina, West Bank, June 1995.

THREE

Woman's Body, Nation's Honor: Rape in Pakistan*

Shahla Haeri

In a rare moment in the history of Pakistani society, a few raped women decided to go public and shake their society out of its long and complacent stupor.[1] Pakistani women have for centuries buried in their hearts the rage and anguish of rape. In the interests of family honor and for fear of ostracism, they were (and still are) forced to keep quiet or face further humiliation and abandonment by their families. Pakistani families customarily hide the "shame" of their women whose honor (*izzat*) has been "looted." Society has actively discouraged public disclosures of rape, and until very recently it preferred not to know about it. With courage and determination and a little help from their friends, the women discussed in this chapter broke this long-standing taboo. The year was 1991, a year after the ouster of prime minister Benazir Bhutto by then president Ghulam Ishaq Khan.

One of the women described her ordeal in the following manner:

> The CIA (Crime Investigating Agency) treated me like a notorious criminal. Repeatedly they pulled my hair and slapped me on the face. They wanted me to make false sexual allegations against Asif Zardari (Benazir Bhutto's jailed husband) and wanted me to

55

say that Benazir had given me [and the party's student wing] weapons to create chaos in Karachi or that she had passed on national security tips to Rajiv Gandhi. I refused it. They tortured me again. I was terrified and cried in my heart. A policewoman warned me about my interrogator's bad behavior. She said, "You are not married. They make you married." (statement of Rahila Tiwana, a Pakistan People's Party (PPP) student activist)[2]

I have lost my home. I know what my husband will do to me. I know that I am a *bayghairat* (without honor, loss of one's self-respect) in the eyes of my *khandan* (family), which has disowned me. I have been sentenced for life for the crime of being raped, but this is not the end. I know that there is only humiliation in it for me now. Only God can grant me justice, but I must speak, so that maybe other women can be prevented from meeting a fate similar to mine. (statement of Khurshid Begum, a poor washerwoman whose husband used to be a PPP supporter)[3]

I know that a lot of dirt is going to be flung at me. But I have decided to take them on. And I hope I have the courage to see it through to the end or I will kill myself. (statement of Veena Hayat, a woman of the elite class and a close friend of Benazir Bhutto and her husband)[4]

What is culturally and historically specific about these rape cases that sets them apart from similar cases happening in Pakistan or in other parts of the world? What gives them their uniquely Pakistani flavor? My objective in this chapter is to situate these particular cases within the sociopolitical context of Pakistani society. I argue that what is unique to the rape of these three women is that they all happened in the year following Benazir Bhutto's ouster in 1990, that one of the women was a personal friend of Benazir Bhutto, one was a supporter of Bhutto's Pakistan People's Party, (PPP) and the other was an activist in the PPP. The rapes took place in Karachi, the capital city of Sindh province, from where the Bhutto family hails. Theoretically, I argue that "political rape" is a modern improvisation on the theme of "feudal honor rape."[5] Symbolically, political rape in Pakistan draws on its feudal heritage and in this sense manifests its cultural specificity. The target of humiliation and shame is not necessarily a specific woman. It is rather a political rival—an old enemy on whom revenge is to be taken. In its modern context, political rape has the tacit and at times explicit legitimation of the state, just as honor rape has continued to have cultural support and collective sanctions.[6]

In the following pages, I introduce each woman and her case, followed by a brief discussion of the concepts of honor and political rape. My concern here is not so much with providing the details of each case as it is with identifying the ultimate target of the rape and the motivations behind it. I briefly review the political situation in Pakistan and consider some implications for human rights for women.

THE POLITICS OF RAPE

On December 7, 1991, Pakistanis awoke to the public lamentations of an aged father, who, obviously in pain and weeping, revealed at a crowded press conference that his daughter, Veena Hayat, had been gang raped two weeks before. This was an unprecedented act in Pakistan, particularly so for a man of his stature. He was Sardar Shaukat Hayat, a member of the landed aristocracy and the political elite and an old colleague of Pakistan's foremost leader, Muhammad Ali Jinnah (d. 1948). No "dishonoring" of women had been made public, let alone broadcast via the electronic and printed media. It had never happened before, at least not in this dramatic fashion and in such a public forum. Sardar Shaudat Hayat accused Irfanullah Marvat, the Karachi head of Pakistan's notorious Crime Investigating Agency (CIA),[7] the son-in-law of then President Ghulam Ishaq Khan. He was quite clear about the motive behind his daughter's rape. She was punished, in his view, because she was a close friend of the opposition leader, Benazir Bhutto. He had no doubts that this act was the "handiwork of the Sindh authorities."[8]

At the time, Veena Hayat was a divorced woman who lived in a prosperous neighborhood of Karachi. She had two teenaged sons. One of them was studying in the United States at the time, and the other was at a friend's house. Her ordeal involved an evening raid by five masked men who gagged and tied her two servants and then waited to ambush her when she arrived home. When Veena's car drew up, they pulled her out of it, beat her up, and dragged her up by her hair to the upper floor of her house where they humiliated and raped her. The masked men did not loot much but stayed in her house for twelve hours, terrorizing, taunting, and torturing Veena and her domestic workers. Clearly, they were not ordinary dacoits[9] or thieves, as was later claimed by the Sindh authorities. In the words of an observer, "The Veena Hayat case had literally come to knock at the very gates of power."[10]

Supported by the chief minister of the Sindh provincial government, Jam Sadique Ali, Marvat dismissed the allegations, countering that the PPP used their "ladies" for political gain, hinting at a "relationship between Veena and Asif Zardari (Benazir Bhutto's husband)."[11] Veena Hayat's case also polarized the complex and layered systems of justice in Pakistan. Her case was referred to the court, but she and her father refused to cooperate with the investigation, stating their lack of trust in the judiciary's impartiality. Their apprehension was confirmed when the judge exonerated the head of the CIA (the president's son-in-law) of any wrongdoing. Falling back on a tribal honor system[12] instead, Sardar Shaukat Hayat sought justice through his tribal *jirga* (consultative assembly), asking his brethren to restore his daughter's and his family's honor. Ironically, the head of the CIA himself, the man responsible for law and order, also seemed to trust tribal justice more. He too called on his own tribal jirga for support to counteract possible attacks by Sardar Hayat's fellow tribesmen. The political drama reached its peak when Sardar Shaukat Hayat, as if vindicated by their regression to "tribal justice," made a ritualized public appeal: "We welcome his jirga. I hope his own community will take care of him. If there is a Marvat [the name of his tribe] code of honor, as I know it, they will."[13]

There was an immediate outcry by the Pakistani women's rights and human rights organizations, which organized demonstrations and teach-ins in major cities of Pakistan, including the capital city of Islamabad. There were numerous smaller gatherings and consciousness-raising events, including several hunger strikes in which Benazir Bhutto herself and some members of the opposition participated. The religious fundamentalist parties,[14] some of which were part of the government coalition, remained mute. Only after much taunting by outraged journalists, women, and human rights activists did the Jama'at-i-Islami and a few other smaller parties condemn the act in measured language, taking care not to antagonize the government or to appear to be jumping on the opposition's bandwagon.

Had it not been for the publicity surrounding Veena Hayat's case, perhaps the plight of Khurshid Begum would have gone unnoticed—except by a handful of women activists. Khurshid Begum was a poor washerwoman who just a few days before Veena Hayat's ordeal had also been raped, but her ordeal took place in police custody. Khurshid Begum's husband was a PPP supporter who was jailed for an unsubstantiated political allegation regarding the state's national security. Returning home on the night of November 13, 1991, from a visit to her husband, she was grabbed, she said in an interview, blindfolded, and thrown into a car "like a bag of trash" by some policemen. She recalled opening her eyes to find herself in a dark room with a few tables, chair, and a picture of Muhammad Ali Jinnah.[15] She said that two uniformed women removed her blindfold, but they left the room quickly when "a fat, drunk man with three stars" came in.[16] According to Khurshid Begum,

> The fat man was reeling, and he laughed out loud on seeing me. Then they closed the door and one man dragged me to the table

by the hair. The fat policeman fell on top of me. I started scream-
ing and struggling. I got up and ran around inside the room with
one man hurtling me toward the other, grabbing me now by my
hair, now by my breasts. My shirt tore from the middle. Then the
fat man overpowered me, and in the presence of those two other
beasts, satisfied himself of me. I felt like I was about to die.[17]

She too believed that the primary reason for her ordeal was
political. "I was victimized because my husband used to be a
PPP supporter. . . . I don't work for the party. I wash clothes for
people and feed my children. . . . Of course they attacked me for
political reasons. The fat police officer said after he was through
with me: 'Ask Benazir to help you now.'"[18]

Unlike Khurshid Begum, Veena Hayat was shielded by her
family and given moral support. Veena hardly appeared in public
and did not give many interviews. Khurshid Begum's family, on
the other hand, distanced themselves from her and, in her words,
"wanted her 'blood'." Apparently ashamed of what had happened to Khurshid Begum, her brother-in-law summed up their
family's collective sentiment when he told her to "commit sui-
cide." "I fear for my life," lamented Khurshid Begum. "The
Baloch [her ethnic affiliation], as you know, combine ignorance
with pride. I don't know if even my husband would accept me
once he is out of prison."[19] Luckily for Khurshid Begum, she was
given full moral, legal, and material support by several Pakistani
women's and human rights organizations.

Before Khurshid Begum and Veena Hayat, yet another young
woman suffered the fury of some political "operators" in Karachi. Rahila Tiwana was a devoted twenty-four-year-old political
activist who belonged to the student wing of the Pakistan People's Party. I interviewed her several times in Karachi in May of
1993 and had long discussions with her psychiatrist, Dr. Haroon
Ahmed, with Rahila's knowledge and consent.[20]

The beginning of the year 1991 coincided with her arrest,
torture, and subsequent hospitalization in a psychiatric ward for
over nine months. Rahila's father is a civil servant, living with
his wife, his four daughters, among whom Rahila is the eldest,

and one son in a comfortable state-owned house in a colony just outside of Karachi. All her family members are devotees of Benazir Bhutto and activists on behalf of her party. Repeatedly, she told me how much she loves Benazir and how worried she was for her leader's life because while in jail she had heard her interrogators, including a cousin of the head of CIA, the same man accused by Veena Hayat, threatening to "kill" Benazir Bhutto.

Before her arrest her house was searched, and she was arrested on the pretext that she had been given weapons and ammunition and had passed on secret messages to Indian agents. When she refused to cooperate with Sindh authorities to fabricate charges of sexual misconduct and national security allegations against Benazir Bhutto and her husband, her interrogators turned savage. So severely was she beaten and tortured that at some point she lost consciousness.[21] Regaining her senses, she was horrified to find herself "bloodied all over." She does not remember what happened to her. She does not think she was raped, though all her descriptions lead one to that conclusion. But whether she was actually raped or not, her ordeal was horrendous enough to require her long rehabilitation in a psychiatric ward. Dr. Haroon Ahmed shared with me the videotape of his conversation with Rahila, taken nine months after she was jailed and tortured. Rahila sobbed throughout her long interview, her face expressing the terror she had felt, her body shaking uncontrollably.

A BRIEF HISTORICAL AND POLITICAL BACKGROUND

Before moving onto an analysis of honor rape, I briefly discuss the political and historical mediating structures, setting the context for an understanding of the dynamics of honor rape in Pakistan.

A former British colony, Pakistan is a young nation-state, partitioned from India in 1947. Having gone through several bouts of military dictatorship, its present form of government is democratic,[22] though besieged by vigorous fundamentalism and a well-entrenched feudal system. Added to the mélange is Pakistan's complex ethnic and linguistic diversity.[23] The structural, cultural, and ideological interaction of these phenomena constitute the specificity of government in Pakistan, coloring the public's world-view and expectations. As the religious backlash to modernism and modernity gains momentum, Pakistan, like many other Muslim nation-states, seems to be sliding through the quagmire of crises of *identity* (ethnic and linguistic) and *legitimacy* (religious, secular).

With the sudden demise of General Zia ul-Haq in the summer of 1988, Pakistani politics has become ever more complex and cunning. Political tensions, kept under tight control by General Zia's military regime, now burst furiously into the open, polarizing the nation along ethnic, religious, ideological, and political lines. These alliances, however, shift constantly, making rather unreliable any clear determination of who is where in Pakistan. Nonetheless, at the core of Pakistani sociopolitics is a major divide between deeply rooted aristocratic feudalism and corporate business, with the fundamentalists and the military throwing their support behind this or that alliance, as the political situation may demand. In real life, the boundaries of these realms are much more porous and permeable than this observation might imply, but it nonetheless provides a useful analytic perspective.

Within this framework, one may identify Benazir Bhutto as representing the interests of the feudal aristocracy. She learned the rudiments of politics from her father, Zulfiqar Ali Bhutto (1928–79), who was overthrown in a military coup by General Zia ul-Haq in 1977 and hanged in 1979, despite strong international pressure for his pardon. A protégé of Zia ul-Haq and politically his "adopted son," Nawaz Sharif, Benazir Bhutto's rival, rose quickly through the political hierarchy to become the Punjab's chief minister (1984–90). Benazir Bhutto hails from Sindh, and Nawaz Sharif from the more populous and prosperous province of Punjab. Traditionally, with few exceptions, Pakistan's federal power elite have come from the Punjab—hence the traditional political rivalry between the Sindhis and Punjabis (Alavi 1987, 25).

The high political drama created after the unraveling of Zia's military dictatorship brought Benazir Bhutto to national limelight and to the center of political stage. She won the election of 1989, only to be booted out barely a year and a half into her five-year term. In her first term in office, the young and somewhat inexperienced Benazir Bhutto had to contend with contemptuous religious fundamentalist parties, who saw her unfit to become the head of a Muslim state, issued various *fatwas* against her, and even sued her in court for having referred to her late father as a martyr (*shahid*).[24] She also had to face stiff challenges from the opposition, headed by Nawaz Sharif and supported by the president, both of whom were backed by the military. Unable to deliver on her campaign promises, Bhutto was eventually dismissed in August 1990 by the president, who invoked the Eighth Amendment to the Constitution (the handiwork of Zia, this gave the president executive power to dismiss the prime minister and to dissolve the parliament). He brought charges of financial impropriety against her.

The caretaker government of Mustafa Jaoti was asked by President Ghulam Ishaq Khan to remain in power while both Nawaz Sharif and Benazir Bhutto prepared for an electoral showdown later that year. Supported by the president, the military, and the fundamentalist Jama'at-i Islami, Nawaz Sharif defeated Benazir Bhutto to win the election of October 1990. Nawaz Sharif, however, was toppled in April 1993 when the president evidently felt that the prime minister was surreptitiously looking for ways to repeal the Eighth Amendment—the sword of Damocles that every Pakistani prime minister feels is hanging over his or her head. Nawaz Sharif faced daunting challenges not only from an offended president and dissatisfied fundamentalist allies but also from Benazir Bhutto and a strong popular opposition.

It is against this highly complex background of superimposing political, ethnic, and ideological rivalries that I look at the politics of honor rape.

POLITICAL RAPE, HONOR RAPE

Although the idea that "rape is fueled by cultural values that are perpetuated at every level of our society" (Brownmiller 1975, 389) was first ventured in relation to Western societies, it can be generalized to other cultures. In the context of Pakistani society, Khalid Ahmed (Ahmed 1992, 36–37), the noted Pakistani journalist observes,

> Feuds are settled through rapes. Men avenge themselves on each other by raping each other's mothers, wives, daughters and sisters. A brave adversary is supposed to break down under the grief and dishonor of the violation of his womenfolk. At times, women are gang raped, then paraded naked in the streets to show to the society that terminal revenge has been taken.

No one intervenes. Many may feel sad and sorry, but all know the rules of the game.

"Honor," argues Stewart, "is a notoriously paradoxical topic, and one of its most famous puzzles is the effect that women's behavior can have on men's honor" (Stewart 1994, 107). In Pakistani society, the concepts of political rape and honor rape are inextricably linked. In this context, honor (izzat) is intimately tied to a sense of a "natural" masculine right to possess and control his womenfolk. Objectifying honor in the person of a woman, men possess honor, just as they possess gold and land— the three elements that are said to be the most sought after in Pakistan and thus at the root of all conflicts. Logically, it follows, women cannot possess honor in the same way as men. They represent honor; they symbolize honor; they are honor.[25] Objectified into manipulable possessions, symbolic or otherwise, women lose a sense of individuality in the eyes of the community. Raping a woman robs a man of his most prized possession, his honor, but it obliterates a woman's whole being. Once a man's honor is violated, all he can do, all he is expected to do, all he should do is seek revenge. As for the raped woman, no one cares—or dares to care; she does not exist as an individual.

Perhaps the modern political rape resonates historically with the development of separatist political opposition in Pakistan in which some women also participated. Politics, revenge, and humiliation of the "enemy" was in the minds of a losing Pakistani army during its civil war with East Pakistan, now Bangladesh, in 1971 when Pakistani soldiers sexually assaulted and raped a large number of Bengali women just as their troops were retreating (Brownmiller 1975, 78–86). Symbolically, too, it was the rape of a nation that had dared to defy her big "brother," wishing to assert her autonomy and demanding recognition of her distinct identity (Sisson and Rose 1990).

With the passage of the Hudood Ordinance in 1979 legalizing punishment for adultery, theft, drinking, and false accusations, the number of women in police custody has increased dramatically (Jahangir and Jilani 1991; Kennedy 1987, 307–19). Under the Hudood Ordinance, the boundaries between rape and adultery or fornication (*zina*) have become rather blurred. The women of Pakistan are thus caught in a double bind: if they report a rape case—assuming that they can overcome all familial and cultural barriers that militate against disclosure—not only may they not get justice, but the chances are great that they themselves may be accused of adultery.[26] Despite the rape, torture, and abuses that women face in police custody, many are reluctant to speak up or to file charges against the responsible officers for fear of police reprisals. Women's predicament in such situations and their fear-inspired reluctance to pursue justice is complex and multifaceted. This is due partly to the shame many raped women feel, partly to intimidation by the agents of "law and order," and partly to the equation of rape with adultery under the Hudood Ordinance. This strongly discourages many women from seeking help, rendering "sexual justice" practically ineffective in Pakistan.

Theoretically, variations of violence against women have been conceptualized in terms of controlling female sexuality, restrict-

ing women's autonomy, keeping them in their place, and maintaining male guardianship and dominance (Brownmiller 1993;
Hanmer and Maynard 1987; Omvedt 1990). Concurring with
these perspectives and drawing on my ethnographic field work
in Pakistan, I submit that in the case of the women mentioned
above, the act of rape is more than a show of dominance through
brute force to keep women in their place. It is also more than an
instrument of oppression to restrict women's movement and
control their bodies. Nor is it used merely to make public examples of raped women in order to strike fear in the hearts of other
women, thus forcing them to obey the rules of the male power
structure and to remain within certain culturally and religiously
specified boundaries. While sharing aspects of these elements,
the specific cases of these three women involve an act of *revenge*
aimed at humiliating and dishonoring a powerful and potentially
threatening rival. Here the "enemy" was none other than
Benazir Bhutto. How is that possible, one might ask, if she
herself is a woman? This is precisely the point. When female
members of her party are raped, not only are individual women
dishonored, but also, symbolically, Benazir Bhutto, leader of the
opposition and the model of womanhood, is herself "raped" by
association. How could a nation, any nation, choose to have a
raped leader? Conversely, how could a leader who is unable to
protect herself or her followers protect her country from being
invaded by its "enemies," real or imagined?

Although out of power in 1991, Benazir Bhutto was considered a great threat by the authorities, particularly in the Sindh
province. She was a force to be reckoned with. She had to be
brought to her knees. It was not enough that the president had
brought lawsuits against her, all of which were eventually
thrown out. Still very popular with the masses, she had to be
taught a proper lesson, a lesson all too meaningful for a woman.
She had to be dishonored, symbolically and actually.

The unfortunate women who are caught up in this archaic
cultural and political feud become the conduit for political action and a culturally meaningful medium for sending the mes-

sage to a political enemy or rival. It is at the level of individual experience that Pakistani women share the horror of "bodily violation" with women from other cultures. The premises of human rights are based on the sanctity of the individual and the inviolability of this sanctity. So long as the prevailing tribal and feudal ethical system remains strong in Pakistan, chances of meaningful human rights changes for women on a large scale are dim. On a positive note, painful as the experiences of these women have been, they have confronted Pakistani society with moral tension, leading to greater public awareness of the issue of violence against women. They have also strengthened the resolve of many Pakistani women activists who are poised to reclaim their bodies and their voices. They are determined to speak out, realizing that remaining silent any longer is a "crime."

NOTES

* This chapter is a slightly modified version of my article (Haeri 1995) in Afkhami (1995).

1. Although news of rape, violence, and abuses against women had become more or less a part of the daily news by then, women themselves were seldom involved in such publicity.
2. Personal communication, Karachi, May 22 1993.
3. *Herald*, January 1992, 42; *Shirkat Gah's Newssheet* 4(1), 1992, 4.
4. Ibid.
5. By *feudal*, in the Pakistani context, I mean a relatively small group of politically active and powerful landowners. It is also a moral category in the sense that Pakistanis often talk of a *feudal attitude,* meaning "a combination of arrogance and entitlement" (Richard Murphy, personal communication). Honor rape is not limited to feudal vendetta and occurs in society at large. See also Shah (1993, 36) and her interview with Miriam Palojo, a female leader of the Sindhi movement, on the plight of Sindhi peasant women (46).
6. Rape of Pakistani women as a form of "feudal vendetta," states Zohra Yusuf, is widespread. The most famous—or rather infamous—case is that of Nawabpur, "when three women of a family were forced by the sons of a local landlord to parade naked in the

street. This was a form of vendetta against their brother, who had
wanted to marry a woman from the landlord's family" (see Yusuf
1992, 47–48).

7. Irfanullah Marvat also held the portfolio of home affairs advisor
to the Sindh Chief Minister, Jam Sadique Ali.

8. *Herald,* January 1992, 38–39.

9. According to Yule and Burnell (1886 [1989]), a dacoit is a robber
who belongs to an armed gang. The term was current in Bengal
and found its way into the penal code. By law, to constitute dacoity
there must be five or more in the gang committing the crime. In
1817, Sir Henry Strachey observes, "The crime of dacoity has, I
believe, increased greatly since the British administration of justice" (ibid., 290).

10. *Herald,* January 1992, 41.

11. Ibid.

12. Pakistani kinship and political social organizations vary according
to ethnic groups and from region to region. As such, "tribal" social
organization finds different manifestations and structure in Pakistan. For an analysis of Pakistan's political structure as it relates
to "tribal" system, see Lindholm (1977, 41–66).

13. *Herald,* January 1992, 45.

14. Whether the Islamic revivalist parties or movements should be
identified as fundamentalist is a dispute beyond the scope of this
chapter. However, the Jama'at-i Islami in Pakistan printed the term
fundamentalism in its own English political posters during the
October 1993 election.

15. *Herald,* January 1992, 43; *Newsline,* December 1991.

16. *Herald,* January 1992, 43.

17. Ibid.

18. Ibid.

19. Ibid.

20. I am thankful to Dr. Haroon Ahmed and his wife, Anis Haroon,
for their generosity in sharing with me their knowledge and insight
about this case.

21. For a description of violence and abuse of women prisoners, see
the report by Asia Watch and the Women's Rights Project, Human
Rights Watch (1992).

22. Whether or not the Pakistani form of government is democratic
has been the subject of some debate. Given the fact that Pakistan

has been under military rule for most of its young history, some skepticism regarding its fledgling democracy is understandable. Nonetheless, one may categorize it presently as a democracy, however imperfect, because of its functioning parliament, free press, and relative existence of individual and civil rights.

23. It is interesting to note here that Urdu, Pakistan's national language, is not native to a vast portion of the population. Linguistically, Pakistan is diverse, with the majority of the population speaking their own native tongues (Sindhi, Punjabi, Pushto, Sarieki, Baluch, and so on) at home. Urdu, however, is taught at schools. English is spoken even less and is primarily the language of the elite.

24. The court dismissed the case.

25. Like many complex concepts, *izzat* has multiple connotations and involves overlapping meanings, including respect, honor, esteem, dignity, and reputation. As such the term may be gender neutral; both men and women can have dignity and honor, but the main component of their honor is affected differently domestically and publicly. Women's honor is often a component of their chastity (Stewart 1994, 107). As custodians of women's chastity, women's loss of honor bears directly on their primary male kin's honor. In the case of political or honor rape, a woman's own izzat is perceived by the perpetrators as immaterial if not irrelevant, giving the trauma of rape greater poignancy. What is relevant is how it reflects on her men's honor. It is in this sense that the victimized women represent honor or *are* honor.

26. Asma Jahangir, the human rights lawyer, wrote in the *Herald*, January 1992, 52b:

> *Zina* includes all forms of extramarital sex which, after the promulgation [of the Hudood Ordinance], is punishable with imprisonment and whipping. . . . A victim of rape is caught in a snare: if she complains of rape, she has to make out a watertight case, or else she in turn can be accused of *zina*. . . . If a woman who has been raped fails to report the crime, she may well be arrested for *zina* in any case, if the crime is discovered.

FOUR

Gender and Sexuality: Belonging to the National and Moral Order *

Julie Peteet

Nationalism has long been a privileged frame for discussing and theorizing about Palestinian political and social life. Similar to standard texts on nationalism (Anderson 1991; Hobsbawm 1990), those on Palestinian nationalism (Cobban 1984; Khalidi 1997; Muslih 1988; Quandt, Jabber, and Lesch 1973) have not highlighted sexuality or the gendering of nationalist practice or ideology as analytical issues. Yet, sexuality has been endowed with a nationalist meaning and subjected to nationalist regulation.

The recent literature on gender and nationalism (Enloe 1990, 1993; Mosse 1985; Parker, Russo, Sommer, and Yaeger, 1992; Thapar 1993) rejects the idea that social or political life is organized in bounded public-private spheres. The notion of the national subject as a preconstituted singular category of analysis, experience, and action has given way to a much more complex rendering of a multiplicity of subject positions. In a different vein, Mosse points to the intimate relationship between European nationalisms and respectability when he states, "Nationalism helped control sexuality yet also provided the means through which changing sexual attitudes could be absorbed and tamed into respectability" (1985:10). The juxtapositioning of control

70

with the management of change is highly relevant to a discussion of Palestinian nationalism and sexuality.[1]

In this chapter I argue that the construction, deployment, and meaning of sexuality is intertwined with Palestinian nationalism, both secularist and Islamist. The Palestinian Resistance Movement (PRM) and more recently Hamas, the Palestinian Islamist movement, have, explicitly and implicitly, taken up the public management of sexuality—female sexuality, in particular. The approach taken here is to flesh out the ways in which these categories—sexuality and nationalism—can be constitutive of one another. Several questions can be posed. How was sexuality scripted and managed during the Resistance era in Lebanon? How has sexuality been positioned in the Intifada? Furthermore, how are these positionings of sexuality constitutive of gender and nationalism? Is Palestinian nationalism male and heterosexual? Is the nation a fraternity? These are the sorts of questions that contemporary reflections on nationalism, sexuality, and gender raise.[2] Drawing on ethnographic research in Palestinian communities in Lebanon (1979–82 and the 1990s) and the West Bank (1990), this chapter proposes that the Palestinian nationalist struggle has opened spaces in which gender and sexuality could, in a very subtle way, become subject to experimentation while at the same time bringing them under the purview of the PRM.

Elsewhere I have argued that Palestinian nationalism contains a contradictory potential (Peteet 1991). It constituted a legitimate spatial arena in which a women's movement could thrive, and yet it strove to contain that movement. It could be an arena in which gender was rescripted in progressive fashion, but equally it could rescript it in traditional ways. Within this new space, nationalism, sexuality, and gender intersected in a particular field of power. Palestinian nationalism begrudgingly recognized the multiple aspects of identity and their articulation with the national but has denied them the status of either independent agency or accepted them as a basis from which to launch political organizing. It encouraged a hierarchical arrangement of forms of subjectivity, subordination, and struggle that privileged the national.

LEBANON 1968 TO 1982: SECULAR NATIONALISM[3]

The PRM operated in Lebanon (1968–82) as a political, military, and social force in the daily lives of the Palestinian community. As a self-styled political as well as social movement, the PRM's goal was to struggle for Palestinian rights to a homeland and, in the process, to mobilize the mass of people to participate. A concern with and a reformulating of cultural notions and practices of gender, generation, and class were inevitable consequences of a program of mass mobilization. The younger generation leading the movement in Lebanon engaged in a critique of traditional culture that was seen as partly responsible for the defeat in 1948. One should not underestimate the power of this critique to lend legitimacy to the sorts of social and cultural experiments the resistance movement and an atmosphere of intense and prolonged crisis jointly engendered. The notion of honor residing in women was an integral if not defining component of this critique, and the sarcastic statement "We left to save women's honor" was directed at both Palestinian culture and the older generation who experienced the events of 1948.

Gender experimentation unfolded within a national framework that both legitimized and yet constrained the potential for radical social transformation in two ways. First, it hierarchized forms of identity and political struggle. Second, it assumed control over and defined legitimate sexualities while simultaneously constructing a space in which notions of tradition were often subject to intense scrutiny. It was a space in which young women felt emboldened enough to engage in sexual experimentation. The traditional framework of intense surveillance and control of female sexuality by the family was being supplanted by a nationalist movement less concerned with a concept of honor tied to women's sexual behavior and one more caught up with national self-determination. As resistance movement cadres took over the refugee camps and set new standards of social behavior, their authority and influence were beginning to displace that of the elders, both men and women, who had traditionally been the guardians and arbiters of proper female conduct. The resistance movement may have harnessed women's sexuality and honor to the nationalist cause, yet they also weakened the control over women by assisting them in challenging their families and protecting them in the advent of violent reaction.[4]

A brief overview of Palestinian domestic service in Lebanon is one particular intersection between gender, sexuality, class, and nationalism. Until the advent of the PRM and a surge in the standard of living as a consequence of the regional economic boom associated with oil in the late 1960s and early 1970s, it was not uncommon for women from the refugee camps to work as domestic servants in Lebanese (or Palestinian) households.[5] Intimately associated with poverty and subordination, domestic work signaled sexual vulnerability.[6] Once in power (1968), the resistance called for Palestinian women to discontinue domestic service and offered alternative employment as well as welfare services, which eased the margins of poverty. Palestinian domestics signified an intertwined national and familial humiliation. The call for women to leave domestic service publicly declared the Resistance's inclusion of Palestinian female sexuality in its domain of moral authority and influence and signaled the end of refugee subordination to upper-class Lebanese and Palestinians. With the more recent resubordination of Palestinians in the wake of years of conflict, sieges, and massacres, the decimation of the Resistance movement in Lebanon, and and extreme impoverishment, some Palestinian women have again taken up domestic service in order to feed their families, a very clear indication of the economic marginalization of this community and the precipitous decline of nationalist politics in everyday life.

Militarization poses a problematic for the construction and reproduction of gender identities and their deployment during sustained conflict. Western feminist literature on militarization points to the intimate relationship between militarized masculinity and a feminized and subordinate other (Enloe 1993; Norton 1991); such a relationship may, however, not be as clear-cut in nationalist movements that are neither expansionist nor narrowly defined in terms of ethnic composition. In such instances, the assumed relationship warrants some rethinking. Thus, while militarism and sexism can be closely linked, the relationship, I would argue, is culturally and politically specific. One cannot flippantly and summarily argue that notions of Palestinian masculinity have been constructed against a female other in all aspects. The consequences of women in the military for male gender identity were hardly uniform. Few people publicly opposed it, many welcomed it, and most did not react either way. The implications of women in the military for sexuality were highly ambiguous. Military activities offered a space and a veil of legitimacy to sexual experiments engaged in by young women and men. Militancy was a critical component of Palestinian culture, but men did not have a monopoly on it by any means, and thus it is difficult to see it as an arena in which masculinity was reproduced and asserted against a female other.

Unlike women's peace movements in Europe and the United States, Palestinian women in Lebanon did not demand an end to militarization in Lebanon or the uprising in the Occupied Territories, both situations that claimed the lives of significant numbers of young people. In the aftermath of defeat and resubordination in Lebanon, while there is a critique of the leadership, it does not encompass the notion of armed militancy and the era of its heyday.[7] The critique is most virulently voiced by the mothers of the martyrs who previously made sense of the loss of their children by politicizing their reproductive activities in a sort of contract with the Resistance (Peteet 1991, 1997). The resistance was to support them financially and endow them with an honored position in the social order. With the effective abandonment by the PLO of the Palestinian community in Lebanon, both financially and politically, mothers of the martyrs direct their wrath at the resistance for breaking their implicit promises (Peteet 1995).

The daily experience of conflict and crisis should be forefronted in attempts to understand why there was no mobilized women's opposition to militarization. The mundaneness and routinization of military assault and the accompanying chronic fear fostered an atmosphere where in daily life, national identity was put into stark relief. This diluted the potential of militancy to define masculinity against a female other.[8]

Under conditions of conflict femininity can be highly ambiguous. Women were expected to be militants in a number of capacities that ranged from carrying arms to mass work (such as mobilization of the community and social work) to exemplifying steadfastness by remaining in the camps during assaults. Whether carrying the gun or engaged in mass work, women activists expanded the parameters of what constituted the feminine and thus revealed the potential for fluidity in the gendered order of society. Feminine status was most ambiguous when women carried arms, which could encode a range of meanings—from being a beloved member of the community to being a woman of dubious moral reputation. An exemplary reputation could signal a gender-neutral position. Therefore, caution should guide attempts to argue that militarization necessarily constructs a masculinity formed against a female other.

The relationship between nationalism and sexuality is put into relief if we look at the resistance's intervention in domestic, sexual, and marital affairs and the way it endowed them with political meaning and consequences. The resistance positioned itself as a source of control over women's sexuality, marriage, and reproductive potential. In Lebanon, the resistance encouraged and indeed members took on themselves the task of trying to arrange marriages between fellow members of resistance factions. The resistance identified itself as an endogamous space and defined its outer boundaries in terms of membership or affiliation. Yet the direction of endogamy was highly gendered: women members' exogamous marriages signaled a sort of national betrayal. Women who married exogamously had doubts cast on their political worthiness and trust, while men's out-marriage, which tended to be more frequent, occasioned little comment and hardly affected their political standing and credibility. The intertwining of nationalism and sexuality is also suggested by the linkages between women's moral, sexual, and political reputations. Evaluations of a young woman's moral comportment often played a prominent role in assessments of her political standing.

The resistance can often be said to have replicated family control and management. While nationalizing its meaning, it also cleared a spatial arena in which women and men were able to explore alternative sexual mores and practices. This was spatially and ideologically distinct from the family and carried within it its own forms of protection and empowerment as well. While not flaunted, sexual relations between members were hardly uncommon. The resistance could offer moral, emotional, and often financial support to women who faced parental opposition to marriages of their own choosing. Parents might have a visit from several high-ranking members to try to persuade them of the soundness of their daughters' choices and their right to make them. In cases of a total breakdown in family relationships, young women could seek sanctuary with the resistance.

THE INTIFADA: NATIONALISM, GENDER, AND THE MORAL ORDER

The direction of the relationship between nationalism, gender, and the moral order took a significant turn with the Intifada, the Palestinian uprising in the occupied West Bank and Gaza Strip that broke out in the late 1980s. Initially, women's high levels of activism, well noted in both press coverage and academic accounts, could be attributed to a ten-year period of grassroots organizing and mobilization by women's committees (Hiltermann 1991) and to the mass nature of the uprising, which mobilized broad sectors of society. However, the Intifada only temporarily and contingently diluted gendered domains, activity, and norms.

In the first year of the Intifada, committees organized on a neighborhood basis absorbed much of women's energies and activism. The committees again point to the contradictoriness of women's nationalist participation to effect change in the context and meaning of gender. While the committees were a space of activism, they were also an extension of traditional domesticity in both locale and function. By the summer of 1988, the committees were banned by the Israeli occupation authorities and had lost much of their momentum. Their demise, along with a steep drop in the spontaneity of protests, reduced mass participation in the uprising, and ideological shifts in the Palestinian political arena, signaled the beginning of women's demobilization and a serious challenge to the secular ideology that had guided women's activism and Palestinian national politics.

The political culture of the Intifada called forth and valued personal qualities of stoicism (*sumud*), austerity, and moral rectitude. Specific to the political culture of self-denial and stoicism was an absence of frivolity, bodily adornment in the form of cosmetics and fashionable dress, merriment, celebration, and popular expressive forms such as song and dance. Weddings were a primary target of an enforced austerity. The political culture of stoicism was highly gendered; women were central to its embodiment and public performance. As sites for the display of conspicuous consumption and the enactment of frivolity, their bodies were adorned and decorated in public displays of the cultural aesthetic. Thus, the culture of denial and austerity took aim at women; to enact the culture of stoicism, women were asked to show restraint in public dress and the organization of celebrations.

The Israeli ban on popular neighborhood committees, which dampened one potential avenue of women's culturally legitimate participation in politics, coincided with a significant development in the Palestinian political and social arena. The most serious challenge to the secular leadership of the national movement has come from Hamas (*Harakat al-Muqawama al-Islami-yya*), a Palestinian Islamist movement that emerged in the late 1980s. While women are not forefronted in Hamas texts, they initially played an important role as the grounds on which a secularist-Hamas tension was played out.[9] In the late 1980s in Gaza, Hamas launched a campaign to impose the veil. Hamas's charter states that before Palestine can be liberated, society has to be reformed along Islamic lines. With few resistance activities to establish its political credentials, Hamas set out to construct a moral society through a campaign of forced veiling. In this vision of a new moral order, veiled women were to embody and display the qualities not only of an Islamic morality but of a Palestinian nationalism, thoroughly imbued with Hamas's notion of an Islamic morality. With the Islamic veil reinterpreted to signify a new and more moral nationalism subsumed by Islam, the enforcement of veiling by young men was endowed with national meaning (Hammami 1990). Women resisting the veil received little support from the secular national movement whom they accused of offering the woman issue as a concession to the Islamists. They were acutely aware of the extent to which they were the initial grounds of a struggle between the secularist and the Islamist and the associated dangers. With veiling equated with nationalism and morality, women's resistance could be equated with collaboration and treachery.[10] In short, a conflated nationalism, morality, and religiosity were inscribed on women whose comportment and dress were now subject to an intense surveillance (Hammami 1994, 62). In this atmosphere of conservatism and cultural retrenchment, women produced a critique of the PRM and its inability to adequately deal with the question of gender and the Islamist movement (Kuttab 1994a; Hammami 1994).

CITIZENSHIP

Curthoys's (1993, 34) reference to the "recent reorientation within feminist debates from theorizing the state to theorizing citizenship" raises a number of issues because there is as yet no Palestinian state. So how does one theorize in such a situation? The positioning of women within the national movement, their spheres of activity, and nationalist thought on identity are points of departure for thinking about possible relations to a future state. How relations to a state are gendered is still central, but must be transfigured to encompass how one relates to a fragmented national community[11] and political entity and the possibilities these relations entail in the event of a state and citizenship.

For most women in the region, relation to the state cannot easily be conceptualized in terms of the European Enlightenment-based notion of the universal citizen. Nor is the matter as seemingly simple as stating that a woman's relationship to the state is dependent on her relationship with a male. The world of kinship and the life cycle are pivotal points of departure in any discussion of gender and citizenship in the Arab Middle East.[12] As minors, the citizenship of both males and females derives from their fathers, a relationship based on notions of blood and descent. Unlike men's citizenship, which can be transmitted to their children, a woman's citizenship ends with her: it is terminal. She can transmit it neither to her children nor to a nonnational husband. If she marries a Palestinian with a similar legal status, the issue of citizenship both for herself and for her children does not arise. If she marries someone with a different legal status, particularly with a non-Palestinian legal identity, her children are not considered to be Palestinians either in terms of belonging to the community or to a possible political entity. In short, access to citizenship and national identity is contingent on a relationship to a male, whether by descent or marriage.

In the context of post-Enlightenment Europe, McClintock has argued that "a woman's *political* relation to the nation was submerged as a *social* relation to a man through marriage" (1993, 65, emphasis in original). What needs to be inserted into this equation is descent—woman as a daughter and woman as mother. Descent and marriage are the defining categories in the assigning of citizenship. A Palestinian woman can keep her citizenship or identity card even if she marries a non-Palestinian. But a daughter or son of a Palestinian mother and a non-Palestinian father cannot claim the same sort of belonging. A child is not considered by the Palestinian community as Palestinian unless his or her father is. The patrilineal categories of blood and descent are conceptualized as somehow immutable categories of affiliation and belonging.

For the past several decades, the Palestinian resistance movement has been the arena in which women have been politically active and in which overall Palestinian political policy has taken shape. In the absence of a state and citizenship, women's positions in and relations to the resistance movement take on a certain analytical prominence. The resistance movement could be described as a unit in which kinship constituted a kind of boundary. Terms of reference and address were indicative of a kin ethos. Leaders were commonly referred to as *fathers* and addressed as *"father of* . . . [the name of his first-born son or a nom de guerre]." Young unmarried women were *sisters*. Married women were often addressed as *"mother of* . . . [either their own first sons' name, a martyr, or the female form of their husband's nom de guerre]. Mobilization often proceeded through kin structures, locales, and relations (Peteet 1991). As an endogamous unit, women who married out could have doubts cast on their political commitments and worthiness. Framing resistance in a family trope conferred on the movement and affiliation with it a sense of the "naturalness" of kinship and called forth kinlike obligations and sentiments of loyalty.

The Palestinian nation may be represented symbolically as female (the land and its products, Palestine as the lover), but so far its privileges of full and complete belonging and its transmittal are male preserves. In the Palestinian National Covenant (1964, and the 1968 amended version), identity and belonging are based on patrilineal descent. Article 5 of the 1964 document states that the Palestinian identity is "transferred from fathers to sons." In Article 6, Palestinians are defined as Arab citizens who lived in Palestine before 1947 and "every child who was born to a Palestinian father after this date." Will the new stage of autonomy open new possibilities for formulations of identity? Official discourse and popular sentiment have located women as transmitters of Palestinian cultural identity but not of formal belonging to the nation. While women are expected to reproduce the nation demographically[13] through their reproductive potential and ideologically through the maternal task of socializing youth as nationalists and in cultural heritage, in the realm of law and citizenship their role is neither recognized nor validated. Only males embody the qualities necessary to transmit formal national identity and belonging to the nation. The issue is the relationship of blood, bodily substances, and their gendering to the construction of national belonging. Women's blood and milk infuse raw human material into the national body, and their nurturing transmits the emotional sentiments of national belonging. But men's blood gives formal belonging. Men's blood not only signifies belonging through descent, but also its shedding for the sake of recovery of the land through martyrdom. Thus, there is a distinct, hierarchical, gendered binary in terms of ways of relating to the national body.

The intersection between gender, morality, and the nation is quite apparent in the issue of collaborators. During the Intifada, hundreds of collaborators were attacked or killed. Women were accused of collaboration, and some were killed, although much less often than were men. However, what is noteworthy is how these killings were framed and how knowledge of them circulated. Since 1967, Israel has attempted to recruit Palestinians as collaborators (sometimes successfully, sometimes not), often from a prison population that has included drug dealers and prostitutes. A somatized discourse intertwining the elements of treason, gender, sexuality, and morality surrounded discussions and Palestinian media presentations of the killings of women accused of collaboration. Morally illicit female behavior, which could range from prostitution to sexual relations outside the bounds of marriage, was recoded as national betrayal. Simultaneously, national betrayal by women was couched in a discourse of moral deviance. What was hard to discern in this conflation of female immorality with treason was what had actually occurred. Were prostitutes, who were not necessarily collaborators, being killed because of moral house cleaning undertaken in the name of nationalism? Is prostitution a betrayal of the nation? Were women collaborators prostitutes? What is significant for my purposes is the public presentation and understanding of these killings. Women killed as collaborators were usually deemed to have been prostitutes.

Although Hamas has not broached the issue of citizenship, it hardly takes a stretch of the imagination to envision their concurrence with the notion that a secular policy of citizenship for women is contingent on their relation to a male. Kinship terms, particularly male kinship terms, run through the Hamas Charter. Members are known as "Sons of the movement" (Ahmad 1994, 39). Critiques of Fatah contain an element of kinship as well. In an interview, Hamas leader Jamil Hamameh said, "Fatah, because of its hegemony and because of its belief that it was the mother of Palestinian people, adopted a cortical stand as it did not accept any other claims of parentage" (Ahmad 1994, 61). To describe the relationship between Hamas and the secular, nationalist organizations, the Charter deploys a gendered discourse—as "of a son toward his father and the brother toward his brother" (Article 27).

An article in the charter discussing *jihad* states that the "woman is allowed to go fight without the permission of her husband and the slave without the permission of his master" (Article 12). Thus the state of jihad suspends the usual relations of subordination and allows women, like slaves, to be active subjects in a highly circumscribed temporal zone but only in the fight against the enemies of Islam. In the battle for liberation, women play a role equal to men yet different. A woman's role revolves around her reproductive capabilities, "for she is the factory of men." The Hamas Charter also takes up the issue of women who unknowingly are coopted by the enemies of Islam.

The role of Hamas is to regain the beguiled women from these enemy organizations. Thus women have almost no subjectivity or agency. They are simply unwitting dupes or, in their loyalty to Islam, akin to slaves. They are the grounds on which enemies destroy Islamic communities, and to regain those communities women must be regained.

In the construction and maintenance of national belonging, men and women have been assigned different and somatized tasks. Men transmit formal, blood-based belonging, which confers citizenship, while women reproduce the community physically. And most significantly, women's sexuality now has implications well beyond familial ones.

CONCLUSION

The Palestinian Declaration of Independence (Palestinian National Council 1988) could well become the site for a contentious debate over the nature of national belonging, citizenship, and gender. It included an article specifying equal rights for women.[14] There are concerns that this article could be removed in order to appease the Islamists. Yet new spaces of autonomy may facilitate the proliferation of organizing poles around a plurality of subject positions that a nationalist frame had muted and subsumed. Whether the post-peace-accord period is a first step toward statehood or the consolidation of occupation and the working out of a relation of subordination and dominance, for women the legal structure of autonomy and the content of the law are key issues. What kind of a legal system will prevail in the new acutely fragmented spaces of autonomy in Gaza, Jericho, and other parts of the West Bank?

Taking into account the transitional nature of the present, how are women moving to fill the newly crafted political spaces? The old formula of ranking struggles as primary and secondary has been displaced and marginalized by the discourse of democracy and human rights in which women are locating their own struggle. The relationship between feminism and nationalism has undergone a gradual shift from the early nationalist era, when feminism was marginalized if not indeed rejected. A discourse of hierarchy of struggle located a feminist consciousness and struggle as threatening to national identity and unity and as a secondary struggle in both time and space.[15] Palestinian nationalism supposed a predetermined national identity standing above and subsuming other forms of identity and social position such as gender and class. Gender issues were to be addressed after national liberation and within the structure of a state. It was not the case that nationalism did not recognize other subject positions. It did, but it ranked them and privileged nationalism. Mouffe argues that only by de-essentializing the homogenous and coherent subject can we be "in the position to theorize the multiplicity of relations of subordination" (1992, 372). However, the nature of the linkage between the women's movement and the national movement effectively precluded serious theorization of the multiplicity of subject positions and relations of subordination and ways of politically organizing around them.

During the course of the Intifada, feminism as a way of understanding and acting on the world gained some currency as women moved beyond the national frame of ranking subject positions and setting up nationalism and feminism as competing spheres of interest, identity, and loyalty. The prior insistence on one or the other imposed a fragmentation of women's identity, forcing a multiplex, dynamic, and however self-contradictory phenomenon into bounded, unidimensional categories. A decidedly vocal Palestinian feminist-democratic discourse emerged that was critical of nationalism's tendency to collapse aspects of identity, privilege the national, and subsume alternative or dissonant interpretations of the social order.

With some form of autonomy on the horizon, however limited, Palestinian feminist discourse enmeshed itself in the discourse of democracy,[16] which avoided the dead-end trap of the either-or approach (feminism or nationalism) and located women's issues as issues of democracy and human rights. For example, women activists critiqued the Islamists' imposition of veiling by framing it within a democracy discourse rather than one of women's rights. Kuttab wrote that involuntary veiling contradicted political pluralism and a democratic spirit (1994a, 72). Feminist agendas and discourse may have been in a tense relationship with the national movement, but the women's movement seemed to be committed to a both-and relationship and to be willing to work with these tensions and contradictions. Framing demands for equality in a democratic vision does not preclude organizing around the category of women. In the General Union of Palestinian Women's Declaration of Principles, women engaged in a critique of the Palestinian nationalist movement's past where "national concerns were prioritized over social issues. Bitter experiences, however, have made Palestinian women conscious of the specificity of women's issues that are linked to the struggle for justice, democracy, equality, and development" (General Union of Palestinian Women 1994, 137).

Women activists seemed to be advocating a form of citizenship in which sexual difference and the kinship status of women were irrelevant, where women related to the state as rights-bearing individuals and not through kin-based relationships with males.[17] With the advent of a limited form of autonomy in the Occupied Territories, women activists formed "lobbies" to work on issues such as the Constitution and women's participation in the elections.[18] The Declaration also demanded "equality in civil rights, including the right to obtain, maintain, or abdicate citizenship and in a woman's right to grant it to her spouse and children" (Lipshitz 1994).

The women's movement and national movement have been rather quiet but certainly not inactive on the issue of sexuality. It was still categorized as being in the realm of the private and referred to euphemistically—by Hamas in commands to veil and be moral and in the nationalist conflation of sexual activity and national betrayal. The GUPW's Declaration referred to women's mobility and autonomy but did not mention sexuality. We need to be looking at the ways in which women may be claiming the management and control of sexuality from both Islamic and nationalist appropriations. With their demands for equality in personal status laws and intervention in violent practices, they clearly signaled that the private is public and that intervention, from a secular and democratic authority in which women are full participants, was in order.

NOTES

* An earlier version of this chapter was presented at Harvard University's Colloquia on Women and Gender in the Middle East in February 1995. I would like to acknowledge with gratitude the support provided by a Fulbright Faculty Research Grant in Islamic Civilization and the Joint Committee on the Near and Middle East of the American Council of Learned Societies and the Social Science Research Council with funds provided by the National Endowment for the Humanities.

1. The ethnographic literature on sexuality in Muslim Middle Eastern contexts is still in its infancy, and sexuality has seldom been the focus of sustained research. See Abu-Lughod (1993), Combs-Shillings (1989), Farah (1984), Geertz (1979), Mernissi (1975), *Middle East Report* (1998), and Sabbah (1984).

2. See Joseph Massad (1995), who has also been working on this topic and raises a number of similar issues.

3. The Palestinians in Lebanon were expelled or left their homes in northern Palestine during the 1948 to 1949 Arab-Israeli war and have since been denied return or compensation. The number of Palestinians residing in Lebanon is subject to much dispute. The current United Nations figure of 346,000 registered refugees is contested by figures such as 189,000 proposed by a leading Lebanese newspaper *al-Safir.*

4. Rosemary Sayigh (1994) has observed a somewhat different situation. She writes that honor killings rose during the era of resistance control in Tel al-Zaater refugee camp. My observations in Chatila and Ain-al Helwah camps were rather contrary. It may depend on which camp and which faction was in control of that camp as well as the exact historical period. She was talking about the brief period in the early 1970s when the resistance was in

control and the civil war had yet to engulf them. I did my fieldwork during the latter period.

5. Since the late 1970s, foreign domestics have all but replaced local domestic workers in the Arab world. Foreign servants (from Sri Lanka, the Philippines, Thailand, and India) are preferred over Arab women because they accept lower wages and cannot easily leave if dissatisfied.

6. The positioning of domestics as sexually vulnerable knows few cultural borders. Guatemalan activist and Nobel Peace Prize winner Rigoberto Menchu (1991) offers a poignant and harrowing account of a period in her life as a domestic servant in urban Guatemala; sexual services were often expected of young servant girls.

7. The critique is aimed at a leadership that they feel used and then abandoned them. The heavy losses of life are considered wasted since they were intended to bring a modicum of political gain.

8. A similar situation prevailed among the indigenous population resisting the Guatemalan military. Under attack as a group and responding as communities, masculinity was not forefronted in defining militancy or activism.

9. See Hammami (1990, 24–28) and Taraki (1989, 30–32).

10. See Hammami (1990, 1994) for the earliest and most solid analyses of the veiling campaign.

11. Palestinian national identity has a fundamental point of difference not always highly relevant in other nationalisms. Scattered in exile in various countries for nearly fifty years, Palestinian have developed exilic, nationalist identities highly bound up with particular places. For example, the Palestinians of Lebanon have experienced exile differently than the Palestinians of Syria or Jordan. Their place-specific experiences of exile form another layer of Palestinian identity. In addition, Palestinians live under differing legal systems, which has implications for their legal status, identity, and rights. With the recent peace accords, there is now a further category of Palestinians legally and in terms of relationship to the homeland— the Palestinians of Jericho and the Gaza Strip.

12. See Joseph (1993) on the state, gender, and kinship in Lebanon.

13. In the context of Singapore and its exhortations to educated upper-class Chinese women to produce more children, Heng and Devan suggest that nationalism was so gendered that "a sexual-

ized, separate species of nationalism . . . was being advocated for women" (1992, 348). They argue that women's relation to the nation was "uterine nationalism" (as opposed to a male phallic nationalism) (349).

14. The document states: "Governance will be based on principles of social justice, equality and nondiscrimination in the public rights of men or women, on grounds of race, religion, color or sex under the aegis of a constitution that ensures the rule of law and an independent judiciary" (Palestinian National Council 1988, 6). Included in the text was a "special tribute to that brave Palestinian woman, guardian of sustenance and life, keeper of our people's perennial flame" (8).

15. For discussions of how the politics of national liberation and national security have deployed the notion of priorities of struggle and development to deflate women's demands for equality, see Peteet (1991) and Sharoni (1993, 65–66).

16. On feminist-democratic discourse, see Kuttab (1994a). Palestinian women are not alone in this avenue. In the early 1990s, Tujan Faisal, woman member of Jordan's Parliament, concerned herself with questions of human rights and democracy. She argued that women's rights are within the domain of human rights. She has submitted amendments to the Passport and Nationality Law to permit women to obtain a passport without the consent of a male relative and to be able to transmit citizenship to their children. Faisal frames these concerns as human rights issues.

17. See note 12.

18. See comments by Rada Zeraid, director of the Palestinian Link Center, reported by Oded Lipshitz in *al-Hamishmar,* January 21, 1994; reprinted in Lipshitz (1994).

FIVE

"Gendering the Nation": Reconfiguring National and Self-identities in Azerbaijan*

Nayereh Tohidi

On August 30, 1991, the parliament of the Republic of Azerbaijan became one of the first among the Soviet republics to adopt a resolution of independence during the disintegration of the Soviet Union. That resolution revisited on the Azeris some of the serious challenges that they had faced during their first republic in 1918 to 1920. Its current post-independence problems, however, are exacerbated by the international rivalries over Azerbaijan's vast oil reserves and by the armed conflict with Armenia over the disputed territory of Nagorno Karabagh. At present, 20 percent of its territory is under occupation, which has led to the internal and external displacement of one out of every seven Azerbaijanis; 55 percent of these displaced people are women and children (Commission on Security and Cooperation in Europe 1996, 5–14). This war has proved destructive to the economy and morale of both nations.

In this milieu of inter-ethnic rivalry and war-induced dislocation, both physical and mental, women and men in Azerbaijan may be said to be going through a semi-decolonization process that impels them to reassess, reimagine, and redefine their identities, which are nationally and internationally contested. In this search for a cohesive national identity, a gendered process is inevitably underway. The place of women in this period of transition has acquired great relevance against the backdrop of intense soul-searching on questions of national identity, ethnic loyalty, Islamic resurgence, and cultural authenticity.

A striking visual corroboration of the tensions and competing definitions inherent in these reconfigurations of self- and national identities may be offered by the following example. During my first year of field work (1991 to 1992) in what was then Soviet Azerbaijan, I often encountered posters of a glamorous, blond, smiling Turkish beauty pasted on the walls of many stores, offices, and private homes. This particular image of a beauty queen from Turkey promoted certain gender-related messages. At the same time, it conveyed a certain political orientation undergirded by a growing ethnic and nationalist consciousness.

In less than four years, however, I would encounter another female image in competition with and sometimes even superseding the above. This second picture was that of a demure young woman, with a white head scarf, whose downcast eyes were focused on a set of prayer beads that she held in her hands. The caption on the picture was a *hadith* (prophetic tradition) extolling the merits of prayer. Clearly, the subject of this new image is gender roles and the national identity of Azerbaijan that is emerging out of the postindependence crucible. The juxtaposition of these two images underscore an underlying tension between the values of the post-Soviet, post-Communist "culture of exhibitionism," emphasizing physical beauty, Western fashion, and consumerism (as represented by the first poster) and the more Islamically oriented values of modesty, morality, and disdain for conspicuous materialism embodied in the second. The popularity of the two contrastive images is suggestive of, first, the complexity, diversity, and fluidity of national and cultural identity in post-Soviet Azerbaijan and, second, an assumption that in present-day Azerbaijan, as in other colonial and postcolonial contexts, gender issues intersect with those of class, nationality, ethnicity, and religion.

The rest of this chapter is concerned with what has been termed the "woman question" and a discussion of the variables that have foregrounded this question and that continue to shape a distinctive gendered discourse with broader ramifications for an overall national Azerbaijani identity. A major purpose of my analysis is to present the current dysfunction in post-independence Azerbaijan and at the same time the vast potential of this country in sharper focus in correlation to previous Soviet policies of social engineering in general and of gendered socialization in particular (whose repercussions are still strongly felt today). I highlight both the differences and continuities between the Soviet and post-Soviet eras. In addition, I take into account ethnoreligious factors to provide a more balanced perspective on the cultural, political, and gender dynamics at play today. My discussion, arranged under broad rubrics, consecutively deals with the legacy of the Soviet modernizing experience in present-day Azerbaijan; the role of Islamic conservatism and modernism; the role of the intelligentsia, the bourgeoisie, and workers, with special attention devoted to the role of women in formulating a national, Azerbaijani identity; and finally, the continuing relevance of family values and the code of honor in defining cultural authenticity. The chapter concludes with some tentative prognostications for the future based on the larger social and economic trends that are currently discernible.

THE SOVIET LEGACY OF MODERNIZATION

In principle, women's emancipation was declared to be one of the national, foundational objectives of the Soviet Union. This policy was also applied to Azerbaijan during the seventy years of Soviet rule there. The Soviet policy of gender equality was predicated on a Marxist economist perspective that women's emancipation would directly result from their participation in social and productive labor in the formal economy. Their entrance into the labor force on a large scale was consequently encouraged. Universal access to education and gainful employment along with the establishment of equal rights in social and political domains—especially egalitarian reforms in family law—did contribute to a rise in the overall socioeconomic status of women in both public and private spheres.

Education is one area in which the state socialism of the USSR deserves undeniable credit. In contrast to many Muslim societies elsewhere, Azerbaijani women are universally literate. With the introduction of a market economy in the post-Soviet era, conventional higher education is losing its appeal, and male students tend to enter private business before finishing their education. Women are thus beginning to exceed men in certain fields and in levels of educational advancement. As of 1994, 46 percent of secondary-level students are women, but they are less numerous in educational fields that lead to better-paid and higher-level employment. Although women constitute over 65 percent of primary and secondary educators, for example, they comprise only 22 percent of school administrators.

In the Soviet era, the health statistics of Azerbaijani women used to be better than those of its neighbors, Turkey and Iran, and far superior to many other Muslim states. Female life expectancy in 1989, for instance, was 74.2 years compared to 69.4 in Turkey and 67.1 in Iran. Their fertility rate was lower at 2.7 (compared to Turkey at 3.6 and Iran at 6.1), while the maternal mortality rate of 29 per 100,000 live births compared to a rate of 200 for Turkey and 250 for Iran. In reality, however, in terms of access to health and reproductive services, the picture was somewhat grim. In Azerbaijan, as throughout the Soviet Union, the state's pronatal policy, its lack of attention to family planning, and its provision of minimal access to contraceptives rendered abortion the primary means of birth control. The prevalence of abortion, usually carried out in abysmal conditions, and the frequency of induced and incomplete operations in particular remains major gender-related health issues neglected by Soviet and post-Soviet statesmen alike (Tohidi 1991, 1994).

Compared to most other Muslim societies, the massive integration of women into the formal economy of Azerbaijan has been identified as another success story of Soviet state socialism. Yet a female participation rate of 44 percent conceals a different story when subjected to gender-sensitive evaluation. Women's heaviest participation remains in agriculture and manual farm labor (52 percent in 1989 and 49 percent in 1993). On collective farms, moreover, women's labor is concentrated in nonmechanized areas since less than 10 percent are appropriately skilled. Only 1.3 percent hold managerial or administrative positions. Urban industrial women workers, 45 percent of the total, are also concentrated in the lower-paid, lower-ranked, and lower-skilled categories. Even officially conducted surveys report that only half of employed women are satisfied with their work (Tohidi 1991, 1994).

With the advent of *perestroika* and *glasnost* in the Soviet Union, it became an open secret that despite protective labor legislation a widespread pattern of gender discrimination in favor of men existed. Many women were laboring under hazardous working conditions. The situation has been worse in the environmentally devastated areas of Central Asia and in some urban industrial regions of Azerbaijan such as Sumgait and Baku. According to the laws of the Soviet state, male-female wage differentials should not have existed, but as a consequence of horizontal and vertical occupational segregation by sex, women's average earnings throughout the USSR have been estimated at about 30 percent lower than those of males (Lapidus 1982).

The situation was not much better in the realm of Azerbaijani politics. Based on the quota system, a proportional presence of women at local, regional, and national levels of formal politics was maintained in all three branches of government. In 1989, 39 percent of deputies in the Supreme Soviet of Azerbaijan were women, and until 1991 the parliament's speaker was a woman, yet their mere representation in the Soviets failed to translate into women's empowerment. Not only were female and male deputies usually selected by the ruling Communist Party, but women deputies held much less prominent positions than male deputies, suffered a higher rate of turnover, and were less likely to be Party members (Buckley 1987, 229–37).

The course of socioeconomic progress for women was uneven as Soviet state policy and gender strategy changed from a strict ideological commitment to Marxist-style gender egalitarianism to a later more pragmatic attitude to women's rights based on economic productivity. With little regard for sustainable human development, the Soviet state pursued, especially under Stalin, a strategy of modernization based on heavy and military industrial growth. This strategy called on women to mobilize and take an active part in social production. But in the sphere of reproduction, the need for quality child care, labor-saving household appliances, food-cycle technology, and daily consumer goods, for example, did not constitute priorities for the state.

Personal status law was reformed to be consonant, at least in theory, with gender egalitarian aims. However, the state paid only lip service to effecting fundamental changes in gender roles, the patriarchal structure of the family, and the gender-based division of labor in domestic and reproductive domains. In their daily lives, women remained heavily dependent on their male kin (*arkha*),[1] who continued to have a large say in their conduct.

During the post-Soviet transitional period, however, women's overall status has declined as women and children are hurt the hardest. A small segment of women as well as men have taken advantage of the new market economy by starting private enterprises and family-run businesses and benefited considerably, being among the few able to afford the abundant consumer goods and home appliances. But for the impoverished majority, merchandise in the new colorful shops and fully stocked department stores and meals in the restaurants of major cities like Baku are well beyond their means. There is progressive deterioration in the health-care system. A recent tendency toward privatization of higher education and a decline in the quality of public schools may result in unprecedented rates of illiteracy and school dropouts, especially among the refugees and internally displaced people.

With regard to political participation, following electoral reform and the elimination of the quota system during perestroika in 1989, women's presence in formal politics actually declined drastically, falling in Azerbaijan to 4.8 percent, then recovering to 6 percent in 1992 and 13 percent in the 1995 election. Any real change in women's political roles, however, cannot be gauged from such quantitative shifts in state-oriented "high politics." In post-independence Azerbaijan, a new civil society is emerging with an increasing number of informal and nongovernmental organizations (NGOs) for women, and women are active at the informal level as well. As of 1997, eighteen women's organizations were officially registered. Given the urgency of the war-stricken situation and the priority of basic needs for the majority of people, most of these new women's NGOs started functioning as apolitical charity groups and support networks. Yet a number of these women's groups have politically partisan natures and in reality function as the women's wings of certain political parties. For example, the Women's Council of the New Azerbaijan Party represents the dominant party of President Aliev, and the Association in Defense of Women's Rights represents the Popular Front of Azerbaijan, an opposition group. A few of these women's groups, however, have maintained a rather independent position, and through their praxis some of them are gradually evolving into semi-feminist-oriented activists advocating women's rights and gender-conscious democratization and development. For instance, the Center for Human Rights in Azerbaijan has a women's group that periodically publishes a very useful Information Bulletin on women's status. The Women and Development Center also stands out as a most active and internationally engaged group.[2]

THE INTERPLAY OF ISLAM AND STATE SOCIALISM

The majority of Azeri Turks (about 83 percent of the total population) are Shi'i Muslims (the Shi'a and the Sunna, also referred to as *Sunnis* in English usage, are the two main denominations of Islam). Some Soviet scholars (for example, Poliakov 1992) maintain that Islam or Islamic traditionalism is responsible for the continuity in Azerbaijan of certain cultural ideals, gender-related ethos, and specific feminine behavioral traits shared with those in Muslim traditional communities elsewhere despite two centuries of Russian influence. I propose that this argument is rather specious. Neither Islamic determinism (that is, an essentialist approach to Islam still popular among some Orientalists) nor the economic reductionism informing the gender-based ideology of Marxist-Leninists and the advocates of developmentalism adequately takes into account the diversity of the Azerbaijani context and the interplay of religion with other social factors. Islam is implicated in the construction of a particular sociocultural ethos to the extent that it is in active engagement with indigenous customs, state ideologies, socioeconomic policies of particular governments, and quasi-colonial— an inter-ethnic dynamics that allows for considerable diversity in women's situations in the Muslim world. This argument in relation to Azerbaijan is elaborated on in the following discussion.

A short history of the uneasy relationship between Muslim functionaries and the Soviet state is in order here. At the time of the Russian conquest of Azerbaijan and other Muslim communities, the ulema (religious scholars) and the *mullahs* (broadly, clerics) were seen as the most likely leaders of opposition to Russian rule. In order to control and coopt the ulema, the tsarist regime created the Sunni and Shi'i Religious Boards under state control. Each board had a director (called *mufti* for the Sunnis and *shaykh al-Islam* for the Shi'a) appointed by the government.

Traditionally, mullahs have played important roles in Muslim society as prayer leaders, administrators, judges (*qadis*), and scholars. The Russians, however, removed the qadis from the realm of civil and criminal law; by the twentieth century, their functions had become reduced to the recording of births, deaths, and marriages. During Bolshevik rule, civil organizations carried out registration of marriages. But even before then, Russians had succeeded in curtailing the power or coopting the support of the ulema and the mullahs either by military force or administrative cooperation and by granting them rank and privilege: land, titles, and tax exemptions, for example (Alstadt 1992, 57–62).

Hence, a century of Russian rule in Azerbaijan had considerably undermined Islam long before the beginning of Bolshevik de-Islamization. This, along with a higher level of industrialization and modernization, may in part explain why secular nationalism rather than religion has played a larger role in opposing the Soviet regime in the country. It is important to distinguish between "official Islam" and "unofficial Islam" here and to note how each operated in the daily lives of Muslim women and men in both the tsarist Russian and Soviet contexts. Tension and distrust between many Azeris and the religious authorities (representing "official Islam") have long been apparent due to the latter's prostate position, even extending to confrontations with nationalists and democrats.

We cannot, however, claim that there has been a single and predictable Islamic response to the phenomenon of Western modernization whether in the Middle East, in the Russian empire, or in the Soviet Union. In Azerbaijan, the reactionaries and traditionalists, on the one hand, invoked Islam as the most effective and strongest means to resist European-style secular modernization, including the emancipation of women. But on the other hand, several ardent supporters of the emancipation of women emerged from within the ranks of Muslim reformers upholding a modernist and egalitarian approach to Islam, known as the Jadid movement. For most reformers, including secular nationalists, social democrats, and Muslim modernists (Jadidists),[3] the major issues concerning women were their seclusion, illiteracy, the veil, and polygyny. The emancipation of women was for them a prerequisite for the revival of Muslim civilization and for economic, social, and cultural development in Azerbaijan. The Jadidists, as Muslims, sought reform without detaching themselves from their people. After all, Muslims have long accepted the legitimacy of a periodic "renewal" (*tajdid*) of the community. But what that renewal means and should entail, particularly with regard to gender roles, is open to varying interpretations.

The Bolshevik takeover after the October Revolution of 1917 further intensified pressures on Islam. Most mosques and other religious institutions were closed. Many Muslim nationalists and Jadidists who made up the core of the native elite in Azerbaijan eventually joined the Russian Communists, albeit retaining their own interpretation of Marxism and their own agenda for a socialist Azerbaijan within a "Muslim national communist" framework. This agenda was above all a blueprint for national liberation, which, given the mood of the country, was an eminently pragmatic response to the existing political situation. The Baku oil workers were of a rebellious turn of mind, nationalist fervor was on the rise, and the Azeri elite were advocating modernization at the time of the Bolshevik revolution. The time was indeed ripe for a "Muslim national communism" that would synthesize the purely Russian Marxism of a secular communism with Islamic ethics.

Historically, there has been little animosity between Azeri secular modernist intellectuals and religious functionaries. The former on occasion were critical of the mullahs and derided practices such as veiling and polygyny as incompatible with the true spirit of Islam, but they refrained from denouncing Islam in its totality. To Muslim Jadids, many of the socialist ideas could be easily incorporated into their own reformist agenda. They were of the opinion that "Islamic culture or way of life and Marxism are not by definition incompatible ideologies. On the contrary, they could coexist and even complement one another" (Bennigsen and Wimbush 1979, xx).

Such a "syncretistic" approach inevitably ushered in certain lifestyle paradoxes and attitudinal conflicts, creating a bifurcated cultural identity for many people and turning them into "Soviets in public, Muslim Azeris in private" (Tohidi 1996, 111–23). This bifurcation or duality manifested itself most clearly in the realm of gender ideology, as reflected in the words of Betura Mamedova, an Azeri female professor of English in Baku: "Socialism has affected our life externally; our character and psychology, however, have remained basically unchanged."[4] Another Azeri woman, Rena Ibrahimbekova, a prominent psychologist and director of the Center for Gifted Children in Baku, confirmed this observation while expressing a deep concern about many Azeri women's

> tendency to avoid practicing their officially constituted equal rights. . . . I am worried that in the post-Soviet era, we may go back to our *adat va an'aneh* [traditions] at the official level as well as in practice, hence eventually resolving the present duality in favor of its premodern regressive side.[5]

REFORMIST INITIATIVES:
THE ROLE OF THE INTELLIGENTSIA,
THE BOURGEOISIE, AND THE WORKERS

As a people, the Azeri Turks have been divided for the last two centuries between Iran and the Russian empire and its successor, the Soviet Union. With the exploitation of the Baku oilfields and consequent modernization, Azeri intellectuals were influenced by nation-state formations in Europe and revolutionary movements in Russia, Iran, and Turkey in the early twentieth century. Thus, with the collapse of tsarist Russia, the first independent People's Republic of Azerbaijan emerged in 1918. In 1920, however, the

Bolsheviks, supported by the Russian Red Army, conquered the republic and eventually renamed it as the Soviet Republic of Azerbaijan, one of the fifteen republics of the USSR.[6]

During this period of great social change and ideological fervor, Azeri intellectuals—journalists, writers, educators, and social reformers—were often outspoken in their criticism of the social and political ills that beset their society. Among the social reformers were Mirza-Jalil Mammed-Qulizadeh (1866–1932) and his wife, Hamideh Javanshir (1873–1955),[7] who used their very influential and popular journal *Molla Nasreddin* (1906–30) to criticize the establishment, corrupt bureaucrats, and religious conservatives. Through powerful satire and cartoons, the journal played a crucial role in raising women's issues, denouncing forced veiling and seclusion, polygyny, wife battering, violence, and other oppressive practices against women.[8]

In the early years of its publication, depictions of Muslim women were made almost exclusively by male writers. As a consequence, the journal reflected male-oriented Jadid (modernist) approach to the issue of Muslim women's emancipation. As the critical reading of scholars like Evan Siegel (1995, 143–53) puts it in retrospect, the journal's invidious and patronizing comparisons between the "ignorant, passive and victimized" Muslim women and the "sophisticated, active and strong" Armenian and Russian women reflected a variant of the then common male-oriented utilitarian and Eurocentric modernist arguments in support of women's emancipation. This pattern began to change, however, due to a probable direct or indirect feminist and indigenous influence of women like Hamideh Javanshir, mentioned above. Through satirical editorials and letters to the editor written under female pseudonyms, Muslim women were depicted in a more active and at times heroic images who aspired for change and emancipation. In a number of such letters, the conduct of Muslim men and the patriarchal social order were denounced as the main culprits; one letter stated that even "if the Shari'a allows us women to appear bareheaded [unveiled], men don't allow this" (Siegel 1995, 147).

Following these initiatives, the first journal for and by women published in Azeri Turkic was founded by an Azeri woman, Khadija Alibeyova (1884–1961), and her husband in Baku in 1911 as a bimonthly and later as a weekly. Its purpose was to inform women about their rights. While carefully avoiding direct criticism of Islamic authorities, *Ishiq* (Light) quoted and emphasized certain egalitarian passages from the Qur'an and hadith in support of women's education. Although influential and circulating throughout the region, it lasted only a year due to pressures from conservative clerics and lack of financial support.

While *Ishiq* promoted women's education, the first school for Muslim girls had already been founded in 1905 by Haji Zeynolabedin Tagiyev, an Azeri oil millionaire and philanthropist. People like Tagiyev represented the new industrial bourgeoisie, which played an important role in the modernization of Azeri society. Some promoters of women's education pointed to the spread of education among European women and the Muslims of the Volga Tatars as worthy of emulation while advocating a progressive and egalitarian interpretation of the Qur'an (Rorlich 1986b).

Russian colonizers, as in many other colonial contexts, were unconcerned about real emancipation of and improvement in women's status. For instance, Azeris had to petition the city council of the tsarist regime in Baku for money to begin a pedagogical course for Muslim girls at the school for Russian girls. The Tagiyev school, the only existing school for non-Russian Muslim girls, was overcrowded and expensive. Azeri representatives on the city council had to campaign vigorously for the allocation of monies to fund another girls' school for Azeris (Alstadt 1992, 64).

Azeri bourgeois men and their wives were not the only ones campaigning for reform, modernization, and nation building in Azerbaijan. Several women and men from the working class mobilized especially the women for a more revolutionary agenda. As the social-democratic and Marxist movements grew throughout the Russian empire, Azerbaijani workers in the oil industry rallied around a group called *Himmat* (Endeavor).[9] A small, yet active number of Muslim, Christian, and Jewish women from the Tagiyev textile factory and other industries played a leading role in forming a women's wing of *Himmat*. As early as 1904 and 1905, they raised specific demands for "maternity leave for women, time on the job for nursing unweaned children, and medical care for all workers" (Altstadt 1992, 64; Mamedov 1986, 4).

Azerbaijani female and male intellectuals today take pride in their short-lived independent republic of 1918 to 1920, which was formed at the time of the collapse of the Russian empire, characterizing it as "the first democratic republic in the entire Muslim world that provided universal suffrage guaranteeing all citizens full civil and political rights regardless of their nationality, religion, social position, and sex" (Nasibzadeh 1990, 4; cited in Swietochowski 1985, 129). In short, inspiring existence also provided the impetus for later Azeri nationalism.

WOMEN'S CLUBS AND POLITICAL ACTIVISM

Most studies of the role of the Soviet state relating to the "woman question" have been either at an all-Union level or focused on Russian women. One exception to this is the extensive research carried out by Gregory Massell (1974) on the policies of the Communist Party (CP) and the Soviet state toward Central Asian Muslim women. His analysis also applies to Azerbaijan in the Caucasus to some degree, although women's roles and response to Soviet policies have been understandably different in the more urbanized and industrialized context of that republic.

According to Massell, Muslim women were effectively "used" as important allies of Communist elites. They were, assumed the Soviet authorities, the structural flaw in the traditional pre-Soviet order. By considering Muslim women as a potentially "subversive stratum susceptible to militant appeal—in effect, a surrogate proletariat," the Communists generated particularly intense conflicts within Azerbaijani society, providing leverage for its disintegration and subsequent Soviet reconstruction (Massell 1974, xxiii). Such a perception, however, leaves very little room for women's own agency. Many liberal Western scholars and orthodox Marxists routinely portray Muslim women as essentially passive victims. According to my perception of Muslim women's role in the former Soviet Union (FSU), however, women were more than mere pawns and victims of male oppression and more than passive followers of the state and the Communist Party's manipulations. In the specific cases of Tatar and Azerbaijani women—who had backgrounds in the Jadid or Muslim modernist movement and in social-democratic movements as well as in the small yet active educated women's circles—one may argue that some women did at times use the Communists' support for equality and the state's legal protection to fight patriarchy and religious reaction while promoting their own agenda. The story of Almaz by the popular Azerbaijani playwright, Ja'far Jabbarli, though fictional, illuminates the small number of women activists in the 1920s who pursued feminist ideals initially independent of CP influence.[10]

A careful analysis of the Zhenotdel, the women's organ of the CP, both in its Russian and Muslim Azerbaijani contexts, reveals a continuous tension between women members and the male Party leaders. Zhenotdel's brief but stormy existence played a crucial role in the mobilization, socialization, and emancipation of Soviet women in general and Muslim women in particular. It had a mixture of native, local, and Russian leadership in each republic. Besides press organs and publications aimed at literate women, local branches in Azerbaijan as elsewhere used sewing circles, conferences, women's clubs, and even public bath houses for "consciousness raising" and mobilization of women.

The crucial role that local organs and indigenous mechanisms played in such mobilization attests to the native Azeri women's own enthusiastic involvement. Unlike the Party organs dominated by Russian Communists, the women's clubs were almost exclusively staffed by Azerbaijani women. One such club exemplifying Azeri women's agency in this period was the Ali Bayramov Club in Baku, whose press organ, *Sharq Qadini* (Women of the East), played an important role in the political education of women in Azerbaijan. The core cadres of both the club and the journal were Muslim Azerbaijani women. Many Azeris perceived the journal and activities of the club as consonant with their own demands and aspirations, an extension of the Jadid goals, rather than a set of alien or imported colonial ideas.

Historically, the Ali Bayramov Women's Club, which predated Soviet rule, played an enormous role in the social integration of Azerbaijani women. With the spread of revolutionary changes in the Russian empire and increasing participation of both Azeri and Russian women, the club's activities intensified. In 1920, through its seventeen chapters, the club waged a successful campaign for women's literacy and vocational training. It established a garment workshop with a staff of seven women that ultimately grew into a huge textile factory that is still operating in contemporary Baku (Rorlich 1986a, 221–39).

In short, this period in the cultural history of Azerbaijan is distinguished by the emergence of a sense of national identity, modernist and reformist Islamic and secular elites, discourses on the "woman question," and a range of activities in support of women's emancipation.

By 1923, many women had discarded their veils. As part of an anti-veil campaign, certain activists removed their veils at the city theater during a popular play. Yet many others, including some activists of the women's clubs, felt compelled or chose to retain some form of veiling. Instead of the enveloping *charshab,* a compromise version in the form of a headscarf or *kalagaye,* originally part of an Azeri folk costume, was adopted.

The campaign for women's rights and for the abolition of veiling and seclusion occasionally met with resistance from conservative mullahs and other traditionalist segments of society. The women's movement was perceived as having been instigated by the Soviet communists, who were merely continuing the policy of Russification started under tsarist imperialist rule. Increased statist intervention in people's lives and, in fact, the imposition of Sovietization intensified people's resentment if not actual resistance to the idea of women's emancipation. Many Azeris even today express ambivalence toward the women's movement. I noted, for instance, mixed feelings among some Azeri women and especially men toward the prominent statue in a Baku public square of the "Azerbaijan Azad Qadini" (Free Woman of Azerbaijan) erected in 1950 by a popular Azeri artist. Symbolizing women's freedom from the veil, it is a huge Soviet-style figure of a woman in a dramatic unveiling gesture.[11] For some Azeris, notably the more religio-nationalist ones, it signifies the "dishonoring of Azeri Muslims by infidel Russian Communists, a symbol of shame."[12] Among most contemporary male and female elites, even the nationalist ones, the women pioneers of liberation during the early years of Soviet rule are remembered, however, with keen respect. They are praised for their contribution to women's enhanced roles and massive integration into the processes of social modernization and economic development (Abdollazadeh 1994, 3; Ganjeli 1994; Suleymanova 1995).

THE PRIVATE SPHERE: UPHOLDING FAMILY VALUES AND HONOR

The ritualization of belief is frequently a common response on the part of believers who have publicly had to come to terms with an antireligious order imposed by a dominant foreign force. Religion becomes essentially privatized and "domesticated," expressed through certain customs and rituals that are not overly associated with religion but that come to acquire religious flavor and significance. The privatization of religion and other institutions of social life hinges on the compartmentalization of public and private behavior, the latter being more authentic expressions of one's nature and identity.[13]

Islam, like any other major religion, is a multidimensional institution with more than a core of directly spiritual beliefs and rites. It is a complex aggregate of cultural, psychological, and social traditions, attitudes, and customs governing a way of life (Atkin 1989, 13). One can argue, therefore, that the Soviet anti-religious campaigns might have succeeded in minimizing its intellectual and ideological dimensions, but the experiential, consequential, and a certain level of the ritual dimensions of Islam, understood in a broad sense as the Muslim mode of life, have kept their vitality.[14]

Among the attitudes and practices that may be seen as constituting Islamic mores and rituals are the ones specifically associated with gender roles, sexuality, and life cycles; these continued to maintain their relevance in Soviet Azerbaijan. Those related to male circumcision, sex-segregated mourning ceremonies, and means of testifying to a bride's virginity on her wedding night (*yengeh*), for example, might actually have been local customs preceding or superseding Islam but are popularly viewed as Islamic. In fact, in a recent public lecture, Shaykh al-Islam Al-lah-Shokur Pashazadeh, head of the Islamic Directorate of Transcaucasia and the highest religious authority in Azerbaijan, denounced the custom of *yengeh* as non-Islamic and detrimental to marriage and the family.[15]

Unlike gender discourse in many contemporary Muslim countries, gender discourse in the Azerbaijan independence movement has not gained a doctrinal or ideological Islamist ("fundamentalist") tone. So far, ethnicity, language, regionalism, and Islam—in its cultural, spiritual, and ritual forms—have served as the primary sources of national identity in the new republic. Nevertheless, in some respects, the end result for women has been rather similar to the situation in those nations affected by Islamism. By turning the private or domestic domain into a bastion of resistance, gender roles and intra-family dynamics have retained strong traditional and religious characteristics. In effect, women are expected to be paragons of morality and the primary observers of religious rituals.[16]

Appearing in public without a male or an elder female chaperon, wearing pants, smoking or drinking in public, and driving cars are instances of behaviors widely viewed as unacceptable for an authentic Azeri woman, especially in regions outside Baku. Ethnic loyalty and the observance of endogamy by women (but not necessarily by men),[17] the codes of honor (*namus*), chastity, shame, prudery, and virginity before marriage are among the ethno-religious customs prescribed as essential female attributes. Namus, in fact, is an important shibboleth evoked in the shaping of public and private comportment of both men and women. One of the most important connotations of this multi-dimensional and gendered term is women's chastity, even though it is usually used in reference to men, because in both Shi'i Iran and Shi'i Azerbaijan, the responsibility for the protection of namus falls primarily on the men. A woman's misbehavior, especially sexual misbehavior, brings shame and dishonor (*namus-sislig*) not only to her but even more so to her male "protectors" (arkha)—father, brothers, and husband. The findings of my studies in Azerbaijan attest to the continuing strength of the code of namus among Azeris. In my sample, male respondents ranked namus more frequently than females as the most important theme in their early socialization.

Another significant dimension of namus pertains to the homeland and its protection from encroachment. Homeland itself is a gendered concept (Yuval-Davis and Anthias 1989; Kandiyoti 1991b; Sharoni 1993; Peterson 1996). In Azerbaijan, as in many other cultures, homeland is a feminine metaphor, denoted as the motherland (*ana vatan*) whose honor is to be protected and defended by all means. Failure in defending and protecting one's homeland is equivalent to failure in protecting one's female kin-folk and therefore one's namus. This becomes more pronounced in the face of the Karabakh conflict and the occupation of Azerbaijan's territory by armed Armenians. As indicated in the words of Zamfira Verdiyeva, chair of the Women's Association of the Azerbaijan Republic, "homeland becomes more clearly associated with honor" (namus). She says, "Our homeland is our namus. We may give up everything, our wealth, houses, foods, clothings, and even our lives, but not our land."[18]

Compared to Russia and the northern regions of the FSU, the family has remained the most conservative and stable institution in Azerbaijan. Its divorce rate is one of the world's lowest, even though it has risen slightly in recent years to less than 15 percent in 1990.[19] Although the nuclear family is the most common family type, particularly in urban areas, people still rely heavily on extended family norms and networks. Men and women remain deeply family oriented, and women are usually identified by their kin, male kin in particular. Children are the core of people's lives; baby girls are generally welcomed, though with less joy than boys. Mothers have to start collecting dowry materials for a girl at infancy, since marriage remains the essential rite in the lives of Azerbaijanis. Ceremonies associated with marriage are the most joyous yet the most costly and demanding rituals of the life cycle. In addition to an engagement party, two lavish wedding ceremonies (*qiz toyi* for the bride and *oghlan toyi* for the groom) take place. In many regions of the country, traditional customs like *bashlig* (the groom's payment to parents for nurturing the bride), *mahir* (an agreed sum to be paid to women in case of divorce), and *jahaz* (the dowry of household appliances and furniture provided by the bride's parents) are strictly observed.[20]

Divorced women, but even more never-married single women, suffer a social stigma, since mothering is regarded as the primary role of women and their most important source of gratification. Laws protecting mothers—for example, those that make provisions for paid pregnancy and maternity leaves for working mothers—continue to be kept on the books, though they are increasingly ignored in the new market economy. The egalitarian civil family law that replaced the Shari'a when the Soviet state was consolidated has remained in force in post-Soviet Azerbaijan, and it protects women's rights relating to marriage, divorce, and child custody. Enforcement of such laws, however, is becoming ever more difficult in the current transitional society.

As among other nationalities in the Caucasus, like Christian Armenians and Georgians, the primary loyalty of Muslim Azerbaijanis is still centered on kinship groups and intimate friends. This traditional family and kinship system entails paradoxical implications for male and particularly female members.[21] On the one hand, it usually offers solidarity and trust. It can provide economic, political, emotional, and physical support during difficult circumstances, such as during the recent warfare. On the other hand, it operates as a repressive device, limiting women's independence, individuality, and personal growth. The persistence of the extended family structure has reinforced patriarchal norms. Some scholars have attributed the prevalence of the underground economy and corrupt political practices in the Caucasus to this traditional heavy reliance on close familial ties as well.[22] Powerful obligations to one's relatives, clan, and region, especially on the part of women, may have delayed the constitution of citizenship and a national civic identity. This in turn may have contributed to the duality and dissociation in Azerbaijan's modernization in general and women's emancipation in particular. One may even argue that kinship networks have been intentionally organized to resist the state and to function as a buffer against politico-economic pressures. Rather than public versus private binaries, some important parts of public or political life have actually been constructed by family and kin-related private, informal networks.[23]

Political factors aside, certain economic constraints have obviously contributed to the persistence of the traditional extended family structure. As in Soviet Russia, but even more so in the Muslim peripheries of the FSU, the state's productionist emphasis and the reduction of the woman question to its economic base made women's massive entrance into the labor force a priority without corresponding social and economic provisions for transforming the family structure and gender roles. The backwardness in food-cycle technology, the housing shortage that forced young couples to live for years with parents, and the insufficiency of child-care facilities made restructuring of the patriarchal and extended family infeasible. Azerbaijan has especially suffered in this regard; for example, its child-care and preschool education attendance has been one of the poorest in the FSU (16 to 18 percent versus 71 percent in Russia).

Betura Mamedova, mentioned above, speaks for many when she expresses the following sentiments about the significance of the family for the Azeri woman and for the preservation of "authentic" cultural values that promote national cohesion:

> We women are tenaciously clinging to our family, and instead of getting weary of oceans of duties, we are energized by them. We are thought to be the backbone of the family and a buffer when things go wrong spiritually. We enjoy playing this role because this is our life, and it is due to this family tenacity that Azeri people never forget their language, their culture and religion. One Azeri poet called it "blood memory" (*qan yaddashti*).[24]

As one can infer from Betura's comment, women are seen again as the guardians of the nation who have succeeded in playing this role thanks to "family tenacity." Her statement also implies that in a colonial or quasi-colonial inter-ethnic situation, the family would function as the bastion of resistance against assimilation (here Russification). The family, thus, is in effect the *dar al-Islam* (the abode of Islam) to be protected from the penetration of the dominant "other." As happened in Algeria, Egypt, and Iran during their confrontations with colonial domination or foreign intrusion, women's liberation in Azerbaijan has been held hostage to the prescribed roles of women as the primary repositories of tradition, national, and ethnic identities. Certain traditional images, customs, and stereotypes of femininity dubbed as *asil* (authentic) and *ismatli* (chaste) are promoted as markers of Azeri ethnic identity, demarcating its boundaries from those of Russian ethnicity. The assignment of the role of culture bearers to women at a time of insecure political and cultural identity has complicated the process of gender role transformations and impeded progress toward gender egalitarianism.

PROGNOSTICATIONS FOR THE FUTURE

Since the complete takeover of the country by tsarist Russians in the early nineteenth century, the dynamics of modernity and traditionalism pertaining to gender roles as well as other aspects of social life have taken place in a contested realm of Muslim Azeri "us" and non-Muslim Russian/Soviet "them." In this binary system, Azeri women serve as both objects and subjects of nation building and identity politics. This has been true under the colonial rule of tsarist Russia and within the quasi-colonial context of the Soviet regime, as well as during the recent post-Soviet nationalist and independent republic. Women, after all, were primarily associated with the family and religion, two institutions that represented the last bulwark against complete assimilation into a Russianized or Sovietized society. Through the preservation of ethnic traditions (adat va an'aneh) and the Islamic faith, women have become the main agents for sustaining these cultural boundaries. To preserve these lines of demarcation between Azeri society and the colonizing Soviet polity, women remained the main objects of control. Although relegated to the margins of the formal polity, women did play a central role in the informal politics of identity by fostering ethno-cultural and other intangible variables.

Women have not, however, simply passively succumbed to the roles prescribed for them in the post-Soviet Azerbaijani society. Although they do not appear to shun such roles, they are also actively engaged in expanding, reconfiguring, and at times even subverting their image as the signifiers of Azeri identity and moral exemplars of the nation. This is by no means an easy task; this transitional period presents perhaps the most formidable challenges ever for them. Once relatively protected by the Soviet state, women now face the loss of its support together with an inevitably higher economic pressure as they constitute the majority of the newly unemployed in an ever more insecure and violent social atmosphere. Consequently, the need for male "protection" within the context of marriage has intensified the familial and kinship networks. So far, the process of marketization and "democratization" has not only failed to remove the disadvantages for women under the Soviet system; it has actually intensified gender asymmetry. Simultaneously, prior female advantages have been jeopardized due to the disruption of the social safety net, soaring prices, rising unemployment, increasingly open sex discrimination, violence, prostitution, crime, and, above all, the economic and moral devastation created by the war. Such a context may be fertile ground for the revival of extremist ideologies that may declare a divinely or biologically determined patriarchal control over women and a return to strictly gender-based social divisions as a presumed prerequisite for national and spiritual salvation.

However, I find cause for optimism, albeit cautious, in the signs of multiplicity and diversity in almost all spheres of life at the present time that stand in sharp contrast to the Soviet totalitarian past. Despite the current economic vicissitudes, the rich human and natural resources of Azerbaijan hold out substantial possibilities for Azeri women and for the amelioration of their overall social status in the long term. There is fluidity in the way Islamic principles are being socially and politically construed; there is also considerable negotiation and interchange in defining the parameters of national, cultural, and gender identities. The general consciousness of potentially being in charge of their destinies, for both women and men, in a society that is very much in flux and thus amenable to change is at once exhilarating and daunting. Not to rise to this challenge would be a sorely missed opportunity.

NOTES

* This is a substantially revised version of my recent article (Tohidi 1998) in Bodman and Tohidi (1998). I would like to express my

gratitude to the Fulbright Foundation and IREX for supporting the early years of my field work in Azerbaijan and to my departments at the Academy of Sciences of Azerbaijan, the Harvard Divinity School, the Hoover Institution at Stanford, and the UCLA Center for Near Eastern Studies. I am also grateful to the numerous Azerbaijani women and men, particularly my research assistants Elchin Mamedov and Afaq Samadzade, whose generous cooperation has facilitated this research. I would also like to acknowledge the editorial assistance of Asma Afsaruddin in the reorganization and revision of this chapter.

1. The word *arkha* literally means "back," implying kin, primarily male kin, to lean on.
2. The Women and Development Center is directed by a prominent and seasoned activist, Elmira Suleymanova, who is also a professor of chemistry at Baku State University. The Center's ideology manifests an interesting blend of the old Soviet Marxist orientation and the new post-Soviet nationalist rhetoric. I will be offering detailed information on women's groups in Azerbaijan in my book in progress on this topic.
3. *Jadid,* which means "new" in Arabic, was borrowed into Persian and the Turkic languages. *Jadidism,* derived from *usul-i jadid* (new methods), aimed at improving the curricula of the *maktab* (school) and their overall approach to teaching. In opposition to the conservative educators and ulema, known as *qadimists* (old-fashioned thinkers; from Ar. *qadim,* old), jadidism grew into a nationalist modernist interpretation of Islam by the endeavors of the Crimean Tatar journalist Ismail Gasprinski. See Swietochowski (1985, 30–35).
4. Cited from her commentary on "Women in Azerbaijan" written at my request, December 1995.
5. Author's interview in Baku, February 8, 1995.
6. The name of Azerbaijan is a continual point of contention. In this chapter, *Azerbaijani* or *Azerbaijanian* are used in reference to citizens of the Soviet and post-Soviet republic of Azerbaijan encompassing different ethnic groups within this territory. *Azeri,* however, is used only in reference to the majority indigenous ethnic group (Turkic and Muslim) from whom the Republic of

Azerbaijan derives its name. Rather than south or north Azerbaijan as designated by Soviet Azeris, average Azeris in Iran used to distinguish their brethren in Russia and the FSU as the ones living on "the other side" (*otayli*)—that is, the other side of the Aras River that makes up the natural border between the two parts of Azerbaijan.

7. See my book in progress on Hamideh Javanshir (in Farsi), containing her fascinating personal memoirs and observations on Caucasia in the early twentieth century.

8. The journal was named after the legendary Molla Nasreddin (also called Nasreddin Hoja), a figure who appears in clever and didactic stories throughout the Middle East and Central Asia. The journal spanned borders, and its articles were translated from Azeri-Turkic into many other languages. It was most influential in Iran, Turkey, Georgia, and Central Asia.

9. For further discussion and documentation on early social-democratic and workers movements in Baku, especially the role of immigrant workers coming from Iran, see Chaqueri (1985).

10. Almaz was a young radical and devoted teacher in a small Azerbaijani village who organized women around a literacy club and tried to educate them against the oppressive customs of the time (1920s). One of her own male coworkers, the village's mullah, and landlords incited the villagers against her. She eventually escapes from the ordeal by joining the CP. See Jabbarli (1979).

11. The statue is particularly associated with the memory of a young Azerbaijani woman who was set on fire by her father and brothers for dishonoring them by her act of unveiling and joining a women's club in the 1920s.

12. Such extremely negative views about women's unveiling under Soviet rule are rare and came out during my interviews with the leading members of the Islamic Party of Azerbaijan, August 1994.

13. For an analytical elaboration on this, see Johnston (1993, 237–55).

14. My analysis here is based on a socio-psychological definition and theorization of religion originally formulated by sociologists like Glock and Stark (1965).

15. I was present during this lecture delivered in Baku, February 18, 1995, at a conference on Wedding Customs in Azerbaijan organized by the National Committee of Women.

16. For a comparable analysis in the context of Tajikistan, see Tett (1994).
17. See my discussion (Tohidi 1996) on endogamy, inter-ethnic marriage, and nationalism in Azerbaijan.
18. Author's interview, Baku, June 1992.
19. Tohidi (1994, 12).
20. Hassan Quliyev, "Toy Adatlarimiz," paper presented at the Conference on Women and Wedding Customs in Azerbaijan, Baku, February 18, 1995.
21. For patterns similar to the Caucasus, see Joseph (1994).
22. Suny (1990, 231).
23. For a related analysis on this, see Singerman (1996).
24. Comments received from Betura Mamedova, an Azeri teacher, in reaction to the author's earlier draft of this article, December 1995.

SIX

Moving Toward Public Space: Women and Musical Performance in Twentieth-Century Egypt*

Virginia Danielson

FEMALE PERFORMERS AND PUBLIC SPACE

When Umm Kulthum—later to become the most famous Arab singer of the century—was a young girl in the 1910s, a local merchant who observed her growing popularity in the towns around her village in rural Egypt proposed that she give a public concert in his town, Abu Shuquq. As the story was told later, tickets were sold for one to five piasters each (five to twenty-five cents at the then current rate of exchange), and the evening began with confusion among audience members and an argument that lasted almost an hour. After Umm Kulthum began to sing, the argument resumed, and she sang for only one-half hour of the four-hour event.[1]

Public concerts were relatively new to Egypt at the time. The audiences were largely, if not exclusively, male. Sometimes alcohol was served, and inebriated audience members caused disturbances. When Umm Kulthum was about fourteen years old, her family performed at a concert during which her father became concerned about drunkenness. After negotiation with a reluctant

116

manager, he elicited a promise that no alcohol would be served while his daughter was singing.[2]

Having navigated events such as these, female performers including Umm Kulthum but also many others came to occupy prominent places in Egypt's public culture. Over the last hundred years Egyptian public space for musical performance expanded as concerts and theatrical performances became more widespread and as the mass media—including commercial recordings, radio and television broadcasts, films, and videos—became rapidly integrated into social life. Professional performers throughout Egypt began to move from community and familial environments, where individuals or families contracted with them to perform at social events such as weddings, to larger and eventually mediated spaces where musicians or their agents negotiated with institutions, such as theater managements or broadcasting authorities. Every performer did not take this path. However, the motivation to do so increased more or less constantly as the material profits and artistic opportunities to be obtained from these media grew. The roles of women in public life developed along with the burgeoning mass media and its new public venues. Now women reside prominently in public space.[3]

Appadurai and Breckenridge's discussion of "public culture" as a useful concept for exploring these performance contexts includes important features that render it apt for the musical repertories performed by women in twentieth-century Egypt. "It appears," they write, "to be less embedded in such highly specific Western dichotomies and debates as high versus low culture; mass versus elite culture; and popular or folk versus classical culture. . . . It allows us to hypothesize . . . a *zone* of cultural debate . . . where other types, forms and domains of culture are encountering, interrogating and contesting each other" (1988, 6). The repertories performed in Egypt during this century manifest a variety of styles that in turn color each other. Virtually all resist categorization under rubrics such as "popular" and "classical" familiar in the West (Racy 1981, 6, 16; El-Shawan 1980, 23–87; Danielson 1988, 142). Thus it is easy to conclude with

Appadurai and Breckenridge (1988, 8) that "current notions of popular, folk or traditional cultural forms simply are not adequate for the interpretive challenges posed by the cosmopolitan forms of today's public cultures."

Arguably, "public space" has been available historically to Egyptian performers and is not new. Weddings, holidays, and celebrations for saints' days were often in some way open to friends, neighbors, and even visitors or passers-by. Many events took place, at least in part, out of doors.[4] However, the social relations—the relations of power—that governed such events were more or less established, proceeding as they did from the relative status of the host family (for a wedding, for instance) or the character of the event as somber or joyous. Participants were usually in the company of family, friends, and neighbors whose expectations informed and constrained behavior.

These circumstances changed in the public concert, for instance, which was held for no seasonal or occasional reason but simply to entertain those who could afford to pay the admission price and to make money for the performer. Whereas musical professionalism was long-standing in many Arab societies, this new performance was cut loose from the moorings of religious or celebratory occasions and removed from familial environments. These performances (and the later recordings, films, and other mediated events) were simply commercial enterprises that, its principals found, could be very lucrative.

MUSICAL PERFORMANCE IN EARLY TWENTIETH-CENTURY EGYPT

Public commercial entertainment establishments began to appear in Egypt during the nineteenth century. Their center in Cairo was the theater district near Azbakiyya Garden, an area long known as a gathering place for entertainment for occasions such as the celebration of the Prophet's birthday. After the arrival of the French in 1798, "local Christians and Europeans . . . started taverns, restaurants, and cafes in the European style"

(Berque 1972, 88–89) in the vicinity. The development of the Garden by Khedive Isma'il in the nineteenth century brought with it public restaurants and open-air music halls. The Garden itself housed entertainment "kiosks" and outdoor music halls and offered working space for fortunetellers, clowns, snake charmers, sorcerers, and other freelance entertainers. According to historian Husayn Fawzi's description, one could also hear marches by John Phillip Sousa, renditions of "Way Down upon the Swanee River," operettas by Gilbert and Sullivan, and whatever was considered the latest fashion from abroad (Fu'ad 1976, 120). The theater district, centered on 'Imad al-Din Street, featured European productions at the Opera House, Arabic adaptations of European plays, and original Arabic productions, some of which included music.

Full-fledged concerts were probably the offspring of Arabic theatrical productions (themselves derived from European practice), where singers entertained during entr'actes.[5] Concerts of Western music followed the colonization of Egypt in the late nineteenth century (Storrs 1937; Racy 1982). By 1920, concerts of Arabic song were familiar and accessible venues for performers and audiences in Cairo and also in provincial cities and towns. Women appeared as solo singers and actresses in plays (sometimes playing men's roles).

The commercial environment presented many more problems for entertainers than did private homes or community gatherings: audiences were larger, they usually were unknown to the performer, and patrons were occasionally rowdy. In some cases, singers employed by the music halls were required to socialize or drink alcohol with patrons (Fu'ad 1976, 158). The association of performance with vices such as gambling, prostitution, and the consumption of drugs and alcohol was particularly strong in the arena of public commercial entertainment. The presence of foreign soldiers at entertainment venues in cities during the first half of this century, particularly during the two world wars, exacerbated the situation because these men had relatively large amounts of money to spend and few restraints.

Nahid Hafiz summarized commonly felt sentiments, writing that Cairo during this period "was a place of many vices, for example, gambling, licentiousness, usury, drunkenness, drugs and prostitution, all of which resulted from colonialism" (Hafiz 1977, 216).

This "downtown," a new contruction in the nineteenth century, differed in the public eye from the older, "traditional" Cairo represented, for instance, in Najib Mahfuz's novels. The characters of his famous trilogy know about it, are sometimes tantalized by it, but avoid it.[6] For them as for many Egyptians, this quarter of the city was different, Europeanized, not "normal."[7] Indeed, the entertainment quarters were foreign to people of Umm Kulthum's class and background, and most Egyptians shared her class and background.

Entertainment certainly did not attract the ponderous argumentation of "modernization" pervasive in contemporary Arabic debates about philosophy, science, government, or women's rights. Yet it was in this space that solutions to the dilemma of the usefulness of European culture were tried out, adopted, modified, and abandoned—quite literally acted out—with participants from all strata of society. By the mid-1920s, local Egyptian entertainers had moved squarely into the domain of concert and theater, occupied it, dominated it, and proceeded during this century to do likewise with films, recordings, radio, and television. Many performers were women who had to solve the problems of how to behave, what to perform, and what to do with this public space, problems illustrated by the story about Umm Kulthum above.

This chapter begins with the assumption that in patriarchies, whether in Egypt, Europe, or North America, women rarely constitute the primary candidates for inhabiting public forums. It explores the extent to which women have been able to occupy this space and the strategies they used in order to "live" in it while maintaining viable positions in Egyptian society.

Viability was constantly negotiated. Young singers often took more social risks than did other girls and women, but their conduct was at the same time constrained by social practices. The realities of the patriarchy, the ideals of moral society (as locally defined), and the responsibility of the patriarchy to sustain such a society were and are salients in Egypt. Whether one was (or is now) Muslim, Christian, or Jewish, to live in a moral society was a desideratum perhaps as strong as the concept of privacy or of the separation of church and state have become in the West. For women, morality often involved not only sexual virtue but also a reputation of modesty. A local formulation is illustrative: "For us, girls are like eggs. Once [their reputations] are broken, they can't be fixed. *Sharaf* (honor) is more important than any official law."[8] Judging from a reading of Egyptian criticism, written and verbal, over the century, these common social values colored views of public entertainment. While entertainers stretched the boundaries of respectability and good reputation, to be really successful in public venues over time a woman had to appear to be reasonably respectable. The problem, then, became how to sing and dance modestly yet attractively and how to separate oneself from one's competitors at the same time. In complex Egyptian society, the solutions women found were predictably varied, incorporating elements from the increasingly familiar international stage with qualities linked to "good" women locally.

UNDERSTANDING MUSICAL PRACTICE

Understanding how women in Egypt handled the circumstances confronting them requires a fluid social theory that comprehends non-discursive behavior and the complicated patterns of a complex society. The foundation of the analysis here derives from performance theory, anthropological theories of "practice," and the large corpus of literature that has come to be known as cultural studies. Simply put, I view Egyptian singers as informed participants in their society who act to produce Egyptian culture while at the same time they are produced *by* that culture. This model is particularly compelling in the instance of musical performance because definitions of Arabic song historically include the responses of listeners as a component of the concept of song. Arabic song does not exist in its entirety without response from listeners, and the singer—even the singing star—is never isolated from her society. Meaning, in artistic work, is not simply "expressed"; it is produced and reproduced by performers and listeners. Art, here music, does not "reflect" society; it helps constitute society.[9]

The behavior of performers and audiences yields a discourse that indicates ways in which social identities are constructed, enacted, and understood. Speech is the means by which musicians and listeners locate sound, and their talk helps to constitute identities of musical styles. Stephen Blum described this in the following manner:

> The definition of stylistic norms evolves from both the actual practice of performing musicians and the verbal statements, evaluations, justifications which attach themselves to practice. Nonspecialists participate in several aspects of this process: one chooses what he will listen to, what he will attempt to reproduce, and what he will say about it. . . . Recurrent traits or patterns which result from such procedures for music-making might be said to constitute a style.[10]

Listeners' interpretations define the identities of styles and of performers. Distinctions among performers and styles depend not simply on what is performed but also on what is heard and how it is identified.

With musical sound, poetry, appearance, and speech, female singers perform public roles that are subject to modification in response to audience reaction. The behavior of performers, their musical style, speech, presentation, and dress; published reviews, gossip columns, and other printed commentary about performances; and talk—conversation—about musicians together produce musical culture. The process of developing public personae has involved not so much choosing from an array of possible identities but evolving an identity in consort with colleagues and listeners. The public identities—in some cases the stardom—that have emerged are socially situated, linked inextricably to time and place.

The examples that follow manifest alternatives developed by Egyptian women in the public eye: the young Umm Kulthum in the 1920s; the folk singer Khadra Muhammad Khidr in the 1950s and 1960s; the mature Umm Kulthum of the 1960s; and a young singer, 'Ayida 'l-Ayyubi, in the 1990s. Their objectives, as far as one may know, include attracting a particular audience and then maintaining their positions as popular, widely accepted good performers in their chosen milieux.

DRESS

Dress is, of course, one salient in the projection of a public persona, and female singers used clothing to signify affinity. Seeking association with Turkish court music in the 1920s, Fathiyya Ahmad wore bejeweled Ottoman ornaments in her publicity pictures. At various times during this century, women Qur'an readers and singers of religious song have worn head coverings and face veils. More recently, young women who seek international work in nightclubs and don tight-fitting, bejeweled dresses and sports clothes risk thereby a portion of their local identities.[11] The young Umm Kulthum wrapped herself in black veils. Eventually she set a standard of conservative yet stylish dress that many other singers copied: she generally wore long dresses with sleeves, conservative versions of European fashions, or elaborate versions of Egyptian robes (*jalalib*). The European aspects of such costumes conveyed newness; its "coveredness" bespoke the propriety of local values. This combination was borrowed from the styles of the elite women of Cairo, many of whom exhibited a desire to pair the fashion of the dominant European with a personal presentation commensurate with Egyptian social values. Richness of fabric and decoration associated singers with wealth and the upper classes, a status sought by most and used by them to assert their own value in an

Figure 1
Umm Kulthum, ca. 1924 (publicity picture)

Figure 2
Fathiyya Ahmad, ca. 1926, wearing a "Turkish" headdress
(publicity picture)

Figure 3
Umm Kulthum, 1969 (courtesy, Farouk Ibrahim)

Figure 4
A group of upper middle-class Cairene women at the opera house
(courtesy, Dar al-Hilal)

increasingly consumerist society. This model separated the singer from dancers and actresses, whose costumes looked less like the attire of wealthy Cairene women. At the same time, singers wishing to attract attention by exposing more flesh did so under the guise of theatrical costume or in genre photographs in magazines under themes such as "Our Singers at the Beach."

Khadra Muhammad Khidr, who performs *mawawil* (sing. *mawwal;* short verses often in the colloquial language featuring puns) and whose audiences in the 1950s and 1960s were largely working class, wore the simpler *jalalib* and embroidered headscarves of her patrons. 'Ayida 'l-Ayyubi's appearance is modest but contemporary, sporting the casual dress and hairstyle of those college girls who, like herself, do not cover their hair or adopt decidedly Islamicist dress. (Al-Ayyubi's audience, however, includes young women in Islamicist garb; this difference presents no apparent disconnection or contradiction.) Al-Ayyubi appears as an appropriately modest, entertaining, and new young singer.

THE POETIC VOICE

Other tools for establishing style and identity came from concepts about expressive culture that have historical importance. The salience of sung poetry is one of these: one who sings difficult poetry well as Umm Kulthum did, or one who is clever with colloquial texts as Khadra Muhammad Khidr is, attains a much greater level of respectability than a dancer can ever hope to reach. Many of Umm Kulthum's songs were *qasa'id,* sophisticated, literary odes constructed following historic models. Her rendition of so many of these lent a neo-classical color to Umm Kulthum's life work.

Additionally, historical precedent lives in the contemporary memory of gifted, accomplished, and captivating female singers from Arab history. Singers including Sallama, 'Arib, and 'Ulayya bint al-Mahdi (the half-sister of Harun al-Rashid) performed in the courts of the Islamic empire (Sawa 1987 8, 93–95), and their stories have been told and retold. In this century, Arabic films

Figure 5
Khadra Muhammad Khidr and her ensemble, ca. 1970
(courtesy, Dar al-Hilal)

Figure 6
Working-class women buying and selling vegetables at the Fayyoum
Market, 1982 (photo by Virginia Danielson)

Figure 7
Ayida al-Ayyubi, ca 1995 (publicity picture)

have been made about them. Thus modern singers have actually used the stories to advance the discourse. The memory and discourse surrounding it help enable historic resonance for contemporary performance.

Khadra was a master of the clever text, the pun, the punchline of the verse, clearly delivered to the delight of her audience. She sang many occasional poems—often intended for weddings or other celebratory events—with colloquial Egyptian texts that were easily understood. Khadra extemporizes, punning and playing on words. Her listeners then attend to her clever and entertaining artistry; they respond enthusiastically to the wit and joyfulness of the local entertainer in community gatherings.

In a recording made in 1991, 'Ayida al-Ayyubi uses her lyrics to situate herself as an Egyptian Arab: dialectical expressions such as *'ala bali* (on my mind) and *al-maya wa-'l-hawa* (water and breeze) remind the listener of local Egyptian images; the lyric "if I were rich" suggests that she is not; *'ashiqt al-fann* (I loved art) identifies the singer as a proper artist, and lullabies and songs for mothers place her in a long line of singers, male and female, with locally determined ideals of children and family.[12]

THE SINGING VOICE

A singer's voice, however, comprises more than just the lyrics she sings and words she (and others) use to describe her. Her musical style—her non-discursive sound—operates as the most significant marker of identity. The mastery of the modal system of Arab music and historically Arab aesthetics of singing grounded Umm Kulthum in local ideals of artistic accomplishment. Incorporating the sounds of words into the sound of melody moved her away from European *bel canto* and Turkish court singing and toward the ideals of Qur'anic recitation and religious song. This in turn resulted in the popular assessment of her as authentic or genuine (*asil*), motivated by local Egyptian precedents, and not unduly influenced by the West. *"Ma li Futint"* (How I've been captivated) recorded by Umm Kulthum in 1924 and *"Kam*

Ba'athna ma' al-Nasim Salaman" (How often have we sent greetings with the breeze, ca. 1924) offer good examples of historically Arab virtuosity married to careful rendition of significant texts. By contrast, Fathiyya Ahmad's recording of *"Kam Ba'athna"* (ca. 1926) exhibited a florid, melodic virtuosity that overwhelmed articulation of the text but did not disguise the mistakes she made in phrasing and grammatical articulation. Fathiyya's configuration of skills was certainly formidable, and her use of these skills earned the assessment that she was a good singer "in the Turkish style"—an evaluation that she accepted and promoted in the late 1920s.

Khadra's musical artistry could communicate its identity with no words at all. A *mawwal* she recorded on a cassette of wedding music is a good example.[13] The decided nasality of her vocal tone, evident on the first syllable she sings in an improvisation on the words *ya layl, ya 'ayn* (O night, O eye; words that function as syllables for vocal improvisation) locates Khadra as a working-class singer of *mawawil* and related repertories. This sound, *khanafa* in Egyptian Arabic, consists of frontal resonance in the nasal region, moderated so as to be compelling but not overly nasal, a quality regarded by listeners as crude and uncontrolled. It is a distinctive sound valued as local (*baladi*) and folk (*sha'bi*) that marks the identity of the singer. The melodies she sang are relatively limited in range compared to almost anything Umm Kulthum or Fathiyya Ahmad sang; the songs often feature refrains with which untrained listeners can (and do) sing along. A single drum (*darabukka,* or hour-glass drum), a spike fiddle (*rababa*), and an end-blown reed flute (*nay*) accompany the song. These are familiar, easily available instruments often used by performers to suggest folk music and pastoral environments. The drummer plays a rhythmic pattern that is distinctively Egyptian and not characteristic of the sung poetry that constituted such repertories as Umm Kulthum's.

The song *"al-Atlal"* (Traces) recorded in 1966 shows that although Umm Kulthum had lost some of the sheer virtuosity of her earlier performances, her artistry had matured well, leaving her with the ability to invent on the spot literally dozens of reiterations of favored lines at the behest of listeners. In so doing she carried the art and ambience of the cognoscenti—an historic world often constituted by small groups of elite male listeners and a few musicians—onto the concert stages of the Arab world and onto international radio broadcasts, recordings, television programs, and videos.

"*Al-Atlal*" was a modern *qasida,* a lengthy love poem, simpler in language than its historic predecessors but elegant nevertheless and possessed of the self-contained hemistitchs that permitted the singer to extract and elaborate on individual lines. The precomposed melody (a composition by the musical neo-classicist Riyad al-Sunbati) was built from an historic but distinctively Egyptian melodic mode called *rahit al-arwah*. Umm Kulthum's reiterations of lines manifest the various possibilities of the mode and led to others. Her vocal color varies, slipping among frontal and palatal resonances but is never so decidedly nasal as Khadra's. These skills locate Umm Kulthum as a singer of historic poetry, or *shiʻr*, and suggests an international, particularly Arab awareness that is (deliberately) greater than Khadra's. Umm Kulthum's rendition retains a careful articulation of words that listeners immediately explain as proceeding from her religious background. Although her accompanying ensemble is large—it is the size of an American stage band—and includes such innovations as electric keyboards and guitars, the instruments never intrude on the singer's art. Umm Kulthum leads the ensemble and shapes the piece and thus perpetuated an historic model of Arabic singing that is riveted on the singer of poetry rather than the instrumentalist. Altogether, Umm Kulthum's performances utilized historic concepts of singers and song in new and sometimes innovative musical structures. Using them, she developed an artistry widely appealing to Egyptian and Arab societies trying to assert the value of their own histories and cultures.[14]

The younger singer ʻAyida al-Ayyubi entered the business of commercial entertaining as a college student with some international experience. During her relatively short performing career, she has adapted a successful *modus vivendi.* Her media are the compact disc, the stadium concert, and the tour abroad as well as the pervasive cassette tape. Her style lies close to historic colloquial song (*zajal*) with an electronic *takht* (small and historic ensemble in Arab classical music), uniting thereby familiar song style with the small, improvisatory ensemble of historic singers. She produces sound with an open, middle-head resonance, familiar internationally in the voices of Arab, European, and American ballad singers. Her ensemble is small, with electronic instruments prominently featured. It produces a few musical lines, widely separated in pitch; performers are competent, even virtuosic. Yet the solo singer is not driven by them. She retains her historic position of primacy as the singer of verse.

LANGUAGE AND SPEECH

"I sing here in Imbaba—only in the coffee houses of Imbaba," Khadra emphatically repeated to a Europeanized television interviewer in 1992, poking at the interviewer's shoulder with a finger as she spoke, as if to emphasize the difference between Khadra herself, a bulky older woman who wore a *jallabiyya* and head covering, and the young broadcaster who wore European dress and coif. "I am not like her," Khadra conveyed to the audience, "and that's a good thing." Beyond her *jallabiyya,* her forceful manner of speech—that of the *bint il-balad*[15]—and her dialect marked Khadra as decidedly Cairene. "I sing in Imbaba" emphasized the value of the local and in this case working-class community over the wealthy patrons of hotels, nightclubs, and stadium concerts. In this way she constructed herself with words, telling listeners directly or by implication who she was. The words—the interviews, the introductions to audiences, the talk from the stage—formed as much a part of the performance as the costume.

Khadra's statements were carefully crafted because despite her large audience in Imbaba, as a performer she, like many others, generally took the opportunities that presented themselves. But this does not imply that her words constituted a false identity. The words manifest what Simon Frith calls the myth at the heart of the life of a star performer, indicating value shared between performers and their audiences (Frith 1983, 276–77). Khadra, like many others, assessed the complexity of her life over time and emphasized certain aspects to construct herself as a premier, respected working-class singer.

Umm Kulthum advanced the view that she was a "real" (*asil*) Egyptian, a daughter of Arab literature and history and a devoted Muslim. Like Khadra, she produced this identity with music and also with words. In the late 1950s and 1960s, the mature Umm Kulthum spent much of her life telling her audience in one way or another that she was a *fallaha,* a daughter of the land, a daughter of a religious family. "My childhood was like most of my countrymen," she would say. "My father was the village *shaykh.*" "We were very poor." "My mother was a good and honest woman who loved God and cared nothing for money." "We are *fallahin,*" she told a journalist late in her life, "or had you forgotten?" Umm Kulthum's image is a complex one for, at the same time that she articulated this grassroots peasant identity and spoke and sang in colloquial Egyptian Arabic, she also sang elegant and difficult poetry in literary Arabic. Using these languages and literatures, she attempted to link herself at once to centuries of Arab literati and scholars and to life on the ground at the moment.

SOME RESULTS

All four of these women draw local feminine models into the public arena, identifying themselves as elegant and accomplished performers in a historically Arab style, as clever working women, and as talented college students. Their attractiveness as performers depends on their cultivation of innovative artistry with local, familiar qualities and on their adoption of local social models that allow them to navigate public space and become not only acceptable but also beloved figures there.

These personae are of course constructed with an audience in mind, understood in terms of class, locale, and time. For Khadra, it was (and is) the Imbaba of the 1950s and 1960s, a bustling community of working-class people, *abna' al-balad* in the heyday of Nasserism. For Umm Kulthum in the 1960s, it was the Arab world at large. She was the Egyptian cultural leader addressing fellow Arabs at a time when political unity was a primary issue. For 'Ayida al-Ayyubi, it is the Cairo soccer stadium filled with young people but also the international Arab diaspora where "world beat" offers opportunities Umm Kulthum never even considered. 'Ayida's tools are the casual clothes that have become international and the songs and language recognizable not only to the Egyptian audience in the soccer stadium but to Arabs abroad less familiar with the newest trends in the Middle East.

Their performances, in turn, help constitute social practice as listeners adopt them as "their" singers, express preferences, seek recordings, attend concerts, and simply talk about the singers and the songs. The Egyptian student in North America is partly constituted as an Egyptian by his or her choice of 'Ayida al-Ayyubi rather than or in addition to Whitney Huston, for instance. The culture of a car mechanic's workshop in Imbaba draws from the sound of Umm Kulthum or Khadra, for instance, rather than 'Ayida al-Ayyubi (although al-Ayyubi might be playing in a cassette store nearby). The meaning of the music is not simply expressed in the singing of the song; it is produced (and reproduced) by performers and listeners. In this way, singers and listeners in their everyday lives together contribute to structures of feeling that manifest attitudes informed by aspects of life not distinctly musical or artistic but more generally social and sometimes explicitly political or economic.

Much of the technology that enabled these women to move into the public eye was foreign. The personae that they developed to occupy the space were usually not. They did not simply mimic the Greta Garbos that were pictured in newspapers and magazines of the 1920s. They invented solutions to the dilemma of moving into the center of the public eye and collectively developing a forceful and persistent presence in daily life, where they are at once agents of cultural production and participants in it.

NOTES

*   I am grateful for helpful comments on an earlier draft of this chapter from Barbara Larson and Jane Sugarman. The opportunity to present an earlier version of the chapter as an invited lecture in the Islamic and Near Eastern Studies Colloquium series at the University of California, Santa Barbara prompted me to rethink some of the issues, and I thank Scott Marcus and Juan Campo for that invitation.

1. The family was paid 1 £E ($5) for their performance and expenses ('Awad 1971, 19; Fu'ad 1976, 80; Shusha 1976, 12; Abu al-Majd 1963, 229).
2. Her father's concern seems to have involved both his daughter's well-being and the propriety of singing religious songs to a drunken audience (Shusha 1976, 14).
3. A discussion of female singers in Cairo in the 1920s appears in Danielson (1991).
4. For historical discussions of such events, see al-Hifni, Shafiq, and Abu 'Awf (1969, 1:58), Raymond (1968), and McPherson (1941).
5. Arabic plays began to be staged in Egypt in the mid-nineteenth century. Descriptions of singers appearing during entr'actes date from about 1884 (Kamil 1977, 9, 12). The famous singer and composer Muhammad 'Abd al-Wahhab as well as numerous others started careers in this way ('Abd al-Wahhab n.d., 27).
6. An interesting account of the culture of downtown Cairo appears in Massie (1992). Mahfuz's trilogy has been translated into English and published by Doubleday under the titles *Palace Walk, Palace of Desire,* and *Sugar Street.*

7. A close friend from the provincial city of al-Minya remarked with clear disapproval that "Cairo is really a European city" (personal communication, January 1996).

8. Personal communication, al-Minya, January 1996.

9. Salient literature that underpins these ideas includes Anthony Giddens's theory of structuration articulated in numerous works including his *The Constitution of Society* (1984) and Raymond Williams's work on the role of artistic expression in societies perhaps best represented by his *Marxism and Literature* (1977).

10. Blum (1972, 4, 5).

11. Sharihan is one example that leaps to mind.

12. 'Ayida al-Ayyubi, "'*Ala Bali,*" Americana AAVCD 505, 1991.

13. *Khadra Muhammad Khidr,* Randafun 1179/78, 1980s?

14. Further discussion appears in Danielson (1997).

15. A creditable discussion appears in El Messiri (1978); see also El Hamamsy (1975).

SEVEN

"The Law Shall not Languish": Social Class and Public Conduct in Sixteenth-century Ottoman Legal Discourse*

Leslie Peirce

Among sixteenth-century Ottoman subjects, there was uncertainty about the definition of respectability for women. Or so it would seem from a series of questions posed to the mufti Ebu Su'ud (d. 1574), principal interpreter of religious law to the empire's ruler and subjects alike. Although the chief mufti might render his opinion on matters of jurisprudence crucial to the conduct of imperial affairs, he, like any local mufti, was also called on to judge matters of everyday social conduct.[1] The series of questions we are concerned with here asked the mufti to clarify who qualified for the status of *muhaddere*. This term, which might best be translated as "respectable," combines what in modern usage are usually separate concepts—a reputation for chaste behavior and the practice of veiling and/or seclusion (Meninski 1780–1802, 4:428). The term thereby links moral status with the controlled visibility of the female body.

The confusion that underlay the queries posed to the mufti in the mid-sixteenth century suggests that the issues of women's mobility in public, their physical appearance, and their contact with men were as contested then as they are in today's debates about Muslim identity. Legal discourse of the period reveals some of the tensions surrounding this debate—for example, the incompatibility between the desire for seclusion on the part of the individual (women or family) and the community's requirement that the individual assume a public role when necessary. The sixteenth-century legal debate about female seclusion and morality affirms Joan Scott's point that normative positions are less the product of social consensus than of social conflict and, I would emphasize, also of ambiguity and uncertainty (Scott 1988, 43).

The questions posed to Ebu Su'ud concerned the degree of seclusion that was necessary for a woman to be recognized as "respectable." The following three fetvas of the chief mufti trace the status of muhaddere through a variety of social venues (Düzdağ 1983, 56):[2]

> Query: Can [a woman] be muhaddere if she handles her own affairs with the people of the village and brings water from the spring?
>
> Response: No.
>
> Query: Can [a woman] be muhaddere if she goes to the public bath or to the countryside [lit. to villages]?
>
> Response: Yes, if she goes in [such a way as to preserve her] honor and dignity and is accompanied by servants and attendants.
>
> Query [perhaps a variant text of the second query above]: Can [a woman] be muhaddere if she goes to the public bath and to weddings and makes excursions to other neighborhoods?
>
> Response: Yes, if she goes with a retinue.

In another fetva, the mufti provides a more comprehensive characterization of the term:

> Query: Can [a woman] be muhaddere if she lets herself be seen by her father's freedmen and by the sons of [these] freedmen and by her sisters' husbands?

Response: It is not conformity to the prescriptions of the noble Shari'a that is the essential element in being muhaddere. That is why non-Muslim women can also be muhaddere. A woman is muhaddere if she does not let herself be seen by persons other than members of her household and does not set about taking care of her affairs in person.[3]

The mufti seems to be saying, "Don't keep pressing me: this isn't about Shari'a!" In other words, Ebu Su'ud implies that the boundaries of the category muhaddere are not as precise as the rules of religious law on the degrees of kinship (including quasi-kinship relations among family members and household servants) within which females and males might enjoy each other's company without impropriety.[4] Although the mufti's rule of thumb on who can be muhaddere is rather close to Qur'anic prohibitions on male-female contact outside of specified degrees of kinship, he evades giving the category the sanction of Shari'a. By including non-Muslim women in the category, Ebu Su'ud avoids assimilating it to a catechism of Islamically prescribed conduct. (Indeed, the attribution muhaddere figured prominently in the honorific titulature that opened imperial diplomatic missives to Queen Elizabeth of England, who was hailed as "the pride of the muhaddere of the Christian faith.")[5] At the same time, however, the mufti acknowledges the importance of clarifying the social and legal implications of the category by answering the persistent questions about its boundaries.

If the mufti gave the category muhaddere a definition, imperial law endowed it with material consequences. According to the statute books (*kanunname*) issued by the sultans, penalties for illegal behavior might differ according to whether a woman was muhaddere or not. For example, the following statute in the kanunname of the sultan Süleyman, probably issued around 1540, states (Heyd 1973, 109):

If women fight with each other, pull each other's hair, or strike each other severely, the penalty for those who are not muhaddere is a severe flogging and a fine of one *akche* [the standard Ottoman silver coin] for every two strokes; the penalty for those who are muhaddere is that their husbands will be upbraided and fined twenty akches.

Because the severity of a flogging was determined by the local authorities, who could in theory prescribe up to eighty strokes, the monetary penalty for a non-muhaddere woman could exceed the penalty of twenty akches imposed on the muhaddere woman's husband. In other words, the non-muhaddere woman might suffer a severe flogging and a substantial fine, while the parallel punishment for the muhaddere woman was the public humiliation of her husband and the imposition of a comparatively lesser fine.

In addition to disparities in the actual punishment, the sultan's law further underwrote a hierarchy of social status through its assignment of responsibility for a woman's conduct and thus the locus of personal honor. In the eyes of the sultan's law, the non-muhaddere woman was in charge of her own behavior and its consequences, while it was the husband of the muhaddere woman who was publicly accountable for her actions and who was publicly dishonored by her transgressions. Whether or not the non-muhaddere woman had a husband or was chaperoned by a male relative in her dealings with the court, in the formal discourse of the law she was directly answerable for her conduct, unlike her muhaddere counterpart. No wonder then that people were anxious for a definition of the boundaries between social categories, since the sultan's law declared that justice for women—and possibly for their husbands—varied according to their social status. In endorsing the social variability of justice, the imperial statute books may have merely reflected widespread customary practice, but by (re)inscribing such practice in a regulatory program for the whole empire, they gave it high authoritative sanction.

Ebu Su'ud's fetvas, through their equation of social standing with seclusion from the public gaze (whether through domestic

confinement or carefully managed public appearance), defined
the category muhaddere as a privilege of high socioeconomic
status. Only wealthy women or women with wealthy husbands
could afford servants or retainers to act as retinues for their
public excursions and agents for their business dealings. The
notion that seclusion was a privilege as well as an obligation of
the elite was rooted in ancient Middle Eastern and Mediterranean social practice. However, it was repeatedly reconstructed
by texts of the Islamic period, beginning with the Qur'an, to
reinforce contemporary social hierarchy. From this perspective,
Ebu Su'ud's fetvas can be seen as an attempt to redefine the
parameters of seclusion in the language of the mid-sixteenth-
century Ottoman social environment.

The definition of female honor in terms of public conduct
created a powerful incentive for women to shape their behavior
accordingly. But to what extent were women arbiters of their
own conduct in a society that linked female assertion of moral
and social status with male accountability for female integrity
of character? And what of women excluded from the category muhaddere? What of those who in effect established the
category by being the non-muhaddere against whom the privileged group could define its different identity, its claim to innate
superiority of moral character? What, if anything, did legal discourse have to say of their situation? I want to explore these
questions by further examining Ottoman legal texts of the mid-
sixteenth century and the ways in which they confront the tensions surrounding the problem of social class and public
conduct.

THE LIMITS OF SECLUSION

Just as there was confusion about the degree of seclusion that
was required to qualify for muhaddere status, so was there
uncertainty about what might jeopardize that status once
achieved. One of the most vocal debates about the boundaries
of seclusion was the degree to which a husband could prevent

his wife from leaving home. According to the Muslim contract of marriage, obedience to her husband was a principal duty of the wife. In exchange for a guarantee of material comfort appropriate to the husband's social status, the wife was expected to maintain the domestic household and to obey her husband. Women's mobility outside the home appears to have been an area where husbands particularly insisted on their wives' compliance with their wishes. Accordingly, Ebu Su'ud answered many queries on the degree of a husband's control in this area.

On the one hand, the mufti supported the husband's right to wifely obedience (Düzdağ 1983, 54):

> Query: If Zeyd strikes his wife Hind for going to her father's house without permission, what must be done to Zeyd?
>
> Response: Nothing much.[6]

On the other hand, he set limits to the husband's authority by upholding the wife's right to leave the house a minimum of once a week in order to visit her parents (Düzdağ 1983, 56). Other rulings underlined the importance of a woman's contact with her natal family by limiting the ability of the husband to establish a home distant from that of his wife's family (Düzdağ 1983, 53). That religious duties were another aspect of women's lives entitling them to leave the home is demonstrated in the following fetva addressing a woman's desire to make the pilgrimage to Mecca:

> Query: If Hind's husband Zeyd refuses to take Hind on the pilgrimage, and Hind says, "I'll go with my mother's [brother's] son," can she go?
>
> Response: If he is not within the degree of kinship prohibiting marriage, no. If he *is* within the degree of kinship prohibiting marriage [i.e., if he is a close relative], there is no need for Zeyd's permission.[7]

We must be careful not to blame abuses of the practice of female seclusion entirely on the "oppressive" character of individual husbands. As we have seen, a wife's failure to uphold her reputation as muhaddere might lead to legal consequences and loss of face for her husband. If there *was* oppression, arguably it lay more in the ways in which law and customary practice combined to produce a powerful social compulsion on men as well as women to conform to the norms of gender segregation. This is dramatically illustrated in a clause in Süleyman's statute book imposing punishment on a husband who failed to divorce a wife guilty of adultery (Heyd 1973, 95–96).

> If the husband accepts [this/her], and he is rich, he should pay 100 akches by way of the cuckold tax; but it has become the custom to take 300 akches by way of the cuckold tax. If he is of middle status, he should pay fifty akches, and if he is poor, forty or thirty akches.

Here, the legal standard of the sultan yielded to a harsher customary practice. By penalizing the man who might wish to keep his wife, both community and state asserted that honor was not a private prerogative. The cuckold tax of 300 akches was equal to the fine for adultery prescribed by the statute book for wealthy persons. Customary practice thus insisted that the cuckolded husband who did not publicly divest himself of a shamed and shaming wife was as much a disgrace to the community as the adultress herself.[8]

The extreme embarrassment of an adulterous wife may have been the fate of only a few men. However, that men might risk diminished standing in their community *without* any crime having resulted from their failure to secure the norms of gender segregation was the opinion of Ibn Kemal, the chief mufti from 1525 to his death in 1534 and, like Ebu Su'ud, one of the most hailed of Ottoman religious scholars. When presented with a long list of instances of religiously or socially deviant, delinquent, or deficient behaviors and the query whether such behaviors disqualified an individual from giving testimony in court, the mufti answered in the affirmative. Included in the list, along with thieves, pimps, pederasts, habitual liars, heretics, astrologers, Gypsies, and persons ignorant of the most basic elements of their professed faith, were "those who keep company with women who are not close relatives" and "those who do not prevent their wives from [associating with] men who are not close relatives."[9] In other words, in Ibn Kemal's view, disregard of what we might term muhaddere standards of behavior disqualified a man from one of the marks of full citizenship in the community and of an upstanding moral reputation—acting as witness in court.

The category muhaddere had implications for legal practice beyond the punitive. It also raised questions about women's access to legal institutions. For the muhaddere woman, pressure on both her husband and herself to restrict her public exposure could result in an unwillingness for her to appear in court. That this might infringe on the operation of the law as a communal process is the concern of a number of Ebu Su'ud's fetvas. These fetvas are noteworthy in revealing the extent to which the social structure of a community and of individual households within it conditioned the practice of law. In the following fetva, the mufti insists that the muhaddere woman must somehow be represented at court (Düzdağ 1983, 56):

> Query: If Zeyd has a legal suit against the muhaddere Hind, can Hind's husband legally prevent her from going to the kadi's court herself and say, "I won't act as her proxy, nor will I consent to anyone else's acting as proxy for her?"
>
> Response: He cannot prevent the appointment of a proxy if Hind is muhaddere. This is because it is not permissible for the law to languish. If she does not come [to the court] in person, the Shari'a authorities must obtain a proxy for her by ordering that a proxy be appointed.

Here Ebu Su'ud has framed his answer in terms of the priority of a general interest in the integrity of the law over the right of the husband to control his wife's movements or the right of a woman to engage in the practice of seclusion. The mufti, therefore, does not need to address explicitly what may in fact be a ploy of the couple to avoid the legal suit by manipulating the fact of the wife's seclusion.

As Ebu Su'ud noted in his definition cited above, the muhaddere woman might have "affairs to take care of," affairs that could fall subject to litigation or other court procedures. Given females' control of their own property under Islamic law, the necessity for women of high social status in particular to participate in legal proceedings may have been rather frequent. The disinclination of the muhaddere woman to appear in court herself meant that she needed to rely on agents on such occasions. The act of appointment of an agentas legal proxy (*vekil*) required witnesses (almost always male), an apparently tricky procedure when it was muhaddere woman making the appointment. In a fetva concerning the proper means for appointing a proxy, Ebu Su'ud once again asserts the priority of correct legal procedure over the practice of seclusion:

> Query: If [the males] Amr and Bekr come to witness the muhaddere Hind's appointment of Zeyd to be her proxy in some matter, is Amr and Bekr's testimony that Zeyd is Hind's proxy legally acceptable if they only hear her make the appointment from the other side of a door and do not see Hind's face or do not know whether or not there is another woman in the house in which Hind speaks?
>
> Response: No, [their testimony] is not [valid], unless they see her person.[10]

Another situation addressed by the mufti, this one concerning a muhaddere woman's apparent attempt to deny the validity of a marriage contracted on her behalf, demonstrates the role opened up for female witnesses in the problematic area of proxy appointment:

> Query: Hind denies that she made Zeyd her proxy for contracting marriage. The witnesses of the proxy appointment say, "We didn't see Hind's face; a woman behind a curtain spoke [making the proxy appointment]. We testified to the proxy appointment trusting that it was Hind." If Amr, who has brought a suit claiming

that Hind is legally his wife, brings two women who testify con-
currently that the person who appointed Zeyd proxy was Hind,
is Hind legally Amr's wife?

Response: Yes, she is.[11]

The two female witnesses are probably servants or retainers in
the household where Hind is resident; as such, their status is
apparently not elevated enough to exempt them from appearing
in court. However, *as witnesses,* their status is enhanced: where
typically the testimony of two women was required as substitute
for that of a single male, strict observation of the rules of gender
segregation rendered women the only reliable witnesses in a
purely female environment.

The fetvas of Ebu Su'ud discussed above were principally
concerned with delineating the category of muhaddere through
definitions and legal sanctions. The mufti's rulings focused on
managing the practice of female seclusion—that is, preventing
abuses both to the individuals concerned and to communal relations when seclusion interfered with community members' re-
sponsibilities toward one another. These outcomes of the law in
practice emerge from the mufti's role as interpreter of legal
principles within the context of a particular social environment.
In the matter of muhaddere, Ebu Su'ud played a balancing act,
attempting to reconcile a tenacious social practice, itself en-
dorsed by legal discourse, with other requirements of social
order upheld by the legal system. The mufti's fetvas on the
practice of female seclusion illustrate the point that the process
of forging a normative position involves the accommodation of
contending interests, if not the more elusive goal of their recon-
ciliation.

SOCIAL STATUS, MORAL ACCOUNTABILITY, AND LEGAL SANCTION

Ebu Su'ud's attention in his fetvas on the public conduct of
females was drawn more to the muhaddere than the non-muhad-

dere woman. The preoccupation of this eminent jurist with the problems stemming from a practice reserved for the elite reflected a conception of society in which classes of people were distinguished from one another according to their capacity for moral learning and moral excellence. In this view, those who derived status from notable lineage or wealth, for example, were thought to have greater awareness of ethical norms than the common folk (*'avamm*, sing. *'amm*) and, therefore, might be expected to hew to higher standards of conduct. Accordingly, their claim to privilege carried with it an obligation to engage in morally distinguished behavior—for example, practicing female seclusion. While such standards of conduct were aimed at defining the behavior expected of elite groups, they inevitably acted as a normative referent for the entire society and thereby functioned as a moral model for *all* Muslims and, as suggested by the debate over the meaning of muhaddere, for non-Muslims as well.

The view that moral accountability differed from person to person was further articulated in criminal penalties set out in sixteenth-century fetvas and imperial statutes. Penalties frequently varied according to an individual's status within the community. This does not mean, however, that members of elite groups were consistently treated more harshly or more leniently. At times penal law imposed more severe sanctions on them; at times it protected their status.

In the area of sexual crime, for example, persons of privilege were more heavily penalized for adultery and fornication. The imperial statute books used a complex calculus of punishment, factoring in both an individual's wealth and basic aspects of civil status—whether he or she was married or single, Muslim or *dhimmi,* and free or slave. In theory, the fine for adultery imposed on a rich Muslim was six times greater than that imposed on a poor Muslim and twelve times that imposed on a poor non-Muslim or a slave (Heyd 1973, 102–3).[12] The apparent rationale for these wide gaps was that the well-off, free married Muslim enjoyed the greatest blessing possible in life and that failure to honor this blessing should, therefore, suffer correspondingly high penal sanction (al-Marghinani 1840, 2:5).

Another area where criminal penalties varied according to a person's social standing was bodily injury, ranging from minor scuffling to killing another. As with fornication and adultery, standards of wealth and civil status figured in the determination of punishment, with the exception that no distinction between married and unmarried persons was made. For example, in the case of a fight where two persons ripped out each other's hair or beard, a rich person was fined twenty akches and a poor person ten akches; if the fight led to a head wound requiring surgery, the person inflicting the wound paid 100 akches if rich, fifty akches if moderately well off, and thirty akches if poor (Heyd 1973, 104). Slaves and non-Muslims were to be fined at half the rate of free Muslims. In the sultanic statute books, brawling and physical assault were depicted as aspects of male society, unlike sexual crime, where women inevitably figured as perpetrators or victims. In Süleyman's kanunname, fighting among females was the subject of only a single statute, cited above. But by prescribing different standards for muhaddere and non-muhaddere females guilty of brawling and bodily injury, the statute preserved the principle of differential accountability by social class. The difference was that their status was signaled not by a monetary index of wealth but by a behavioral one.

In contrast to these examples of socially privileged persons suffering heavier penalties, in other areas distinctions between "the common people" and the privileged resulted in the imposition of harsher punishments on the former. For example, the following fetva of Ibn Kemal pardoned a religiously distinguished person while punishing a commoner for what appears on the surface to be an equal, even lesser, offense:

Query: If a person who is descended from the Prophet Muhammad [a *seyyid*] says to someone, "You idiot! You cur!," and that person in turn says "That's what *you* are!," legally what must be done to the two of them?

> Response: The seyyid is pardoned; the other is sentenced to punishment by the judge.[13]

The ruling implies that the commoner had in fact committed the greater violation, by insulting a communally honored individual, whereas the seyyid's membership in a distinguished lineage appears to have afforded him immunity from a penal judgement. In another fetva, Ibn Kemal exempted those who were not "common" from the drastic consequences of a broken vow:

> Query: If Zeyd says, "If I drink wine, may I no longer be the slave of God and a member of the Prophet's community," and subsequently he does drink, what must be done according to the law?
>
> Response: If he is a common person, he must renew his faith.[14]

In this instance of the widespread practice of the "conditional vow"—calling down an undesired outcome on oneself if one were to do what one vowed not to do—the speaker risked his Muslim faith and was now, if he was "common," an apostate, requiring that he formally (re)convert to Islam.[15] Underlying this ruling may be the assumption that privileged persons do not need to be subjected to the same stringency of religious conformity as commoners because they "know" the rules by virtue of their status, whereas legal sanctions are necessary to instruct ordinary individuals in publicly desirable behavior. In other words, privileged persons are protected by their *class* identity from the consequences of any violation they may commit as individuals, whereas commoners enjoy no such immunity, lacking as they do any claim to shared moral distinction.

Immunity from the sorts of punishments imposed on commoners did not necessarily imply a license for loose behavior among the privileged. Rather, different kinds of sanctions were deemed effective for different classes of individuals. A statute in Süleyman's kanunname stipulated that religious functionaries who break the law should be exempted from the standard penalties and instead reprimanded verbally (Heyd 1973, 129):[16]

> If those who by virtue of an imperial appointment hold the office
> and receive the salary of judge, seminary teacher, *waqf* adminis-
> trator, waqf supervisor, dervish elder, mosque preacher, prayer
> leader, and the like become liable to punishment, they shall not
> be punished. To prevent them from doing [the same thing] again,
> it is punishment enough for such people for the judge to speak
> harshly to them.[16]

This statute negotiates the tricky status of members of the religious establishment (*ilmiye*) who are in the employ of the sultan.
They must be disciplined, yet—given the status deriving from
their religiously oriented careers—it is not seemly to subject them
to the same sanctions as ordinary folk.

But is the verbal sanction delivered to them a "light" sentence?
For possessors and purveyors of the highest form of knowledge,
to be publicly reprimanded with words may be more humiliating
and, therefore, more punitive than the public imposition of a
monetary fine. Perhaps the judge's pardoning of the seyyid who
cursed the commoner was not as benign an act as we might at
first assume. The notion of a hierarchy of punishment in which
the highest-ranking members of society receive only a verbal
reprimand may have been a feature of Islamic jurisprudence
from its formative period. The legal handbook of the twelfth-
century Hanafi jurist al-Marghinani, popular among the Ottomans, cited the renowned ninth-century jurist al-Shafi'i on the
four degrees of chastisement, of which the first was restricted to
"the most noble of the noble," in al-Marghinani's words, and
consisted "merely in admonition, as if the kadi were to say to
one of them, 'I understand that you have done thus, or thus,' so
as to make him ashamed" (al-Marghinani 1840, 2:76).[17]

The moral force of words in the sixteenth-century society of
Ottoman males cannot be overestimated. As we have seen, the
integrity of an individual's word—symbolized in his eligibility to
testify in court—was a principal measure of his communal
status. That the husband of a muhaddere woman guilty of lapsed
social conduct was exposed to the same punishment as a lapsed

religious dignitary—a verbal dressing down in a communal forum—is both an acknowledgment of his and his wife's status and
an affirmation of the moral nature of the failure to conform to
muhaddere norms.

CONCLUSION

It was not an ideal of the premodern Ottoman legal system that
its justice be blind. Not until the mid-nineteenth century was the
idea entertained that the law should encounter the individual as
a notional entity rather than as a particular combination of
social and civil circumstances to be scrutinized and entered into
the calculus of judgment. To distinguish among groups of individuals, the fetvas and imperial statutes examined above employed such criteria as material wealth, aspects of civil status,
religious lineage, and employment in religious careers. All of
these can be linked to a fundamental social distinction between
the privileged and the common (in the vocabulary of Islamicate
societies, the *hass* and the *'amm*).[18] Corollaries of this distinction
such as claims to moral superiority and social honor were less
tangible measures of status, but as this discussion of the category
muhaddere has demonstrated, the semiotics of honor—the public signaling of one's pretensions to elite status—precipitated
concrete and complex legal issues.

The major focus of the fetvas dealing with female conduct
considered here is on the elite and the tensions among the rules
establishing their world. The fetvas are notable for their lack of
attention to potential conflicts between legal principles dealing
with the milieu of non-muhaddere women and their families
(hence the limited scope of the discussion in this essay, which
explores only a portion of the spectrum of legal discourse). The
social world of Ebu Su'ud's fetvas was one of privilege, whose
code of moral conduct was often beyond the reach of the non-
privileged. This does not mean that the Ottoman legal system
ignored these sectors of society: local court records of the period
abound in cases negotiating the dilemmas of ordinary individu-

als. A question then that must be posed in regard to the court records is the extent to which the opinion of prominent jurists were reflected in the day-to-day operation of local courts.[19] Recent scholarship has argued that fetvas were not without their impact on the practice of the courts, and some local muftis may have served as a forum for dispute resolution in lieu of courts (Hallaq 1994; Gerber 1994; Masud, Messick, and Powers 1996; Tucker 1998). The fetvas of chief muftis such as Ibn Kemal and Ebu Su'ud, even if issued in response to particular local questions, inevitably functioned as normative statements through the process of their dissemination and the creation of a widespread audience for them.

What, then, was the message of Ebu Su'ud's corpus of fetvas on the practice of muhaddere? Can we speak of a coherent code of conduct embedded in what were piecemeal responses to individual queries rather than the sustained and internally coherent arguments typical of a legal treatise? The fetvas of Ebu Su'ud suggest an acute awareness of the tensions surrounding the practice of female seclusion. This was perhaps inevitable, given that the specific situational basis of queries presented to muftis characteristically cast social practices in a problematic aspect. Otherwise, what need was there for a judicial arbiter? Accordingly, the mufti's job was to mediate the tensions articulated to him by individuals caught in what seemed a conflict of legal rules or societal expectations. In his fetvas on female seclusion, Ebu Su'ud appears less a legal and moral theoretician than a troubleshooter trying to bring some principled order to a confused world. This is borne out in his insistence that the practice of muhaddere was not a matter of Islamic belief or an element in a prescribed catechism of conduct.

One of the legal dilemmas presented by the practice of female seclusion was how to discipline an individual whose honor depended on her unavailability to the public sphere. As we have seen, the solution was to make her male guardian responsible. The emphasis on humiliation of the male guardian as a punitive tool was in line with the principle that effective discipline for the elite, whose distinguishing claim was a superior degree of moral honor, was dishonor through words or other personal exposure. Within the marital relationship, the coercive powers of state and society (often hard to distinguish in the premodern period) encouraged a husband's control of his wife by exposing him to public censure should her conduct violate accepted norms. In other words, public accountability of male for female might encourage the exercise of undue authority by male over female. Ebu Su'ud's response to this dilemma was, not surprisingly, to uphold the husband's right to control his wife's public conduct but at the same time to set limits to it.

In his fetvas on female seclusion, Ebu Su'ud attempted to mediate the relationship not only *within* the marital unit but also between the domestic household and society at large. In terms of the relationship between the individual and the community, the mufti worked to prevent violation of legal practice incurred in the name of seclusion as well as manipulation of the practice of seclusion to avoid the law. In the formulation of his fetvas on proxy appointment and witnessing, he defended the integrity of public law against the presumptions of the privileged. Ebu Su'ud's insistence that "it is not permissible for the law to languish" in the context of regulating elite female behavior suggests that the cultivation of elite status in the midsixteenth century was in part an attempt to ward off the public regulatory mechanisms whose scope was expanding under the sultan Süleyman, known to later generations as "the Legislator," and his chief mufti.

NOTES

*   I would like to thank the staff of the Süleymaniye Library for facilitating my research in the fetva collections housed there. I am grateful to the American Philosophical Society, the American Council of Learned Societies, and the Institute of Turkish Studies (Research Travel Grant) for funding that research. An early version of this essay was presented in 1992 at the Dayan Center for Middle Eastern and African Studies, Tel Aviv University. I would also like

to thank the Speaker Series of the Committee for the Study of Women and Gender in the Middle East and Islamic Societies, Harvard University, for twice inviting me to present my work. The present chapter has benefitted considerably from the comments of these audiences.

1. For a study that situates Ebu Su'ud in both a legal and an historical context, see Imber (1997) and Mandaville (1979, 289–308).
2. Following is the Turkish of the three fetvas cited:

   - *Karye ehlinden maslahatın kendi görüp pınardan su getiren Hind, muhaddere olur mu? Olmaz.*
   - *Hamama ve kuraya giden Hind muhaddere olur mu? Olur, ırz u vakarla ve hadem ü haşem ile giderse.*
   - *Hamama ve düğüne ve ahar mahalleye seyrana varan Hind, muhaddere olur mu? Olur, eğer haşmetle varır ise.*

3. In Turkish: *Babası 'utekasına ve evlad-ı 'uteka ve hemşireleri zevcine görünen Hind, muhaddere olur mu? Muhadderelikte mu'teber olan, hudud-i şeriat-i şerifeyi ri'ayet değildir. Onunçün kafirelerde dahi muhaddere bulunur. Ele görünüp mesalihine bizzat mübaşeret eder değil ise, muhadderedir.*
4. Surat al-Nisa', 4:23–24.
5. Public Record Office, London: S.P. 102/61/237 (letter of the grand vezir Siyavush Pasha dated Ramazan 1000 {1592}; S.P. 102/61/81 (victory letter dated Rebi'ul-Ahir 1009 {1600}, at the conclusion of the Kanisza campaign.
6. *Çok nesne lazım olmaz.*
7. Ebu Su'ud Efendi, *Ba'z ul-Fetava*, Süleymaniye Library, Ms. Yeni Cami 685/3, folio 179a.
8. These themes are the subject of Turkish director Yılmaz Güney's widely acclaimed film *Yol.*
9. Ibn Kemal (Şemseddin Ahmed b. Kemal Paşa), *Fetava*, Süleymaniye Library, Ms. Dar ul-Mesnevi 118, folios 78b–79a.
10. Ebu Su'ud Efendi, *Ba'z ul-Fetava*, folio 170b.
11. Ebu Su'ud Efendi, *Ba'z ul-Fetava*, folio 167b.
12. This is possible because punishment for adultery and fornication is determined for each of the guilty parties by his or her civil status rather than by the particular circumstances of the transgression: a

male slave and a freeborn Muslim female will receive quite different punishments for engaging in a mutual act of adultery (according to Süleyman's *kanunname,* the slave receives one-quarter the punishment of the woman and perhaps even less if she is quite wealthy).

13. Ibn Kemal, *Fetava,* folio 33a.

14. "*Tecdid-i iman lazım olur, 'avammdan ise;*" Ibn Kemal, *Fetava,* folio 74a.

15. For discussion of the conditional vow, see Imber (1993) and Peirce (1998b).

16. The statute goes on to state: "and if they deserve to be imprisoned, they shall, if someone stands surety for their person, not be imprisoned and the matter shall be submitted and officially notified by the judge to My Sublime Court. If, however, their offense is a grievous outrage and there is a likelihood of their resorting to flight, and furthermore, there is nobody standing surety for them, they shall be imprisoned."

17. For similar views of the Hanafi jurists al-Kasani (d. 1191) and Ibn Humam (d. 1457), see respectively, Schneider (1995, 163) and Imber (1997, 211–12). I thank David S. Powers for the reference to Schneider's citation of al-Kasani. For an illuminating discussion of hierarchy and social class in medieval Islamic thought, see Marlow (1997).

18. On the distinction between *hass* and *'amm* (*khāṣṣ* and *'āmm* in Arabic transcription), see Beg (1978, 4:1098–99).

19. For further discussion of this question, see Peirce (1998a).

EIGHT

Toward Islamic Feminisms:
A Look at the Middle East*

Margot Badran

Muslim women's engagements with modernity in its diverse forms from the nineteenth to the late twentieth centuries have both produced and been driven by new forms of consciousness about gender that surfaced at various moments. The basic argument of this chapter is that Muslim women's feminisms in the Middle East have emerged in the context of encounters with modernity and that Islam has been implicated in the construction of these feminisms, as have notions of transnationality. This chapter considers how women, through their own reinterpretations of religion, culture, and modernity, informed by experience and referenced by sacred scripture, have constituted their own subjectivity within transnational contexts.

Feminism as a new consciousness of gender and women's subordination first emerged among the upper and middle classes in the crannies of unevenly gendered modernity at different moments in various countries of the Middle East (Sharabi 1988). Feminism, especially in stages of open activism, constituted uncomfortable challenges to masculinist scrambles to control the construction of modernity—its processes and its class and gender privileges. Men of the middle and upper classes would "get to modernity first," control the space, transfer power and privi-

159

leges, and, in short, define (a patriarchal) modernity (Sharabi 1988). It has often been argued that women were made to constitute or preserve "the traditional" at moments when customary ways were in danger of disappearing. I think it was not so much that women should act as symbols of an endangered old order so that men could be less (culturally) anxiously "modern," as that women must not compete for the benefits of modernity and define it in egalitarian terms.

In the late nineteenth and twentieth centuries, pioneering women constructed new feminisms out of attempts to engage more fully with modernity, appropriating the discourses of Islamic modernism and secular nationalism.[1] In the final third of the twentieth century some women, as recent beneficiaries of or aspirants to a new modernity, are questioning mainstream masculinist positions and developing a "feminist" consciousness from within Islamist movements. Historically, women have both created their own independent movements and have participated in male-dominated movements, while they critiqued them and also subverted them in certain ways. This gives rise to certain analytical challenges. How do we talk about women's activism within independent feminist movements without exaggerating the notion of free agency (Ortner 1996, 16)? How do we talk about women's agency as "feminists" within masculinist movements without underestimating the possibilities of their independent agency?

Permeating projects and processes of modernity in Middle Eastern societies has been the chiaroscuro—the light and shadow—of "the West." In the Middle East, modernity has always been complicated by association with a colonializing and imperialist West and has played out differently across class and gender lines. The earliest beneficiaries of modernity were the upper strata and more specifically men. Women were both more restricted in their access to the benefits of modernity and more tainted by its Western associations. The uneven gendering of modernity and its implications cast deep shadows on women's modernist discourse, especially their feminist discourse: it was

"Western" and therefore nonindigenous. During the colonial and early postcolonial periods, its Western associations implicated feminism as nationally subversive and treasonous.[2] There was also a dichotomy that was set up early (by opponents of Islamic modernism within the Muslim Middle East) between Islam and modernity, constructed as an East-West antagonism. This opposition has been sustained not only within certain quarters in Middle Eastern societies but by Westerners hostile toward or ignorant of Islam.

In the Middle East, Muslim women who have claimed a feminist identity did so as one of a number of identities, such as Muslim and nationalist. There have been other Muslim women who have claimed a single public identity such as nationalist, socialist, or Islamist, adamantly refusing any other label. While everyone possesses multiple identities, making a particular identity visible or invisible is a political decision. This political decision is often controlled by the dominant discourse, whether it is nationalism, socialism, or Islamism, which makes the articulation of a simultaneous identity a treacherous act. Late nineteenth-century Islamic modernism opened up space for multiple identities, so that one could be, for example, an Islamic reformer, a secular nationalist, and a feminist. Late twentieth-century Islamism, certainly the patriarchal mainstream, is in contention with other identities, especially nationalism and feminism, which it subsumes in the case of the former and aims to obliterate in the case of the latter.

Relations between Muslim women as feminists and Islamists have been uneven. At certain moments, they have been highly polarized, with each viewing the other as implacable adversaries (Badran 1994b). I think, for example, of second-wave feminists and Islamists in Egypt in the 1970s and 1980s or of feminist and Islamist women in Algeria or Sudan today. There has also been another pattern of relations between some, more open, Muslim feminists and Islamist women. This is a tolerant strand that acknowledges some common ground and mutual concerns, fostering space at certain moments for shared struggle. During the period of first-wave feminism in Egypt in the 1930s and 1940s, there were cordial relations between feminist and Islamist women who shared many goals. Recent instances include the following three examples. One, in the "head-scarf debate" in Turkey in the mid-1980s, second-generation feminists supported emergent Islamist women's right to wear *hijab,* in the form of a head scarf at the university and in other public sites (Olson 1985) Two, Yemeni feminist and Islamist women's recent common activism has promoted women's participation in parliamentary elections, with both sets of women using the discourse of Islam to politically mobilize women.[3] Yemeni feminist and Islamist women have also banded together to fight reactionary items in the new draft for a revised personal-status code or family law, which is based on the Shari'a or religious legal corpus (Badran 1998). Three, the first feminist book fair in Cairo in 1995 displayed books of feminist and Islamist women and drew women together in panel discussions across the feminist-Islamist spectrum.[4] Some third-wave Islamists have unprecedentedly admitted that there are lessons to be learned from Egyptian feminist history and even from critical readings of Western feminist literature, in the effort to construct an Islamic theory of women's liberation (Rauf 1996).[5]

While the nationalist dimension of Muslim women's feminisms has been recognized widely, this has not been true of the Islamic dimension. I argue that the feminisms of most Muslim women have historically been more Islamic than commonly alleged. (First-wave Turkish feminists have been the major exception to this tendency.) This argument intersects with the notion of plural identities and loyalties that is operative in everyday life but is often obscured at the level of public discourse and in the politics of positioning. In trying to understand Muslim women's feminisms we have to a certain extent been imprisoned by an inadequate vocabulary. A word for feminist (used adjectivally) first appeared in Arabic in 1923 (in Egypt) but this word, *nisa'iyya,* ambiguously connoted "feminist" or "women's." Its meaning had to be discerned from the context or from feminists' direct translations of the Arabic word into French or English. In the early 1990s (in the period leading up to the United Nations women's conference in Beijing in 1995), a new, unequivocal Arabic word specifically for "feminism" began to circulate in Egypt; the word is *nisawiyya* (variant form of nisa'iyya). In Turkish and Persian, there are loan words for "feminism." A lack of critical deconstruction of concepts, especially gendered deconstructions, and sufficient historicization have also hampered understanding of Muslim women's feminisms. Serious debates in public forums have been put off course by a persistent circulation of disparaging and degrading stereotypes of feminism (most frequently turning feminist critiques of masculinist domination into feminism as "man-hating projects sowing discord between genders"). Orientalist notions first articulated around the turn of the century and echoed later in the century by mainstream Islamist contentions that Muslim women "cannot possibly be feminists" have also skewed discussions.

To demonstrate my arguments about feminist-Islamist juxtapositions and imbrications I look at the experience of Muslim feminists in Egypt early this century and of Islamist women in Turkey at the end of the century. I draw on my own historical work on Egyptian feminism, especially my book *Feminists, Islam, and Nation* (Badran 1994a), and on research on contemporary Islamist women in Turkey by Turkish sociologist Nilüfer Göle, recently published in English under the title *The Forbidden Modern* (1996; translation of Göle 1991); both sources reveal strikingly similar gender activist modes, goals, and strategies. I note how early Egyptian feminist and contemporary Turkish liberal Islamist discourses both emerged from within the framework of Islamic movements (early reformist or later resurgent) in which Muslim women, through revisiting sacred scripture, seek to constitute modern lives for themselves. I discuss the divergent public identities that both sets of women have assumed and their positions within the dominant discourses of their respective moments.[6] I conclude this comparative reflection with a broader look at Muslim women's revisioning of Islam through *ijtihad* (interpretive readings of Islamic sacred texts) as part of a more global project feminist and Islamist women are engaged in today. Both Islamist and feminist women are rereading the Qur'an and other religious texts, bringing to bear their own experiences and new critical methodologies to enact readings that are more meaningful to modern women (Wadud-Muhsin 1992).

I speculate on the future to encourage thinking of the broader and longer-term implications of my discussion. I suggest that the new radical feminism in Muslim societies—and I include diaspora societies—as we begin the twenty-first century will be "Islamic feminism." My arguments for this are the following:

1. Islam is becoming a paramount cultural and political paradigm.

2. Muslim women who are more highly educated in greater numbers than ever before have begun gender-progressive readings of Islamic sacred scripture that will achieve— and indeed have already achieved—significant "feminist" breakthroughs.

3. Only the language of an "Islamic feminism" can potentially reach women of all classes and across urban-rural divides, or to put it slightly differently, the majority of Muslims can associate only with a "feminism" that is explicitly "Islamic."

4. Because of increasing globalization and growing Muslim diaspora communities, Muslim women who practice Islam and want to embrace feminism need an Islamic feminism.

5. The globalized media and technology revolution produces a decentered and denationalized feminism and connects Muslim women inside and outside predominantly Muslim nations or communities with each other.

The conceptual and political location of this "Islamic feminism" will occupy a middle space, or independent site, between secular feminism and masculinist Islamism. I suggest that "Islamic feminists" will come to acknowledge plural identities and that "secular feminists" will make more explicit an Islamic dimension of feminism that will link them to other Muslim women as theorists and activists of gender. "Islamic feminists" will acknowledge positionings and linkages beyond those created by religion and cease to shy away from the feminist label but rather will acknowledge such an identity. Globalization and diasporization are producing multiple identities and sliding intersections of "feminist" concern that are increasingly hard to deny.[7] I believe that the new radical feminism in Muslim societies—that is, "Islamic feminism"—will play a salient role in (1) the revisioning of Islam, (2) the constitution of a new modernity in the twenty-first century, and (3) the transformation of feminism itself. Feminism may even get a new name.

Historically, feminism has been implicitly or explicitly part of other discourses, such as religious reformist or nationalist discourses. It gendered these discourses in ways that take as central concerns the constructions and positionings of women and their rights, choices, and opportunities. Feminism is a reformative and transformative strategy. Within Judaism and Christianity, feminist reinterpretations of sacred scripture and activisms have refigured the practice of religious ritual, opening up new roles for women as ministers and rabbis and for "unordained" women as leaders of congregational prayer. These "religious feminisms," appearing in countries with a separation of religion and state or at historical moments when secular discourses hold sway, have been more specialized or compartmentalized; they have not occupied center stage.

As we move toward the close of the twentieth century, the gender-conscious identities of Muslim women—within predominantly Muslim states and societies, in old Muslim minority communities, and in new diasporas—have become increasingly complicated. Muslim women face the conundrum of what to call their gender activism—what is legitimately possible and politically expedient within their diverse ideological and political frameworks. Women's progressive gender activisms across the feminist-Islamist spectrum are blurring as the borders between feminisms and gender-progressive Islamisms are breaking down. Actors and analysts alike face the challenge of how to characterize these gender activisms (Badran 1994b).

A process is now underway to locate a feminism within a more explicit and strenuous Islamic religious paradigm, but as yet there are no center-stage religious feminisms in Islamic societies. As secularism—in the form of privatization or compartmentalization of religion and in the muting of religious cultural symbols—recedes in Muslim societies, and as Islam becomes the predominant discourse, the new feminism will be a religious feminism. A case in point is Iran, where a new Islamic feminism is becoming increasingly visible (Mir-Hosseini 1996a, 1996b; Najmabadi 1998).

The notion of an Islamic feminism is an uneasy one. Its constitution and practice are fraught with issues of power, authority, and legitimacy. The feminisms that evolved within Jewish and Christian religious frameworks emerged in Western societies and are seen as internal, "indigenous," or local critiques. Feminisms that evolved later in Muslim societies in postcolonial contexts were discredited in the patriarchal mainstream as Western and a project of cultural colonialism and therefore were stigmatized as antithetical to Islam.[8] Indigenous patriarchal fear and the penumbra of Western postcolonialism operated to squeeze out space for a feminism as *part* of Islamic discourse.

In the 1990s, the notion of an Islamic feminism and, indeed, the term itself have been surfacing in parts of the Middle East. The term, however, is controversial and not necessarily well thought out, and there is no consensus about its meaning on the part of either advocates or adversaries. Women in Iran who publish a radical paper called *Zanan* are part of what Iranian scholars Afsaneh Najmabadi (1998) and Ziba Mir-Hosseini (1996a, 1996b) call an emergent Islamic feminist movement.[9] Feride Acar (1991, 301) notes the appearance of the term *Islamic feminism* in the Turkish popular media. Saudi anthropologist

Mai Yamani (1996, 263) writes that social circumstances in her country have caused "an identifiable strand of Saudi women to make of Islam the vehicle for the expression of feminist tendencies." The term *Islamic feminist* has occasionally been used by feminist journalists in the Egyptian anglophone press to refer to feminist acts of Islamist women.[10]

ISLAMIC-ISLAMIST MODERNIST PROJECTS, NEW READINGS OF OLD TEXTS

Egyptian women's turn-of-the-century feminism and Turkish women's end-of-the-century Islamist "gender activism," which some call Islamic feminism, have both emerged out of broad movements of Islamic reform or revisioning. This involved women "going back" to religious scripture to purge current practices of "deviations," "accretions," and "omissions" through fresh readings of scripture or ijtihad. Such "going back" was an operation of "going forward." Women and men in Egypt, Turkey, and elsewhere have referenced sacred texts in order to engage with modernity (in the sense of new configurations of the social, economic, political, scientific, and technological). Modernity as process always includes elements of "the before" or "the traditional." Modernity is construed as involving new turns or departures rather than ruptures and is uneven temporally, spatially, and indeed in the experience of individuals themselves.

It seems important at this point that I clarify my use of the terms *Islamic* and *Islamist*. I employ the term *Islamic* in two ways—broadly to signify anything pertaining to Islam and more specifically with reference to the late nineteenth century through the second third of the twentieth century. I use *Islamist* as an adjective or noun to refer to manifestations in the final third of the twentieth century of "political Islam" with hijab (Islamically prescribed head cover and modest dress) as its marker. Göle (1996) uses the term *Islamist women* in a very broad sense to include all women who wear hijab or "those who cover," as they are often called; these are the first generation of women to take up the new hijab. In Egypt today, for example, there are many women who cover who are not part of the male-led Islamist movements. Many women simply wish to conform to what they understand is a religiously prescribed mode of dress, which has by now become a popular social convention.

Islamic modernism's core idea and analytical tool is ijtihad. The pioneering proponent of this early movement of Islamic reform in late nineteenth-century Egypt was Muhammad 'Abduh, a religious scholar and later Mufti of Egypt (Stowasser 1993, 3–28; Haddad 1985). This new movement attempted to ease the way for Egyptian Muslims (especially the more economically advantaged) to reckon with modernity—to be Muslim and modern. Islamic modernism also paved the way for secularism or an increasing privatization of religion and individually interpreted religion. In Egypt, although most law was removed from the direct jurisdiction of Islam, personal status (or family law) continued to be based on the Shari'a or religious law. The emergent secular elites of the late nineteenth and early twentieth centuries, who welcomed a tempering of the hold of institutionalized religion, viewed this revisionist Islam as a positive, forward-looking, modernist project. The British colonial authorities saw Islamic reform as tempering Muslims themselves and thus serving the purposes of colonial rule.[11] It would be because of what was seen as "accommodationist" rather than a more "independent" Islamic reformist move that would prompt late twentieth-century Islamists to reject the 'Abduh-ian modernist project. Islamic modernism, however, provided a basis for a consolidation of a new nation-state with equal room for all Egyptians, irrespective of religion. Secular progressives of the day thus saw 'Abduh's modernist project as liberatory. Women's "feminist consciousness," which had first emerged out of the jolt of contradictory contacts with modernity, took shape as a "feminist" version of Islamic modernism at the end of the nineteenth and beginning of the twentieth centuries. The shadows that fell on Islamic modernism also fell on women's feminism; indeed they were long shadows casting a darkness on feminism to this day.

The current Islamic revisionist project in Turkey, emerging in a highly secularized landscape, is widely seen as an ominous move backward. Ataturk, distancing himself from the previous religiously founded Ottoman imperial state and its defunct multiethnic empire, resolved to build a modern and secular nation-state in the 1920s and 1930s. He explicitly aligned modernization with Westernization, evacuating religion wholesale from his construction of modernity. A fully secular constitution or Civil Code (of 1926, based on a Swiss model) was imposed from on high, bringing both public and private (or societal and family) spheres under the purview of secular state law. Unveiling (dehijabicization) was imposed by the state. Women's new dress and new lives became symbols of state-imposed Westernized modernity. The state-led unveiling, new educational and work opportunities for women, and political rights dispensed from on high constituted what has been called *state feminism*. (Many feminists, however, consider the notion of a state feminism to be an oxymoron; Kandiyoti 1991c). The Kemalist state did not allow for an independent women's movement; when women tried to form an autonomous feminist organization they were prevented by the state.[12] This is not to say, however, that elite women did not benefit from the "rights" bestowed on them (Toprak 1993, 297–98). This rigorous state-led rupture with Islamic culture took hold mainly among urban elites—the designated beneficiaries of the secularized, Westernized modernity in whose everyday lives new transformations played out. The more modest strata and provincial and rural populace were left out of the circumference of the new Westernized modernity. For them Islamic culture remained alive.

It has been argued that the assault on religious culture, and the elitist scripting of Kemalism, planted the seeds for an eventual populist resurgence of Islam among the unsecularized nonelites coming mainly from the Anatolian provinces who did not benefit socially or economically from republican modernization. The populist reappropriation of religion, by women and men alike, half a century later constituted an attack on the legacy of Kemalist modernity with its fervent secularism and exuberant Westernicity. Such a "return" to Islam and its scriptures for a reaffirmation of cultural legitimacy and renewed identity is seen by Kemalist loyalists in Turkey and anxious "Islam-watchers" in the West as retrogressive (Toprak 1981). There are other analysts, such as Nilüfer Göle, Yesim Arat, and other social scientists, for example, who see in the Islamist movement elements of a forward-looking modernist project: a populist attempt to redefine modernity in Islamic terms (Arat 1990; Göle 1996).

GENDERING ISLAMIC MODERNIST PROJECTS: EARLY TWENTIETH-CENTURY EGYPTIAN FEMINISTS (SECULAR AND ISLAMIC)

In *Feminists, Islam, and Nation* (Badran 1994a), I demonstrated how Muslim Egyptian women's reinterpretation of Islam (influenced by the example of the Muslim reformer Muhammad 'Abduh) paved the way for cloistered middle- and upper-class women to gain access to public space, to remove the veils from their faces, to claim a public voice, and to demand educational, work, and political rights. Such maneuvers and claims, legitimized by new readings of Islam, or women's ijtihad, constituted an explicit feminist project through which women aimed to constitute themselves as modern citizens in a modern state and society and, indeed, to help construct the new state and society itself. (If Muslim women in Egypt located their feminism firmly within the parameters of their Islamic religion, Coptic feminists in Egypt likewise evoked a religious justification within their own Christian tradition for the feminist activism they shared with Muslim women. However, there was no Christian reform movement; thus Coptic women's religious arguments for feminist activism remained at a general rhetorical level.)

There was another discourse at work during the originary

moment of feminism in Egypt, which only slightly postdated the emergence of Islamic modernism: this was the discourse of secular nationalism. Following British colonial occupation in 1882, women and men in Egypt created a nationalist movement to expel the British from Egyptian soil. Egyptians constructed "the nation" in territorial terms, grounded in the equality of Muslims and Copts as citizens and common inhabitants of the land. This replaced the older construction of "nation" along religious and ethnic lines (the *millet* system) under the Ottomans (under whose loose jurisdiction Egypt remained until 1914). This nationalism was called *secular nationalism,* expressing another dimension of the term *secular*—inclusivity of persons of different religions as citizens with equal rights. At the same time, this construction of the secular provided space for religious difference and an equality in difference—the equal rights of Egyptian citizens to be different in religion and to be "governed" communally in matters of religion. (It is interesting to note that the Arabic word for "secularism" [*'alamaniyya* or *'almaniyya*] comes from the word for "world" [*'alam*], while *secular* in Latin-based languages comes from the Latin word for "age" [*saeculum*]. The Arabic term has a spatial signification, while the Latin has a temporal one; this suggests two different constructions of the term and a need to consider the possibility of salient differences between the two terms.)

Egyptian women gendered the nationalist discourse; furthermore, as Muslims, they wove it into their gendered discourse of Islamic modernism. Muslim women who, as feminists and as women, struggled to be modern held Islamic modernism and secular nationalism together in interactive tension in the colonial period and in the early postcolonial era, preserving this often torturous link to this day.[13] Meanwhile, secular nationalist men moved farther down the secular road, abandoning religion to the purview of the ulema, the religious scholars.[14]

Egyptian women's feminism has been called secular to signify the inclusivity of Muslims and Copts within its circumference. This kind of secularism mirrored the secularism of (secular) nationalism that articulated the equality of Muslims and Copts as citizens in the land of Egypt. Like secular nationalism, progressive women's articulation of secularism did not connote an evacuation of religion from the feminist project but accorded space to religious difference. Secular nationalist men, with their eyes most fixed on the politics of the public arena, relegated religion to the sidelines and the sphere that it still controlled— the "private" sphere, where personal status codes (with separate codes for Muslims and Christians) regulated family life. While secular nationalist men saw this in general as politically expedient and as advantageous to themselves as men, as secular nation-state builders, and as family patriarchs, (secular) feminist women could not ignore religion and the "private" sphere, which was a site of inequality or inequity—and a location where a continued application of premodern masculinist interpretation of religion was condoned. The preservation of a premodern masculinist hegemony in the "modern era" created conflictual everyday lives for women, thwarting their abilities to access the full rights of modern citizens in the public arena that as Egyptians was their due. Patriarchal authorities in families could, and did, control women's public access.

As feminists, Muslim Egyptian women, therefore, operated simultaneously to modernize the state and society (the public sphere) and to modernize the family (the private sphere) and, in so doing, functioned both as secular feminists and as Islamic feminists. Secular feminists operationalized "secularism" in the public sphere by fighting for the rights of all citizens, keeping a central (but not exclusive) focus trained on gender, irrespective of religious affiliation. Secular feminists operationalized "secularism" in the private sphere, by upholding religious difference and acknowledging the importance of religion and, as Muslims, the need to push Islamic reformist inquiry forward into implementation. Muslim Egyptian women's feminism, to repeat, was at once a "secular feminism," in the sense of being inclusive of both Muslims and Christians and according space to a common struggle of Egyptian women to enjoy their equal rights as citizens, as well as an "Islamic feminism" that placed Islamic reform and modernism at the center of the debates around the regulation of personal status laws, referencing sacred texts in their project to modernize the legal regulation of the family.

In the colonial (1882–1922) and quasi-postcolonial periods (1922–56), Egyptian (secular) nationalism constituted the paramount public discourse but never eradicated Islamic discourse. Muslim women as feminists—who continued to identify with and practice their religion—called themselves simply *feminists,* assuming their affiliation with and upholding of Islam to be self-evident and not in need of public declaration. Women in the late nineteenth and early twentieth centuries could be Muslim, modern, and secular.

GENDERING ISLAMIST MODERNIST PROJECTS: TWENTIETH-CENTURY TURKISH ISLAMIST GENDER ACTIVISTS (ISLAMIC AND FEMINIST)

Unlike in Egypt, where women's secular feminist activism early this century sprang from the ground prepared by the Islamic modernist movement but not directly from within the movement itself, a women's gender-sensitive discourse surfaced from within the Islamist movement in Turkey in the 1980s and 1990s.[15] Contemporary Turkish "gender activists" from the ranks of the Islamists do not identify themselves explicitly as feminists.

The new Islamist women in Turkey, according to Göle's research conducted in the second half of the 1980s, initially sprung from that segment of society that had not profited from the Kemalist secularized Westernized modernity. They had been virtually consigned to a space beyond the pale of this version of modernity, remaining within the circumference of Islamic culture represented in the Kemalist discourse as "backward."[16] Meanwhile, second-wave feminists also made their appearance on the scene in the 1980s; they were the daughters of the elite Kemalist women whose identity and feminism had been designed and delivered by the state. These new feminists were direct heirs of a prepackaged version of modernity and "state feminism," which had curtailed women's agency and cut off these elite women from their Islamic heritage and from the Turkish majority. Kemalist "state feminism" masked the preservation of salient aspects of patriarchal culture hidden under the guise of a so-called progressive Western veneer. It particularly galled this new generation to discover that male headship of the family was inscribed in the Turkish Civil Code, something previously obscured (Z. Arat 1994; Sirman 1989, 1990; Tekeli 1986, 1990, 1995).

Both of these groups of women of the new generation have reacted against the project of modernity and of state feminism imposed from on high. Such rejection constituted women's moves to take the initiative in constructing their own identities and shaping their everyday lives. The new feminists and Islamist women alike were well aware that women's bodies had been sites for signaling Kemalist modernity: the unveiled woman was the symbol of the secular, Westernized modern nation. The new generation made their own bodies sites of opposition to the Kemalist legacy. Islamist women who took up the hijab, in the form of a head scarf, signaled an Islamic modernity through the new symbolism of the veiled body. Meanwhile, feminist women, in defense of their bodies, rallied against the public harassment and domestic violence to which women of all classes were subjected. The defense of the body, problems of identity, the insistence on self-agency and deciding their own agendas, catapulted two different kinds of women onto the activist stage half a century after the introduction of the Kemalist project.

The new Islamist women (as noted coming mainly from ordinary families in Anatolian towns and villages or working class families in the big cities outside the circumference of the Westernized modernity) surfaced in significant numbers in the 1980s in the large urban universities where their reappropriation of the veil, in the form of a turban, signaled their existence. These women, among the high achievers at the university, were part of a broader Islamist movement aiming to restore Islam to public primacy. Inspired by new readings of sacred scripture, they articulated an Islamic modernity as a counterpoise to the "Western," secular modernity scripted by Kemalism. Through their political participation in the Islamist movement, these new activists projected an Islamic modernity for women. They left behind the private sphere of the home—the *mahrem,* the private, hidden, silent, invisible space, the "traditional" space of women (of the middle and upper strata). *Mödern Mahrem* (1991), the Turkish title of Nilüfer Göle's book *The Forbidden Modern,* calls attention to Islamist women's revisioning of the conventional gender symbolism. Thus, in Turkey while Islam was restored to view with the rising Islamist movement, women made themselves publicly visible as Muslims. The two titles seem to display an unresolved tension in an Islamic construction of modernity in Turkey.

Not only were progressive Islamist women important as role models for other women, but their Islamic activism is a path to their own self-reconstruction and practice of agency as well. Yesim Arat (1990) and Feride Acar (1991) in studying Islamist women's journals (*Kadin ve Aile, Bizim Aile,* and *Mektup,* which are closely aligned with men's religious associations) point to contradictory imbrications of the secular and religious in their content. It is not clear to what extent women have editorial control or are conduits for men's gendered Islamist discourse. Along with articulating the standard rhetoric of women's primary roles as wives and mothers, their positioning as believers, and appeals to wear the hijab, women's education is encouraged, even in gender-mixed settings (the existing gender-integrated schools are a Kemalist legacy, economically unfeasible to dismantle). There is a sprinkling of a rhetoric of women's rights and emancipation in Islam. Noting that Islamist women were assuming agency as editors and writers, Arat (1990, 21) speculates that "these activities, in due time, might become secularized sources of power for women." It is not unlikely that some women will take the initiative in constructing a more liberatory discourse out of a confused welter of ideas. It might be that Islamist women will use such journals for enunciating a feminism within the discourse of Islam or eventually create new publications for this purpose.

Göle's study indicates similarities and dissimilarities between contemporary Turkish Islamist gender activists and early Egyptian feminists. The recent emergence on the public scene of the newly veiled (hijab-ed) Turkish women within the Islamist movement is reminiscent of the emergence of still-veiled (so-called hijab-ed but more accurately, *niqab*-ed—that is, "face-covered") Egyptian women on the public scene during the militant stage of the nationalist movement. In both instances women assumed new roles as political activists, learned valuable organizing and oratorical skills, and sought new opportunities in public space. These were both gendered modernist moves.

The arguments for education and work for women that Islamist women in contemporary Turkey advance eerily echo those advanced by the secular feminists at the beginning of the century in Egypt. Progressive Islamist women's rhetoric in Turkey extolling women's roles as mothers also closely reproduces the maternalist rhetoric of early Egyptian feminists articulated within the discourse of Islamic modernism and secular nationalism.[17] For the Egyptian feminists such rhetoric was a preemptive strike on the part of women pioneering in public roles who did not want the public carpet swept away from them on the pretext that they were abandoning their "true religiously ordained" roles. Maternalist rhetoric is freighted with multiple layers of meaning that need to be contextualized. Göle observed that some Islamist women—doing *teblig* (spreading the religious message) or working for pay—confronted their husbands about sharing domestic burdens and thereby refigured (functional) maternalism. Early Egyptian feminists were not that radical in their gender activism and accepted the notion of fuller maternal responsibility in the domestic sphere. But it must be added that these elite women, unlike the Turkish Islamists of more modest circumstances, relied on the domestic labor of other women to free themselves for their new activist forays.

While women are articulating and acting out new roles within the Islamic movement and claiming new rights and opportunities—shored up by scriptural reference—the difficulties women experience and potential threats should not be underestimated. Women face the complicated tasks of helping to restore Islam to cultural prominence, to critique the "old Islam" (in ways not unlike those of the early Islamic modernists in Egypt, yet in a different context) to help create an Islamic modernity, and to gender that modernity. To achieve all of this, they have to manipulate complicated sets of loyalties and engage in complicated gender politics within the Islamist movement itself and vis-à-vis secularists.

HIJAB AND MODERNITY

How does hijab fit into the discourse of modernity?[18] Contemporary Turkish Islamist women's new appropriation of the hijab constitutes a conscious act of religious observance, a reintroduction into the public realm of a symbol of Islamic public identity, and a gendered cultural statement of the right to be present in the collective public polity as Muslims. It is also a (consciously or unconsciously) political statement. Turkish women took up the hijab while already present in the public sphere.

Pioneering Egyptian feminists who entered public space early this century removed what was then called the hijab (but was actually the niqab) as a symbol of the marginality and public erasure of women of the middle and upper strata. For them, the hijab (in the form of the niqab) was not an Islamic requirement but a patriarchal imposition justified in the name of Islam. Huda al-Sha'rawi and Saiza Nabarawi announced the start of the feminist movement by a public unveiling of their faces in 1923 to symbolize the rejection of a culture of female segregation and domestic seclusion. Covering their heads only, they "modernized" the hijab in keeping with Islamic prescription. While al-Sha'rawi, like most other elite women, eventually removed her head covering altogether, it is significant that she wore the hijab for her "official" portrait as a feminist leader. It is not so much the hijab itself as its contextualization and the discourse around it that announces or suppresses Muslim women's agency and signals modernity or its nemesis. Some third-generation feminist and Islamist women in Egypt have remarked on this "feminist hijab."

REFUSING MASCULINIST POLITICS OF POSTPONEMENT

It is often thought that women's "gender activism" within the context of an Islamist movement—whether in Turkey or elsewhere—is a doomed project because women's gender issues will ultimately be subsumed. This is not an unfounded fear. Göle (1996) points out that Turkish Islamist activist women, operating as "missionaries" advancing the interests of the movement, tend to defer solutions to problems that women encounter in their daily lives to the future ideal Islamic society. Moreover, in the examples we have of Islamists in the Middle East moving from an oppositional mode to state power—that is, in Iran and Sudan—women have been initially heavily controlled. Egyptian women's active participation in the nationalist movement early this century—during which they juggled feminist and nationalist goals—was seen at the time as boding well for an eventual women's liberation. Yet after independence (albeit partial) in 1922 when nationalist men came into power, women's full rights—in law and practice—were deferred in favor of the building of a new independent nation-state. This was the moment when Egyptian feminists left the masculinist nationalist party (the Wafd) to found their own independent feminist organization and mount a highly visible movement (Badran 1994a).[19] Gender activists within Islamist states and movements have yet to mount independent movements although some are making judicious maneuvers.

Ultimately, a liberal discourse advanced by a male mainstream (whose words often do not match their convictions) will not save women, and a conservative discourse articulated by a broad masculinist movement will not doom women.[20] What matters is what women themselves do—their own assertive, independent activism. Historically, women have been both seduced by men's liberal discourses and coopted by men's conservative discourses. Women have at different times and places through their gender activisms tried to take charge of their own destinies. Both nationalist and Islamist (mainstream) discourses have delegitimized feminism and especially independent, organized feminist activisms.

GENDERED IJTIHAD:
THE WEB OF FEMINISM AND ISLAM

Ijtihad is a methodology used by feminist and Islamist women to reread the Qur'an and other religious texts to expose patriarchal interpretations of them and to advance more just understandings of Islam. Early this century, women operated within colonial contexts, early postcolonial contexts, and (as in Turkey during the collapsing Ottoman empire) ascendant secular nationalist contexts. Today women are operating within late postcolonial and postmodern contexts at a time when political Islam is ascendant. In both the early and late twentieth century, women met the challenges of modernity and the need to rearticulate culture. Then, women who were part of the educated elites of their day and were from wealthy or comfortable circumstances took the lead in formulating and disseminating their new readings of Islam and gender. Today, however, ideas about elite education, the formation of classes, and the dominant political discourses are different from those in the early part of this century.

In the early moments of confrontation with modernity in the Middle East—for example, Egypt in the nineteenth century—an inherited sense within Sunni Islam that the canon of jurisprudence had been fixed (by the tenth century C.E.) was operative.[21] In popular parlance "the gates of ijtihad had been closed."

Although interpretation did not cease over the subsequent centuries, this notion carried enormous weight.[22] In late nineteenth-century Egypt, Islamic reformer Muhammad 'Abduh advocated an opening of the "gates of ijtihad" to enact fresh interpretations of sacred scripture that took into account contemporary social, economic, and political realities. Through his call, contemporary men and women were exhorted to rethink Islam. Early feminists such as Malak Hifni Nasif, Nabawiyya Musa, and Huda al-Shaarawi in Egypt followed the lead of progressive interpreters like 'Abduh in advancing new understandings of Islam as they tried to forge modern lives for themselves. They used Islamic arguments to legitimize new forms of education and work and to gain access for women to congregational prayer in mosques. Women in this early group had state primary school and teachers' training diplomas, state secondary school and teachers' training diplomas (provided by the colonial state, with courses taught in English by British teachers except for the Arabic language and religion), and private lessons at home (taught by French tutors). Lebanese Nazira Zain al-Din, tutored by her father, who was a religious scholar, embarked on a detailed investigation of religious texts. She published *al-Sufur wa-'l-Hijab* (Unveiling and veiling, 1928) in Beirut, advancing religious arguments against face veiling, segregation of the sexes, and female seclusion. For her efforts in enacting a more gender-sensitive reading of religious texts, she was maligned in print by men of religion. She responded in a second book called *al-Fatah wa-'l-Shuyukh* (The young woman and the Shaykhs, 1929) the following year and subsequently disappeared from the scene.

In the final decades of the twentieth century, highly educated Muslim women, armed with advanced educations, including doctoral degrees, are applying a combination of historical, linguistic, hermeneutic, literary critical, deconstructive, semiotic, historicist, and feminist methodologies in their rereading of sacred texts pushing ijtihad to new limits. They are not treading safe ground. Sudanese scholar of Islamic religion and law Abdullahi an-Na'im (1990, 11) writes:

To attribute inadequacy to any part of the Shari'a is regarded as heresy by the majority of Muslims, who believe that the whole of Shari'a is divine. This widespread view creates a formidable psychological barrier, which is reinforced by the threat of criminal prosecution for the capital offense of apostasy (*ridda*), a real threat today in countries such as the Sudan.

This is borne out in the case of an Egyptian professor, Nasr Hamid Abu Zayd, who taught in the Department of Arabic at Cairo University. When he applied some of these techniques in rereading the Qur'an, certain individuals took it on themselves to declare him an apostate. Third parties (his Islamist detractors) pronounced him divorced from his wife (a Muslim woman cannot, according to religious law, be married to an apostate). The Egyptian higher court upheld this pronouncement (after it had been rejected in a lower court), and eventually he had to take refuge in exile.[23]

Muslim women, however, have pried open space to publicly rethink their religion, exposing false readings of sacred sources and articulating gender equality within Islamic discourse. In the 1980s, Moroccan feminist scholar Fatima Mernissi of Mohammed V University in Rabat conducted research on *hadiths* (sayings attributed to the Prophet Muhammad) exposing the misogyny perpetuated over the centuries through the circulation of false hadiths. She published her work in French under the title *Le harem politique* (1987) and in English translation as *Women and Islam: An Historical and Theological Enquiry* (1991b) and as *The Veil and the Male Elite: A Feminist Interpretation of Women's Rights* (1991a). A progressive Islamic feminist group composed of women of different ideological strands came together to form Sisters in Islam in Malaysia in the 1980s. After mounting their own investigations, they published booklets for wide circulation advancing Qur'anic arguments for gender-egalitarian authority in the family and arguing that the sacred text does not condone wife battery. African-American Muslim religious scholar Amina Wadud has published her work on Qur'anic reinterpretation, in which she opened up a range of gender issues for fresh examination in *Qur'an and Woman* (1992, under the name Wadud-Muhsin). Pakistani religious scholar Rifaat Hassan, who teaches in the United States, is also rereading the Qur'an. One of her earliest articles is "Equal before Allah? Woman-Man Equality in the Islamic Tradition" (1987). In South Africa, bold interpretive and activist work is being done by women such as Fatima Noordien, as well as by men such as Farid Esack at the Gender Desk of the Clement Main Road Mosque in Capetown.[24] Esack has published a persuasive and provocative book that takes up issues of equality and pluralism in Islam called *Qur'an, Liberation and Pluralism: An Islamic Perspective of Interreligious Solidarity against Oppression* (1997).

It is becoming increasingly difficult to talk about feminisms and gendered Islamisms. Seemingly, a salient distinction to make is between those who articulate gender equality within Islamic discourse and those who do not. Heba Rauf, an Egyptian Islamist political science graduate student at Cairo University, does not. Yet unlike Zeinab al-Ghazali and Safinaz Kazim, who adamantly reject a feminism (by that or any other name) within the discourse of Islam, Heba Rauf is trying to articulate a new "women's rights" discourse (she rejects the term *feminism*) within Islam.[25] Her master's thesis, which she recently published in the United States under the title *"al-Mar'a wa-'l-'Amal al-Siyasi: Ru'ya Islamiyya"* (The woman and political work: An Islamic perspective, 1996), uses Islamic discourse, and from within the Islamist movement in Egypt Rauf promotes a political construction of women's maternal role, religiously legitimizing political activism for women. Like early Egyptian feminists she stretches the "private" into the "public," transcending and dissolving the distinctions people have tried to make between these realms. In Rauf's case the holistic space is the Islamic *umma* (polity), and in the case of the early feminists it was the (secular) *watan* (nation-state). However, failing to take up the issue of gender equality as a right of citizens in the holistic umma of the private and public leaves room for masculinist hegemony. Egyptian women who early in the century advocated a political maternal role within the nationalist cum Islamic modernist paradigm witnessed the subsuming of this gendered role within a "larger" (masculinist) nationalist discourse *after* a nationalist state was established. This may well adumbrate the eventual implications of a politicized Islamic maternity if and when an Islamist state is achieved in Egypt.

Before returning to the intellectual activism of Iranian Islamic feminists mentioned earlier in the chapter, I would like to talk about positionality. Much of the innovative interpretive work, employing various feminist analytical techniques, is being published by Muslim women outside the Middle East. While Mernissi and Rauf live and work mainly in the Middle East, their books referred to above were published in France and the United States, respectively. (Both have done graduate work in the West, and both travel frequently to the West to participate in intellectual exchange.) The other new interpreters and activists mentioned above conduct their work outside the Middle East in Malaysia, South Africa, and the United States.

The bold new interpretive work Iranian women are performing and disseminating through *Zanan* is being done inside the Middle East and moreover inside an Islamic state. These women have experienced political and intellectual repression in the name of Islam inside the Islamic Republic of Iran. Only in the post-Khomeini era have they been able to carry on a public debate on gender questions based on their own rereadings of the Qur'an. Enacting their own ijtihad they are articulating an Islamic gender equality. In an Islamic republic where the Qur'an functions as the "constitution" of the land, women have found it possible as citizens to question readings of the Qur'an that do not result in social justice for citizens. These new Islamic feminists—who publicly claim the label—are, moreover, inclusionaries who welcome intellectual debate across an East-West divide (Mir-Hosseini 1996a; Najmabadi 1998). These Iranian Islamic feminists are publicly and explicitly taking independent and risky positions on gender as they reinterpret the religion.

They are not adjuncts to masculinist political projects. Quite to the contrary, they are finding a separate space—between secular feminism and masculinist Islamisms. It is what I call the middle ground, in the sense of "in-between space."

In this chapter I am claiming that the new radical feminism of the future in Muslim societies will be Islamic feminism. In formulating an explicit, independent feminist discourse of gender egalitarianism inside the Middle East, the new Iranian Islamic feminists are in the lead.

CONCLUDING REFLECTIONS ON
FEMINISM AND ISLAM

Is feminism any gender-sensitive project? Is feminism something articulated by a self-declared feminist? Is a person who looks to the religion of Islam for models and messages of gender-sensitive behaviors an Islamist? Is a feminist or Islamist identity something proclaimed, or can it be inferred? If we accept that contextualization is crucial or definitional and that acts are understood in their obvious embeddedness in ideological or political projects, then how can we capture feminisms emerging within Islamist movements? Naming, self-definition, and positioning are important, yet acts do carry multiple inflections or operate simultaneously on different registers. As we move into the twenty-first century, feminist-Islamist overlap on terrains of gender and culture is increasingly discernible. At present, an Islamic feminism seems to most to be an oxymoron. But as constructions (and understandings) of feminism and Islamism continue to shift and become more complex, this perception will dissipate. The middle space I mentioned at the beginning of the chapter as the site for new feminisms in Muslim societies and among many diaspora Muslims will become increasingly populated. It will be a space full of opportunity and full of danger—the location of a new feminist culture and a new Islamic culture.

NOTES

* Earlier versions of this chapter were presented at the Gender and Society Workshop at the University of Chicago; at the Symposium on Gender and Sacred Texts at Northwestern University; and as a public lecture at the University of Notre Dame sponsored by the Mediterranean/Middle East Studies Program, the Department of Classics, and the Program for Gender Studies during the spring of 1997. I profited from the questions, comments, and discussions at these events. In particular, I would like to thank the following for their comments on the versions of this chapter presented on those occasions: Jacqueline Bhabha, Faisal Devji, Gönül Ertem, Mala de Alwis, Ritty Lukose, and Kamala Visweswaran. I thank Tikva Frymer-Kensky and Robert Shreiter for conversations on gender, secularism, and religion.

1. For a general look at the nexus of feminism, religious reformism, and nationalism in the late nineteenth and twentieth centuries in selected countries of the East, see Jayawardena (1986). On Egyptian feminisms, see Badran (1988, 1989a, 1989b, 1991, 1993, 1994a).

2. Basu (1995) notes that women's activism appears to have yielded greater dividends in contemporary nationalist struggles than during the anticolonial movements of the earlier period. In Turkey and Iran, which were not colonized, the state in the 1920s and 1930s dictated a Westernized modernity, an important part of which was "state feminism."

3. The author was present at an audience with Shaykh al-Azhar Muhammad al-Tantawi, February 1997, in the company of Yemeni feminist Raufa Hassan, who taped the Shaykh's confirmation of women's right to vote and his negation of the idea that a woman's voice is '*awra* ("something shameful to be covered;" awra literally means "pudendum"). The taped interview was reproduced on cassettes for wide distribution in Yemen prior to the April 1997 election.

4. On the feminist book fair, see Badran (1995). From the end of the 1980s and into 1990 (before it was closed) the Arab Women's Solidarity Association held public *nadwas* or seminars where some

feminist and some Islamist women gathered, but the general atmosphere between the two was strained. This was especially apparent when Islamist Safinaz Kazim gave a presentation on hijab in 1989.

5. See also Najmabadi (1998, 63), where she refers to a couple of articles by Mahboobe Ommi, an Iranian writer, published in 1991 in a journal called *Zan-i Ruz* (Today's Woman) and says that "Ommi's rhetoric in these articles centered on accepting the historical validity and positive contributions of feminism for 'the West.'"

6. My book in progress on new feminisms in the Middle East will include a closer look at contemporary Egyptian Islamist gender activists, among others. I have explored convergences and divergences in past and present feminist and Islamist women's experience in various writings (see references) and in public lectures such as "Three Waves of Egyptian Feminism: Gender, Islam, and Nation," a paper presented at the University of Chicago, October 1996, and in "Feminists and Islamists in Contemporary Egypt," a paper presented at the University of Toronto, March 1996. I have looked at processes of Islamist women's globalizing projects in "Gender and Islamist Globalization," a seminar presentation on religion in Africa, Northwestern University, March 1997, and in Badran (1996).

7. On the challenges and implications of these contemporary phenomena, see, for example, Rudolf and Piscatori (1997).

8. It has also been argued that "Islam did not share the misogynous underpinnings of Christianity and Judaism" and consequently "there did not seem to be any grounds for feminism in an Islamic country;" see Najmabadi (1998, 63).

9. Kian (1977, 24) discusses the new feminist phenomenon in Iran without using the term *feminism*.

10. The term has appeared in various articles in *Al-Ahram Weekly* that have been widely read in Egypt and abroad by Arabic speakers.

11. A common position among contemporary Islamists is that 'Abduh's Islamic modernism constituted a cooptation by the colonial authorities (he was exiled and then allowed reentry into Egypt and appointed Mufti) or a selling out to the colonial West. 'Abduh, in articulating his Islamic modernism, pointed out that Arabs had perfected Greek science and philosophy before transmitting it to the West.

12. In 1923, the state outlawed the Women's People's Party. The following year the state created the Turkish Women's Federation, which was dissolved in 1935 not long after the vote had been granted to women (Kandiyoti 1991a, 41).

13. Egyptian feminists distinguished between indigenous patriarchal domination articulated often in both religious terms and colonial patriarchal domination. They contested both simultaneously and deftly in "two languages."

14. Nationalists such as Mustafa Kamil, who supported a renewed caliphate and thus a construction of the nation on religious terms, did not hold the day but did bequeath a different legacy, which slowly fermented underground—that is, under secular nationalist ground.

15. On the rise of Islamism in Turkey, see Ayata (1996), Birtek and Toprak (1993), Mardin (1991), and Ahmad (1993).

16. See Keyder (1993), where he shows how the Western invention of nationalism had to be taught from the top down. See also Keyman (1995, 93–120, esp. 102).

17. Malak Hifni Nasif (Bahithat al-Badiyya) and Nabawiyya Musa extolled the primacy of women's roles as wives and mothers while at the same time articulating the importance of new societal roles for women.

18. Arlene Macleod (1990, 14) puts it well when alluding to the problem of analyzing the "new veil" in Egypt, "a form located neither in the traditional nor the modern vocabulary."

19. Other examples of the deferring of women's rights by liberal or progressive rationalist men include Algeria; see, for example, Hélie-Lucas (1990).

20. Bauer (1997, 244) stresses that both fundamentalist and secular patriarchies are "suspicious of women's autonomy."

21. On the gendering of the canon, see Stowasser (1994).

22. Despite a widespread perception to the contrary, ijtihad did not cease to be practiced; see Hallaq (1986).

23. He is presently in exile at Leiden University. For some of his views, see Colla and Bakr (1997, 327–34) and Abu Zayd (1993).

24. Among the young women activists is Fatime Noordien, whom the author met at the International Women's Forum in Khartoum in 1996; see Badran (1996). On the approaches of the Capetown progressive Islamist activist, see Esack (1997).

25. This is not to suggest that al-Ghazali's and Kazim's writings and actions do not indicate elements of "functional feminism." An analysis of this is beyond the limits of this chapter. I have written about these women elsewhere (Badran 1991, 1994b). I shall also deal with their ideas and activism relating to gender in my new book on Islamic feminisms in the Middle East.

Contributors

Asma Afsaruddin is assistant professor of Arabic and Islamic Studies at the University of Notre Dame. She previously taught at Harvard University where she also served as co-chair (with Mary-Jo DelVecchio Good) in 1994 to 1995 and then chair in 1995 to 1996 of the Committee for the Study of Gender and Women in the Middle East and Islamic Societies at the Center for Middle Eastern Studies at Harvard University. She is the co-editor (with A. H. Mathias Zahniser) of *Humanism, Culture, and Language in the Near East: Studies in Honor of Georg Krotkoff,* published by Eisenbrauns (1997), and is the author of several articles on medieval Islamic thought and Arabic literature.

Anan Ameri is currently the cultural arts director of the Arab Community Center for Economic and Social Services. Her doctorate in sociology is from Wayne State University. In recent years, she has served as the acting director of the Institute for Jerusalem Studies in Jerusalem and has been a visiting scholar at the Center for Middle Eastern Studies at Harvard University and a fellow at the Bunting Institute, Radcliffe College. During 1989 to 1993, she was a member of the United Nations North American Coordinating Committee of Non-governmental Organizations on the Question of Palestine. She has researched and written extensively on women's issues, Third World development, dependence theory, social movements and social change, and United States policy in the Middle East.

Margot Badran is a historian specializing in gender who writes, lectures, and frequently participates in public debates on feminisms in

Middle Eastern and Islamic societies. Her doctorate is in Middle Eastern history from Oxford University where she studied with Albert Hourani. She is a contributor to *Islam and Equality: Debating the Future of Women's and Minority Rights in the Middle East and North Africa* (forthcoming, 1999). Her book *Feminists, Islam, and Nation: Gender and the Making of Modern Egypt* published by Princeton University (1995) has been selected for translation by the Supreme Council of Culture in Egypt for the forthcoming Cairo conference commemorating the hundredth anniversary of the publication of *Tahrir al-Mar'a (Emancipation of the Woman)* by Qasim Amin. She recently taught courses on feminisms and Islamisms at the University of Chicago and is currently teaching gender theory and research methodologies as a Fulbright Professor at the Women's Studies Center at San'a, Yemen. At present, she is working on a book on comparative Islamic feminisms.

Virginia Danielson is currently curator of the Archive of World Music and keeper of the Isham Memorial Library at Harvard University. She also lectures by invitation in the Music Department at Harvard. She obtained her doctorate from the University of Illinois, Urbana-Champaign, in ethnomusicology. Her book *The Voice of Egypt: Umm Kulthum, Arabic Song and Egyptian Society in the Twentieth Century* was published by the University of Chicago Press (1997). She is also the author of numerous articles and reviews dealing with Arab music, female performers, popular music, and Muslim devotional music based on more than fifteen years of fieldwork and research experience in Cairo, Alexandria, and Upper Egypt. She is the co-editor of the Middle East volume of the *Garland Encyclopedia of World Music* (forthcoming).

Mary-Jo DelVecchio Good is professor of social medicine at Harvard University and co-director of its Center for the Study of Culture and Medicine. She also teaches in the department of sociology and serves on the executive committee of the Center for Middle East Studies. In 1990, she founded the Committee for the Study of Women and Gender in the Middle East and Islamic Societies and served as its chair until 1995. Her research focuses on cultural and comparative studies of bio-medicine and bio-technology and has done fieldwork in Turkey and Indonesia, among other countries. She is the author of *American Medicine: The Quest for Competence* published by the University of

California Press in 1995 and the editor-in-chief (with Byron J. Good) of *Culture, Medicine and Psychiatry: An International Journal of Cross-Cultural Research*.

Shahla Haeri is assistant professor of anthropology and director of Women's Studies at Boston University. She has written extensively on women, law, and religion in the Muslim world and is the author of *Law of Desire: Temporary Marriage in Shi'i Iran*, published by Syracuse University Press (1989). She has conducted field work in Iran, Pakistan, and India; among her writings on the topic is "Obedience versus Autonomy: Women and Fundamentalism in Iran and Pakistan." At present, she is writing a book on the relationship between Pakistani women, law, religion, and politics.

Leslie Peirce is associate professor in the Departments of History and Near Eastern Studies at the University of California at Berkeley. She taught previously at Cornell University, University of California at Los Angeles, and Boğazici University. Her book *The Imperial Harem*, published by Oxford University Press (1993), was awarded the Fuat M. Koprülü prize by the Turkish Studies Association in 1996. The book has been translated into Turkish, and a Greek translation is currently underway. Among other grants, she has been the recipient of a Social Science Research Council Advanced Research Grant, a Fulbright Scholar Grant, and a National Endowment for the Humanities Translation Grant. She has written extensively on women's legal and social issues in Ottoman Turkey and is currently working on a book about women and the sixteenth-century Ottoman legal system.

Julie Peteet is associate professor of anthropology and chair of the department at the University of Louisville, Kentucky. Her publications include *Gender in Crisis: Women and the Palestinian Resistance Movement* published by Columbia University Press (1991) and articles in various journals such as *American Ethnologist, Cultural Anthropology, Signs, Cultural Survival*, and *Middle East Report*. Her research has been funded by the Fulbright Commission, the Social Science Research Council, the Wenner-Gren Foundation for Anthropological Research, and the Mellon Foundation. She is currently completing a book manuscript on place and identity in Palestinian refugee camps.

Nayereh Tohidi is an Azerbaijani-Iranian-American scholar who has written extensively on women in Iran and Azerbaijan. Tohidi has a doctoral degree from the University of Illinois, Urbana-Champaign and has taught at a number of universities, including Stanford, Harvard, the University of Minnesota, and the University of California at Los Angeles. As a specialist on gender, Islam and identity politics, and gender and development in the Middle East and post-Soviet Caucasus and Central Asia, she has served as a consultant to the UNDP, UNICEF, and ILO. At present, she teaches Women's Studies and Sociology at California State University, Northridge.

Bibliography

Abbott, Nabia. 1942a. 'A'ishah: The Beloved of Mohammed. Chicago.

Abbott, Nabia. 1942b. "Women and the State in Early Islam I." *Journal of Near Eastern Studies* 1:106–27.

Abbott, Nabia. 1942c. "Women and the State in Early Islam II." *Journal of Near Eastern Studies* 1:341–61.

Abbott, Nabia. 1946. *Two Queens of Baghdad: The Mother and Wife of Harun al-Rashid.* Chicago.

'Abd al-Wahhab, Muhammad. No date. *Mudhakkirat Muhammad 'Abd al-Wahhab.* Edited by Muhammad Rif'at al-Muhami. Beirut.

Abdollazadeh, Fatma. 1994. "Qadin va Jamiyyat." *Azerbaycan* (October 15).

Abdul Jawwad, Islah. 1990. "The Evolution of the Political Role of the Palestinian Women's Movement in the Uprising." In *The Palestinians: New Directions.* Edited by Michael C. Hudson. Washington, DC.

Abu-Lughod, Lila. 1986. *Veiled Sentiments: Honor and Poetry in a Bedouin Society.* Berkeley.

Abu-Lughod, Lila. 1990. "The Romance of Resistance: Tracing the Transformations of Power through Bedouin Women." *American Ethnologist* 17:41–56.

Abu-Lughod, Lila. 1993. *Writing Women's Worlds: Bedouin Stories.* Berkeley.

Abu-Lughod, Lila, ed. 1998. *Remaking Women: Feminism and Modernity in the Middle East.* Princeton.

193

Abu al-Majd, Sabri. 1963. *Zakariyya Ahmad.* Cairo.

Abu Zayd, Nasr Hamid. 1993. "Cairo University and Academic Freedom." *Al-Ahram Weekly,* Apr. 8–14.

Acar, Feride. 1991. "Women in the Ideology of Islamic Revivalism in Turkey: Three Islamic Women's Journals." In *Islam in Modern Turkey.* Edited by Richard Tapper and Nancy Tapper. London.

Afkhami, Mahnaz, ed. 1995. *Faith and Freedom: Women's Human Rights in the Muslim World.* London.

Afshar, Haleh. 1996. "Women and the Politics of Fundamentalism in Iran." In *Women and Politics in the Third World.* Edited by Haleh Afshar. London.

Ahmad, Feroz. 1993. *The Making of Modern Turkey.* London.

Ahmad, Hisham. 1994. *Hamas: From Religious Salvation to Political Transformation—The Rise of Hamas in Palestinian Society.* Jerusalem.

Ahmed, Khalid. 1992. "The Sociology of Rape." *Slogan* (February): 36–37.

Ahmed, Leila. 1982. "Western Ethnocentrism and Perceptions of the Harem." *Feminist Studies* 8:521–24.

Ahmed, Leila. 1984. "Early Feminist Movements in Turkey and Egypt." In *Muslim Women.* Edited by Freda Hussain. London.

Ahmed, Leila. 1992. *Women and Gender in Islam: Historical Roots of a Modern Debate.* New Haven.

Alavi, Hamza. 1987. "Ethnicity, Muslim Society, and the Pakistan Ideology." In *Islamic Reassertion in Pakistan.* Edited by Anita M. Weiss. Syracuse.

Alloula, Malek. 1986. *The Colonial Harem.* Minneapolis.

Alstadt, Audrey. 1992. *The Azerbaijani Turks: Power and Identity under Russian Rule.* Stanford.

Alvarez, Sonia E. 1990. *Engendering Democracy in Brazil: Women's Movements in Transition Politics.* Princeton.

Anderson, Benedict. 1991. *Imagined Communities.* Rev. ed. London.

Appadurai, Arjun, and Carol A. Breckenridge. 1988. "Why Public Culture?" *Public Culture* 1:5–9.

Arat, Yesim. 1990. "Islamic Fundamentalism and Women in Turkey." *Muslim World* 80:17–23.

Arat, Yesim. 1994. "The Women's Movement of the 1980s in Turkey: Radical Outcome of Liberal Kemalism?" In *Reconstructing Gender in the Middle East: Tradition, Identity, and Power.* Edited by Fatma Müge Göçek and Shiva Balaghi. New York.

Arat, Zehra. 1994. "Turkish Women and the Republican Reconstruction of Tradition." In *Reconstructing Gender in the Middle East.* Edited by Fatma Müge Göçek and Shiva Balaghi. New York.

Arkoun, Mohammed. 1994. *Rethinking Islam: Common Questions, Uncommon Answers.* Boulder, Colo.

Asad, Talal. 1986. *The Idea of an Anthropology of Islam.* Occasional papers series, Center for Contemporary Arab Studies, Georgetown University. Washington, DC.

Asia Watch and the Women's Rights Project, Human Rights Watch. 1992. *Double Jeopardy: Police Abuse of Women in Pakistan.* Special Report. New York.

Atil, Esin. 1993. "Islamic Women as Rulers and Patrons." *Asian Art* 6:1–12.

Atkin, Muriel. 1989. *The Subtlest Battle: Islam in Soviet Tajikistan.* Philadelphia.

'Awad, Mahmud. 1971. *Umm Kulthum allati la ya'rifuha ahad.* Cairo.

Ayata, Sencer. 1996. "Patronage, Party, and State: The Politicization of Islam in Turkey." *Middle East Journal* 50:40–56.

Badawi, Jamal. 1995. *Gender Equity in Islam. Basic Principles.* Plainfield, IN.

Badran, Margot. 1988. "Dual Liberation: Feminism and Nationalism in Egypt from the 1870s to 1925." *Feminist Issues* 8:15–24. (also translated into Arabic)

Badran, Margot. 1989a. "Feminism as a Force in the Arab World." In *Contemporary Arab Thought and Women.* Second International Conference of the Arab Women's Solidarity Association, Cairo, November 3–5, 1988. (also translated into Arabic)

Badran, Margot. 1989b. "The Origins of Feminism in Egypt." In *Current Issues in Women's History.* Edited by Arina Angerman et al. London.

Badran, Margot. 1991. "Competing Agenda: Feminists, Islam, and the

State in Nineteenth- and Twentieth-Century Egypt." In *Women, Islam, and the State.* Edited by Deniz Kandiyoti. Philadelphia.

Badran, Margot. 1993. "Independent Women: More Than a Century of Feminism in Egypt." In *Arab Women: Old Boundaries, New Frontiers.* Edited by Judith Tucker. Bloomington, Ind.

Badran, Margot. 1994a. *Feminists, Islam, and Nation: Gender and the Making of Modern Egypt.* Princeton.

Badran, Margot. 1994b. "Gender Activism: Feminists and Islamists in Egypt." In *Identity Politics and Women: Cultural Reassertions and Feminisms in International Perspective.* Edited by Valentine M. Moghadam. Boulder, Colo.

Badran, Margot. 1995. "Women of the Pen." *Al-Ahram Weekly,* Nov. 16–22.

Badran, Margot. 1996. "Khartoum's Answer to Beijing." *Al-Ahram Weekly.* Sept. 5–11.

Badran, Margot. 1998. "Unifying Women: Feminist Pasts and Presents in Yemen." *Gender and History* (forthcoming).

Barazangi, Nimat Hafez. 1997. "Muslim Women's Islamic Higher Learning as a Human Right: The Action Plan." In *Muslim Women and the Politics of Participation.* Edited by Mahnaz Afkhami and Erika Friedl. Syracuse.

Barghouthi, Mustafa. 1994. *Palestinian NGOs and Their Role in Building a Civil Society.* Jerusalem.

Basu, Amrita, ed. 1995. *Women's Movements in Global Perspective.* Boulder, Colo.

Bauer, Janet L. 1997. "The Mixed Blessings of Women's Fundamentalism: Democratic Impulses in a Patriarchal World." In *Mixed Blessings: Gender and Religious Fundamentalism Cross Culturally.* Edited by Judy Brink and Joan Mencher. New York.

Beg, M. A. J. 1978. "al-Khāṣṣa wa-'l'āmma." *Encyclopaedia of Islam.* New ed. Edited by E. van Donzel, B. Lewis, and Ch. Pellat. Leiden.

Beinin, Joel, and Joe Stork. 1997. "On the Modernity, Historical Specificity, and International Context of Political Islam." In *Political Islam: Essays from Middle East Report.* Edited by Joel Beinin and Joe Stork. Berkeley.

Bennigsen, Alexandre. 1985. "Islam in the Soviet Union." *Journal of South Asian and Middle Eastern Studies* 8(1):115–33.

Bennigsen, Alexandre, and Enders Wimbush. 1979. *Muslim National Communism in the Soviet Union.* Chicago.

Berger, Sherna Gluck. 1995. "Palestinian Women: Gender, Politics and Nationalism." *Journal of Palestine Studies* 24:5–15.

Berkey, Jonathan. 1992. *The Transmission of Knowledge in Medieval Cairo: A Social History of Islamic Education.* Princeton.

Bernard, Jessie. 1981. *The Female World.* New York.

Berque, Jacques. 1972. *Egypt: Imperialism and Revolution.* Translated by Jean Stewart. London.

Birtek, Faruk, and Binnaz Toprak. 1993. "The Conflictual Agenda of Neo-Liberal Reconstruction and the Rise of Islamic Politics in Turkey: The Hazards of Rewriting Modernity." *Praxis International* 13:192–212.

Blum, Stephen. 1972. "Musics in Contact: The Cultivation of Oral Repertories in Meshed, Iran." Ph.D. dissertation, University of Illinois.

Blum, Stephen. 1975. "Towards a Social History of Musicological Technique." *Ethnomusicology* 19:207–31.

Bodman, Herbert L., and Nayereh Tohidi. 1998. *Women in Muslim Societies: Diversity within Unity.* Boulder, Colo.

Boudhiba, Abdelwahab. 1985. *Sexuality in Islam.* London.

Brownmiller, Susan. 1975. *Against Our Will: Men, Women and Rape.* New York.

Brownmiller, Susan. 1993. "Against Our Will." In *Violence against Women: The Bloody Footprints.* Edited by Pauline B. Bart and Eileen Geil Moran. Newbury Park, Calif.

Buckley, Mary. 1987. "Female Workers by Hand and Male Workers by Brain: The Occupational Composition of the 1985 Azerbaijan Supreme Soviet." *Soviet Union* 14(2):229–37.

Carapico, Sheila. 1996. "Gender and Status Inequalities in Yemen: Honour, Economics, and Politics." In *Patriarchy and Economic Development: Women's Positions at the End of the Twentieth Century.* Edited by Valentine Moghadam. Oxford.

Carrier, James G. 1992. "Occidentalism: The World Turned Upside Down." *American Ethnologist* 19:195–212.

Chaqueri, Cosroe. 1985. *Asnad-i Tarikhi-yi Junbesh-i Kargari/Susiyal Dimukrasi va Kumunisti-yi Iran.* Tehran.

Charlton, Sue Ellen M., Jana Everett, and Kathleen Staudt, eds. 1989. *Women, the State, and Development.* Albany.

Chhachhi, Amrita. 1991. "Forced Identities: The State, Communalism, Fundamentalism and Women in India." In *Women, Islam and the State.* Edited by Deniz Kandiyoti. Philadelphia.

Cobban, Helena. 1984. *The Palestinian Liberation Organization: People, Power, and Politics.* Cambridge.

Cole, Juan. 1994. "Gender, Tradition, and History." In *Reconstructing Gender in the Middle East: Tradition, Identity, and Power.* Edited by Fatma Müge Göcek and Shiva Balaghi. New York.

Colla, Elliot, and Ayman Bakr. 1997. "Silencing Is at the Heart of My Case." In *Political Islam: Essays from Middle East Report.* Edited by Joel Beinin and Joe Stork. Berkeley.

Combs-Shillings, Elaine. 1989. *Sacred Performances: Islam, Sexuality, and Sacrifice.* New York.

Commission on Security and Cooperation in Europe. 1996. *CSCE Digest* 19(1):5–14.

Curthoys, Ann. 1993. "Feminism, Citizenship and National Identity." *Feminist Review* 44:19–37.

Danielson, Virginia. 1988. "The Arab Middle East." In Peter Manuel, *Popular Musics of the Non-Western World: An Introductory Survey.* New York.

Danielson, Virginia. 1991. "Artists and Entrepreneurs: Female Singers in Cairo during the 1920s." In *Women in Middle Eastern History: Shifting Boundaries in Sex and Gender.* Edited by Nikkie Keddie and Beth Baron. New Haven.

Danielson, Virginia. 1997. *"The Voice of Egypt": Umm Kulthum, Arabic Song and Egyptian Society in the Twentieth Century.* Chicago.

Düzdağ, M. Ertugrul. 1983. *Şeyhülislam Ebussuud Efendi Fetvaları Işığında 16. Asır Türk Hayatı.* Istanbul.

Enloe, Cynthia. 1990. *Bananas, Beaches and Bases: Making Feminist Sense of International Politics*. Berkeley.

Enloe, Cynthia. 1993. *The Morning After: Sexual Politics at the End of the Cold War*. Berkeley.

Esack, Farid. 1997. *Qur'an, Liberation and Pluralism: An Islamic Perspective of Interreligious Solidarity against Oppression*. Oxford.

Esposito, John. 1982. *Women in Muslim Family Law*. Syracuse.

Esposito, John, ed. 1997. *Political Islam: Revolution, Radicalism, or Reform?* Boulder, Colo.

Farah, Madelain. 1984. *Marriage and Sexuality in Islam: A Translation of al-Ghāzāli's Book on the Etiquette of Marriage from the Iḥyā.'* Salt Lake City.

Fay, Mary Ann. 1996. "The Ties That Bound: Women and Households in Eighteenth-Century Egypt." In *Women, the Family, and Divorce Laws in Islamic History*. Edited by Amira El Azhary Sonbol. Syracuse.

Fay, Mary Ann. 1997. "Women and *Waqf*: Property, Power, and the Domain of Gender in Eighteenth-Century Egypt." In *Women in the Ottoman Empire: Middle Eastern Women in the Early Modern Era*. Edited by Madeline C. Zilfi. Leiden.

Foucault, Michel. 1979. *Discipline and Punish: The Birth of the Prison*. Translated by A. Sheridan. New York.

Fox-Genovese, Elizabeth. 1982. "Placing Women's History in History." *New Left Review* 133:5–29.

Friedl, Erika. 1991. "The Dynamics of Women's Sphere of Action in Rural Iran." In *Women in Middle Eastern History: Shifting Boundaries in Sex and Gender*. Edited by Nikki Keddie and Beth Baron. New Haven.

Frith, Simon. 1983. "Essay Review: Rock Biography." *Popular Music* 3:276–77.

Fu'ad, Ni'mat Ahmad. 1976. *Umm Kulthum wa-'Asr min al-Fann*. Cairo.

Ganjeli, Sabir. 1994. *Har Satirda Bir Tarikh*. Baku.

Geertz, Clifford. 1968. *Islam Observed*. New Haven.

Geertz, Hildred. 1979. "The Meaning of Family Ties." In *Meaning and*

Order in Moroccan Society. Edited by Clifford Geertz, Hildred Geertz, and Lawrence Rosen. Cambridge.

Gellner, Ernest. 1981. *Muslim Society.* Cambridge.

General Union of Palestinian Women. 1994. "Declaration of Principles on Palestinian Women's Rights." *Journal of Palestine Studies* 24:137–38.

Gerber, Haim. 1994. *State, Society, and Law in Islam: Ottoman Law in Comparative Perspective.* Albany.

Ghadbian, Najib. 1997. *Democratization and the Islamist Challenge in the Arab World.* Boulder, Colo.

Giaccaman, Rita. No date. "Palestinian Women and Development in the Occupied West Bank." Birzeit University. Unpublished paper.

Giaccaman, Rita. 1995. "International Aid, Women Interests, and the Depoliticization of Women." *Gender and Society, Working Paper* 3:53–59.

Giddens, Anthony. 1984. *The Constitution of Society: Outline of the Theory of Structuration.* Berkeley.

Giddens, Anthony. 1982. *Profiles and Critiques in Social Theory.* Berkeley.

Gilmore David, ed. 1987. *Honor and Shame and the Unity of the Mediterranean.* Washington, D.C.

Giovanni, Maureen. 1987. "Female Chastity Codes in the Circum-Mediterranean: Comparative Perspectives." In *Honor and Shame and the Unity of the Mediterranean.* Edited by David Gilmore. Washington, D.C.

Glock, Charles, and Rodney Stark. 1965. *Religion and Society in Tension.* Chicago.

Göcek, Fatma Müge, and Shiva Balaghi, eds. 1994. *Reconstructing Gender in the Middle East: Tradition, Identity, and Power.* New York.

Göle, Nilüfer. 1991. *Mödern Mahrem: Medeniyet ve Örtünme.* Istanbul.

Göle, Nilüfer. 1996. *The Forbidden Modern: Civilization and Veiling.* Ann Arbor.

El Guindi, Fadwa. 1981. "Veiling *Infitah* with Muslim Ethic: Egypt's Contemporary Islamic Movement." *Social Problems* 28:465–83.

Haddad, Yvonne Yazbeck. 1985. "Islam, Women, and Revolution." In *Women, Revolution and Social Change*. Edited by Yvonne Yazbeck Haddad and Ellison Banks Findly. Albany.

Haeri, Shahla. 1995. "Woman's Body, Woman's Honor." In *Faith and Freedom: Women's Human Rights in the Muslim World*. Edited by Mahnaz Afkhami. London.

Hafiz, Nahid Ahmad. 1977. "*Al-Ughniyya al-Misriyya wa-Tatawwuruha khilal al-Qarnayn al-Tasi' 'Ashar wa-'l-'Ashrin*." Ph.D. dissertation, Hilwan University.

Hale, Sondra. 1996. *Gender Politics in Sudan: Islamism, Socialism, and the State*. Boulder, Colo.

Hall, C. Margaret. 1992. *Women and Empowerment*. Washington, D.C.

Hallaq, Wael. 1986. "Was the Gate of *Ijtih*ād Closed?" *International Journal of Middle Eastern Studies* 18:427–54.

Hallaq, Wael. 1994. "From *Fatwās* to *Furū'*: Growth and Change in Islamic Substantive Law." *Islamic Law and Society* 1:17–56.

Hallaq, Wael. 1997. *A History of Islamic Legal Theories: An Introduction to Sunnī Uṣūl al-Fiqh*. Cambridge.

El-Hamamsy, Laila Shukry. 1975. "The Assertion of Egyptian Identity." In *Ethnic Identity: Cultural Continuities and Change*. Edited by George DeVos and Lola Ranucci-Ross. Palo Alto, Calif.

Hambly, Gavin R. G., ed. 1998. *Women in the Medieval Islamic World: Power, Patronage, and Piety*. New York.

Hammami, Rema. 1990. "Women, the Hijab and the Intifada." *Middle East Report* 164–65:24–28, 71.

Hammami, Rema. 1994. "L'Intifada a-t-elle emancipé les femmes?" *Revue d'Études Palestiniennes* 51:59–65.

Hammami, Rema. 1995. "NGOs: The Professionalisation of Politics." *Race and Class* 37:51–64.

Hanmer, Jalna, and Mary Maynard, eds. 1987. *Women, Violence, and Social Control*. Atlantic Highlands, NJ.

Harding, Sandra. 1991. *Whose Science? Whose Knowledge? Thinking from Women's Lives*. Ithaca, N.Y.

Hassan, Rifaat. 1987. "Equal before Allah? Woman-Man Equality in the Islamic Tradition." *Harvard Divinity Bulletin* 17(2):2–4.

Hegland, Mary Elaine. (1991). "Political Roles of Aliabad Women: The Public-Private Dichotomy Transcended." In *Women in Middle Eastern History: Shifting Boundaries in Sex and Gender.* Edited by Nikki R. Keddie and Beth Baron. New Haven.

Heiberg, Marianne, Geir Ovensor, Helge Brungorg, et al. 1993. *Palestinian Society in Gaza, West Bank and Arab Jerusalem: A Survey of Living Conditions.* (Arabic). Oslo.

Hélie-Lucas, Marie-Aimée. 1990. "Women, Nationalism and Religion in the Algerian Struggle." In *Opening the Gates: A Century of Arab Feminist Writing.* Edited by Margot Badran and Miriam Cooke. Bloomington, Ind.

Hélie-Lucas, Marie-Aimée. 1994. "The Preferential Symbol of Islamic Identity: Women in Muslim Personal Laws." In *Identity Politics and Women: Cultural Reassertions and Feminisms in International Perspective.* Edited by Valentine Moghadam. Boulder, Colo.

Helly, Dorothy O., and Susan Reverby. 1992. *Gendered Domains: Rethinking Public and Private in Women's History.* Ithaca.

Heng, Geraldine, and Janadas Devan. 1992. "State Fatherhood: The Politics of Nationalism, Sexuality and Race in Singapore." In *Nationalisms and Sexualities.* Edited by A. Parker, M. Russo, D. Sommer, and P. Yaeger. New York.

Hessini, Leila. 1994. "Wearing the Hijab in Contemporary Morocco: Choice and Identity." In *Reconstructing Gender in the Middle East: Tradition, Identity, and Power.* Edited by Fatma Müge Göcek and Shiva Balaghi. New York.

Heyd, Uriel. 1973. *Studies in Old Ottoman Criminal Law.* Oxford.

Al-Hibri, Azizah. 1982. "A Study of Islamic Herstory: Or How Did We Ever Get into This Mess?" In *Women and Islam.* Edited by Azizah al-Hibri. Oxford.

Al-Hibri, Azizah. 1997. "Islam, Law and Custom: Redefining Muslim Women's Rights." *American University Journal of International Law and Policy* 12:1–44.

Al-Hibri, Azizah. 1998. "A Survey of Womanist Islamic Thought." In *A Companion to Feminist Philosophy.* Blackwell Companions to

Philosophy series. Edited by Alison M. Jaggar and Iris Marion Young. Malden, Mass.

Al-Hifni, Mahmud Ahmad, Ibrahim Shafiq, and Ahmad Shafiq Abu 'Awf, eds. 1969. *Turathuna 'l-Musiqi*. Cairo.

Hiltermann, Joost. 1991. *Behind the Intifada: Labor and Women's Movements in the Occupied Territories*. Princeton, NJ.

Hobsbawn, Eric. 1990. *Nations and Nationalism since 1780*. Cambridge.

Hodgson, Marshall. 1974. *The Venture of Islam: Conscience and History in a World Civilization*. Chicago.

Holt, Maria. 1996. "Palestinian Women and the Intifada: An Exploration of Images and Realities." In *Women and Politics in the Third World*. Edited by Haleh Afshar. London.

Huntington, Samuel P. 1993. "Clash of Civilizations?" *Foreign Affairs* 72:22–49.

Huntington, Samuel P. 1996. *The Clash of Civilizations and the Remaking of World Order*. New York.

Hussain, Freda. 1984. *Muslim Women*. London.

Imber, Colin. 1993. "'Involuntary' Annulment of Marriage and Its Solutions in Ottoman Law." *Turcica* 25:59–69.

Imber, Colin. 1997. *Ebu's-Su'ud and the Islamic Legal Tradition*. Stanford.

Jabbarli, Aydin. 1979. *Ja'far Jabbarli: Lyrika, Hekayalar, Piyeslar*. Baku.

Jad, Islah. 1995. "The Palestinian Women's Movement: New Directions." Birzeit University.

Jahangir, Asma, and Hina Jilani. 1991. *The Hudood Ordinances: Divine Sanction?* Lahore.

Jayawardena, Kumari. 1988. *Feminism and Nationalism in the Third World*. London.

Johnston, Hank. 1993. "Religio-Nationalist Subcultures under the Communists: Comparisons from the Baltics, Transcaucasia and Ukraine." *Sociology of Religion* 54(3):237–55.

Jones, L. Jafran. 1987. "A Sociohistorical Perspective on Tunisian Women as Professional Musicians." In *Women and Music in Cross-Cultural Perspective*. Edited by Ellen Koskoff. Urbana, Ill.

Joseph, Suad. 1993. "Gender and Relationality among Arab Families in Lebanon." *Feminist Studies* 19(3):465–86.

Joseph, Suad. 1994. "Gender and Family in the Arab World." A special *MERIP* publication (October).

Kabbani, Rana. 1986. *Europe's Myths of Orient*. Bloomington, Ind.

Kamil, Mahmud. 1977. *Al-Masrah al-Ghina'i 'l-'arabi*. Cairo.

Kandiyoti, Deniz. 1991a. "End of Empire: Islam, Nationalism and Women in Turkey." In *Women, Islam and the State*. Edited by Deniz Kandiyoti. Philadelphia.

Kandiyoti, Deniz. 1991b. "Identity and Its Discontent: Women and the Nation in Millenium." *Journal of International Studies* 20(3):429–43.

Kandiyoti, Deniz. 1995. "Contemporary Feminist Scholarship and Middle East Studies." In *Gender and Society: Working Paper* (Women's Studies Center, Birzeit University, Palestine) 1:5–16.

Kandiyoti, Deniz, ed. 1991c. *Women, Islam and the State*. Philadelphia.

Kennedy, Charles H. 1987. "The Implementation of the Hudood Ordinances in Pakistan." *Islamic Studies* 26(4):307–19.

Keyder, Caglar. 1993. "The Dilemma of Cultural Identity on the Margin of Europe." *Middle East Review* 17:19–33.

Keyman, Fuat. 1995. "On the Relation between Global Modernity and Nationalism: The Crisis of Hegemony and the Rise of Islamic Identity in Turkey." *New Perspectives on Turkey* 13:93–120.

Khalidi, Rashid. 1997. *Palestinian Identity: The Construction of Modern National Consciousness*. New York.

Kian, Azadeh. 1977. "Women and Politics in Post-Islamist Iran: The Gender-Conscious Drive to Change." *British Journal of Middle Eastern Studies* 24(1):75–96.

Koskoff, Ellen. 1987. "The Song of a Woman's Voice: Gender and Music in a New York Hassidic Community." In *Women and Music in Cross-Cultural Perspective*. Edited by Ellen Koskoff. Urbana, Ill.

Krämer, Gudrun. 1997. "Islamist Notions of Democracy." in *Political Islam: Essays from Middle East Report*. Edited by Joel Beinin and Joe Stork. Berkeley.

Kuttab, Eileen. 1993. "Palestinian Women and the Intifada: Fighting on Two Fronts." *Arab Studies Journal* 15:69–85.

Kuttab, Eileen. 1994a. "Liberation des femmes, liberation nationale." *Revue d'Études Palestiniennes* 51:67–72.

Kuttab, Eileen. 1994b. "The Women's Document: A Tool for Women's Empowerment and Struggle." *News from Within* 9:8–10.

Kuttab, Eileen. 1995. "Fixed Paradigms, Changing Realities: Gender and Development in Palestine." In *Gender and Society: Working Paper* (Women's Studies Program, Birzeit University, Palestine) 3:47–52.

Landes, Joan B., ed. 1998. *Feminism, the Public, and the Private.* Oxford.

Lapidus, Gail, ed. 1982. *Women in Soviet Society: Equality, Development, and Social Change.* Berkeley.

Lazreg, Marnia. 1988. "Feminism and Difference: The Perils of Writing as a Woman on Women in Algeria." *Feminist Studies* 14:81–107.

Leacock, Eleanor. 1986. "Women, Power and Authority." In *Visibility and Power: Essays on Women in Society and Development.* Edited by Leela Dube, Eleanor Leacock, and Shirley Ardener. Delhi.

Lindholm, Charles. 1977. "The Segmentary Lineage System: Its Applicability to Pakistan's Political Structure." In *Pakistan's Western Borderlands: The Transformation of a Political Order.* Edited by Ainslie T. Embree. Durham, N.C.

Lipshitz, Oded. 1994. "La Paix des Femmes." *Revue d'Études Palestiniennes* 51:229–35.

Macleod, Arlene. 1990. *Accommodating Protest: Working Women, the New Veiling, and Change in Cairo.* New York.

Makhlouf, Carla. 1979. *Changing Veils: Women and Modernization in North Yemen.* Austin.

Mamedov, Sabir. 1986. *Put k Progrecu.* Baku.

Mandeville, Jon E. 1979. "Usurious Piety: The Cash Waqf Controversy in the Ottoman Empire." *International Journal of Middle Eastern Studies* 10:289–308.

Mann, Michael. 1984. "The Autonomous Power of the State." *Archives Européenes de Sociologie* 25:185–212.

March, Kathryn S., and Rachelle L. Taqqu. 1986. *Women's Informal*

Associations in Developing Countries: Catalysts for Change? Boulder, Colo.

Marcus, Julie. 1992a. "History, Anthropology and Gender: Turkish Women Past and Present." *Gender and History* 4:147–74.

Marcus, Julie. 1992b. *A World of Difference: Islam and Gender Hierarchy in Turkey.* London.

Mardin, Şerif. 1989. *Religion and Social Change in Modern Turkey: The Case of Bediüzzaman Said Nursi.* Albany.

Mardin, Şerif. 1991. "The Just and the Unjust." *Daedalus* 120(3):113–30.

Al-Marghinani, 'Ali b. Abi Bakr. 1791. *The Hedaya or Guide: A Commentary on the Mussulman Laws.* Translated by Charles Hamilton. Lahore.

Al-Marghinani, 'Ali b. Abi Bakr. 1840. *The Hedaya.* Translated by Charles Hamilton. London.

Marlow, Louise. 1997. *Hierarchy and Egalitarianism in Islamic Thought.* Cambridge.

Marsot, Afaf Lutfi al-Sayyid. 1996. "Women and Modernization: A Reevaluation." In *Women, the Family, and Divorce Laws in Islamic History.* Edited by Amira El Azhary Sonbol. Syracuse.

Massad, Joseph. 1995. "Conceiving the Masculine: Gender and Palestinian Nationalism." *Middle East Journal* 49(3):467–83.

Massell, Gregory. 1974. *The Surrogate Proletariat: Moslem Women and Revolutionary Strategies in Soviet Central Asia (1919–1929).* Princeton.

Massie, Meg. 1992. "Cherry Trees and Lotus Leaves." *Al-Ahram Weekly,* March 9.

Masud, Muhammad Khalid, Brinckley Messick, and David Powers, eds. 1996. *Islamic Legal Interpretation: Muftis and Their Fetvas.* Cambridge, Mass.

McClintock, Anne. 1993. "Family Feuds: Gender, Nationalism and the Family." *Feminist Review* 44:61–80.

McNay, Lois. 1992. *Foucault and Feminism.* Boston.

McPherson, Joseph Williams. 1941. *The Moulids of Egypt.* Cairo.

Menchu, Rigoberto. 1991. *I, Rigoberta Menchu: An Indian Woman in Guatemala.* Edited by Elisabeth Burgos-Debray. London.

Meninski, Francisci. 1780–1802. *Lexicon Arabico-Persico-Turcicum.* Vienna.

Mernissi, Fatima. 1975. *Beyond the Veil: Male-Female Dynamics in a Modern Muslim Society.* Cambridge, Mass.

Mernissi, Fatima. 1984. *Beyond the Veil.* London.

Mernissi, Fatima. 1987. *Le Harem politique.* Paris.

Mernissi, Fatima. 1991a. *The Veil and the Male Elite: A Feminist Interpretation of Women's Rights in Islam.* Reading, Mass.

Mernissi, Fatima. 1991b. *Women and Islam: An Historical and Theological Inquiry.* Oxford.

Mernissi, Fatima. 1993. *The Forgotten Queens of Islam.* Translated by Mary Jo Lakeland. Minneapolis.

Mernissi, Fatima. 1994. *Dreams of Trespass: Tales of a Harem Girlhood.* New York.

El-Messiri, Sawsan. 1978. *Ibn al-Balad: A Concept of Egyptian Identity.* Leiden.

Middle East Report. 1998. Special issue on Sexuality and Power in the Middle East 28. Washington, DC.

Mir-Hosseini, Ziba. 1996a. "Stretching the Limits: A Feminist Reading of the Shari'a in Post-Khomeini Iran." In *Feminism and Islam: Legal and Literary Perspectives.* Edited by Mai Yamani. New York.

Mir-Hosseini, Ziba. 1996b. "Women and Politics in Post-Khomeini Iran: Divorce, Veiling and Emerging Feminist Voices." In *Women and Politics in the Third World.* Edited by Haleh Afshar. London.

Moghadam, Valentine M. 1993. *Modernizing Women: Gender and Social Change in the Middle East.* Boulder, Colo.

Moghadam, Valentine M. 1996. "Development Strategies, State Policies, and the Status of Women: A Comparative Assessment of Iran, Turkey, and Tunisia." In *Patriarchy and Economic Development: Women's Positions at the End of the Twentieth Century.* Edited by Valentine Moghadam. Oxford.

Moghadam, Valentine M. 1998. *Women, Work, and Economic Reform in the Middle East and North Africa.* Boulder, Colo.

Moghadam, Valentine M., ed. 1994. *Identity Politics and Women: Cultural Reassertions and Feminisms in International Perspective.* Boulder, Colo.

Mosse, George. 1985. *Nationalism and Sexuality: Middle-Class Morality and Sexual Norms in Modern Europe*. Madison, Wis.

Mottahedeh, Roy. 1995. "Clash of Civilizations: An Islamicist's Critique." *Harvard Middle Eastern and Islamic Review* 2:1–26.

Mouffe, Chantal. 1992. "Feminism, Citizenship, and Radical Democratic Politics." In *Feminists Theorize the Political*. Edited by Judith Butler and Joan Scott. New York.

Muslih, Muhammad. 1988. *The Origins of Palestinian Nationalism*. New York.

Muslim Women's Georgetown Project. 1995. *Islam: A System of Reciprocal Partnership*. Position paper. Washington, D.C.

Muslim Women's League. No date. *The Spiritual Role of Women*. Position paper. n. pl.

Myrdal, Gunnar. 1968. *Asian Drama*. London.

Myrdal, Gunnar. 1970. *The Challenge of World Poverty*. London.

An-Na'im, Abdullahi. 1990. *Toward an Islamic Reformation: Civil Liberties, Human Rights, and International Law*. Syracuse.

Najmabadi, Afsaneh. 1998. "Feminism in an Islamic Republic: 'Years of Hardship, Years of Growth.'" In *Islam, Gender, and Social Change*. Edited by Yvonne Yazbeck Haddad and John L. Esposito. Oxford.

Nasibzadeh, Nasib. 1990. *Azerbayjan Demokratik Respublikasi. Maqalalar va Sanadlar*. Baku.

Nelson, Cynthia. 1974. "Public and Private Politics: Women in the Middle Eastern World." *American Ethnologist* 1:551–63.

Nelson, Cynthia. 1997. *Doria Shafiq, Egyptian Feminist: A Woman Apart*. Gainesville, Fla.

Norton, Anne. 1991. "Gender, Sexuality and the Iraq of Our Imagination." *Middle East Report* 173:26–28.

Olson, Emelie A. 1985. "Muslim Identity and Secularism in Contemporary Turkey: 'The Headscarf Dispute.'" *Anthropological Quarterly* 58:161–71.

Omid, Homa. 1994. *Islam and the Post-Revolutionary State in Iran*. London.

Omvedt, Gail. 1990. *Violence against Women: New Movements and New Theories in India*. New Delhi.

Ortner, Sherry B. 1996. *Making Gender: The Politics and Erotics of Culture.* Boston.

Palestinian National Council. 1988. "Declaration of Independence." Nineteenth Session. Algiers, Nov. 12–16.

Parker, Andrew, Mary Russo, Doris Sommer, and Patricia Yaeger, eds. 1992. *Nationalisms and Sexualities.* New York.

Peirce, Leslie. 1992. "Beyond Harem Walls: Ottoman Royal Women and the Exercise of Power." In *Gendered Domains: Rethinking Public and Private in Women's History.* Edited by Dorothy O. Helly and Susan Reverby. Ithaca, N.Y.

Peirce, Leslie. 1993. *The Imperial Harem.* Oxford.

Peirce, Leslie. 1998a. "Fatma's Dilemma: Sexual Crime and Legal Culture in an Early Modern Ottoman Court." *Annales: Histoire, Sciences Sociales* 53(2):291–319.

Peirce, Leslie. 1998b. "'She Is Trouble and I Will Divorce Her': Orality, Honor, and Representation in the Sixteenth-Century Ottoman Court of 'Aintab." In *Women in the Medieval Islamic World: Power, Patronage, Piety.* Edited by Gavin R.G. Hambly. New York.

Peristiany, John George, ed. 1966. *Honour and Shame: The Values of Mediterranean Society.* Chicago.

Peristiany, John George, and Julian Pitt-Rivers, eds. 1991. *Honour and Grace in Mediterranean Society.* Cambridge.

Peteet, Julie. 1991. *Gender in Crisis: Women and the Palestinian Resistance Movement.* New York.

Peteet, Julie. 1995. "'They Took Our Milk and Blood': Palestinian Women and War." *Cultural Survival* 19(1):50–53.

Peteet, Julie. 1997. "Icons and Militants: Mothering in the Danger Zone." *Signs: Journal of Women and Culture* 23(1):103–29.

Peterson, Spike. 1996. "The Politics of Identification in the Context of Globalization." *Women's Studies International Forum* 19:5–15.

Poliakov, Sergei. 1992. *Everyday Islam: Religion and Tradition in Rural Central Asia.* London.

Post, Jennifer C. 1994. "Erasing the Boundaries between Public and Private in Women's Performance Traditions." In *Cecilia Reclaimed: Feminist Perspectives on Gender and Music.* Edited by Susan C. Cook and Judy S. Tsou. Urbana, Ill.

Quandt, William B., Fuad Jabber, and Ann Mosley Lesch. 1973. *The Politics of Palestinian Nationalism.* Berkeley.

Quraishi, Asifa. 1997. "Her Honor: An Islamic Critique of the Rape Laws of Pakistan from a Woman-Sensitive Perspective." *Michigan Journal of International Law* 18:287–320.

Racy, Ali Jihad. 1981. "Music in Contemporary Cairo." *Asian Music* 12(1):4–26.

Racy, Ali Jihad. 1982. "Symphonic Music of the Arab Near East: The European Idiom and Local Identity." In *The Arab Cultural Scene, Literary Review Supplement.* Edited by Cecil Hourani. London.

Rai, Shirin. 1996. "Women and the State in the Third World." In *Women and Politics in the Third World.* Edited by Haleh Afshar. London.

Rauf, Heba. 1996. *Al-Mar'a wa-'l-'Amal al-Siyasi: Ru'ya Islamiyya.* Herndon, Va.

Raymond, André. 1968. "Quartiers et mouvement populaires au Caire au XVIIIème Siècle." In *Political and Social Change in Modern Egypt: Historical Studies from the Ottoman Conquest to the United Arab Republic.* Edited by P.M. Holt. London and New York.

Rizk Khouri, Dina. 1996. "Drawing Boundaries and Defining Spaces: Women and Space in Ottoman Iraq." In *Women, the Family, and Divorce Laws in Islamic History.* Edited by Amira El Azhary Sonbol. Syracuse.

Rizk Khouri, Dina. 1997. "Slippers at the Entrance or Behind Closed Doors: Domestic and Public Spaces for Mosuli Women." In *Women in the Ottoman Empire: Middle Eastern Women in the Early Modern Era.* Edited by Madeline C. Zilfi. Leiden.

Rohrlich-Leavitt, Ruby. 1975. *Women Cross-Culturally: Change and Challenge.* The Hague.

Rorlich, Azade-Ayse. 1986a. "The 'Ali Bayramov' Club, the Journal *Sharq Gadini* and the Socialization of Azeri Women: 1920–30." *Central Asian Survey* 5(3–4):221–39.

Rorlich, Azade-Ayse. 1986b. *Volga Tatars: Profile in National Resilience.* Stanford.

Rosa, Kumudhini. 1987. "Organising Women Workers in the Free Trade Zone, Sri Lanka." In *Third World, Second Sex.* Edited by M. Davis. London.

Rosaldo, Michelle. 1980. "The Use and Abuse of Anthropology: Reflections on Feminism and Cross-Cultural Understanding." *Signs* 5 (1980):389–417.

Rosen, Lawrence. 1989. *The Anthropology of Justice: Law as Culture in Islamic Society.* Cambridge.

Roy, Sara. 1994. "'The Seed of Chaos, and of Night': The Gaza Strip after the Agreement." *Journal of Palestine Studies* 23:85–92.

Roy, Sara. 1995a. "Beyond Hamas: Islamic Activism in the Gaza Strip." *Harvard Middle Eastern and Islamic Review* 2:1–39.

Roy, Sara. 1995b. *The Gaza Strip: The Political Economy of De-development.* Washington, DC.

Rudolf, Suzanne Hoeber, and James Piscatori, eds. 1997. *Transnational Religion: Fading States.* Boulder, Colo.

Rugh, Andrea. 1984. *Family in Contemporary Egypt.* Syracuse.

Rugh, Andrea. 1986. *Reveal and Conceal: Dress in Contemporary Egypt.* Cairo.

Sabbah, Fatna. 1984. *Woman in the Muslim Unconscious.* Translated by Mary Jo Lakeland. New York.

Saadawi, Nawal. 1980. *The Hidden Face of Eve: Women in the Arab World.* Translated and edited by Sherif Hetata. London.

Said, Edward. 1978. *Orientalism.* New York.

Sawa, Suzanne Meyers. 1987. "The Role of Women in Musical Life: The Medieval Arabo-Islamic Courts." *Canadian Woman Studies* 8:93–95.

Sayigh, Rosemary. 1994. *Too Many Enemies. The Palestinian Experience in Lebanon.* London.

Schick, Irvin Cemil. 1990. "Representing Middle Eastern Women: Feminism and Colonial Discourse, Review Essay." *Feminist Studies* 16:345–80.

Schiff, Ze'ev, and Ehud Ya'ari. 1989. *Intifada: The Palestinian Uprising—Israel's Third Front.* New York.

Schneider, Irene. 1995. "Imprisonment in Pre-Classical and Classical Islamic Law." *Islamic Law and Society* 2(2):157–73.

Schneider, Jane. 1971. "Of Vigilance and Virgins: Honor, Shame and Access to Resources in Mediterranean Societies." *Ethnology* 10:1–24.

Sciolino, Elaine. 1998. "Explain It Again, Please: Who Says I Can't Wear a Hat?" *New York Times,* February 8.

Scott, Joan Wallach. 1988. *Gender and the Politics of History.* New York.

Shaarawi, Huda. 1987. *Harem Years: The Memoirs of an Egyptian Feminist.* Translated by Margot Badran. New York.

Shah, Nafisa. 1993. "Of Female Bondage." *Newsline,* January.

Sharabi, Hisham. 1988. *Neopatriarchy: A Theory of Distorted Change in Arab Society.* New York.

Sharoni, Simon. 1993. "Gender and Middle East Politics." *Fletcher Forum of World Affairs* 17(2):59–73.

El-Shawan, Salwa. 1980. "*Al-Musika al-'Arabiyyah*: A Category of Urban Music in Cairo, Egypt, 1927–77." Ph.D. dissertation, Columbia University.

Shepard, William E. 1987. "Islam and Ideology: Towards a Typology." *International Journal of Middle East Studies* 19:307–35.

Showstack Sassoon, A., ed. 1987. *Women and the State: The Shifting Boundaries of Public and Private.* London.

Shusha, Muhammad al-Sayyid. 1976. *Umm Kulthum: Hayat Naghm.* Cairo.

Ṣiddīqī, Muḥammad Zubayr. 1993. *Ḥadīth Literature: Its Origin, Development and Special Features.* Cambridge.

Siegel, Evan. 1995. "A Woman's Letters to Molla Nasr od-Din (Tiflis)." In *Press und Offentlichkeit im Nahen Osten.* Edited by Christoph Herzog, Raoul Motika, and Anja Pistor-Hatam. Heidelberg.

Singerman, Diane. (1996). "Civil Society in the Shadow of the Egyptian State: The Role of Informal Networks in the Construction of Public." Paper presented at the Colloquium on the Civil Society Debate in the Middle East, Center for Near Eastern Studies, University of California, Los Angeles, 29 January.

Sirman, Nukhet. 1989. "Feminism in Turkey: A Short History." *New Perspectives on Turkey* 3(1):10–34.

Sirman, Nukhet. 1990. "Feminism and the Discovery of the Self in Turkish Politics." In *Turkish State, Turkish Society.* Edited by Andrew Finkel and Nukhet Sirman. London.

Sisson, Richard, and Leo Rose. 1990. *War and Secession: Pakistan, India, and the Creation of Bangladesh.* Berkeley.

Sisters in Islam. 1991. *Are Women and Men Equal before Allah?* Kuala Lumpur.

Smith, Dorothy. 1990. *The Conceptual Practices of Power: A Feminist Sociology of Knowledge.* Boston.

El-Solh, Camillia Fawzi, and Judy Mabros, eds. 1994. *Muslim Women's Choices: Religious Belief and Social Reality.* Providence.

Spellberg, Denise. 1994. *Politics, Gender, and the Islamic Past.* New York.

Stewart, Frank Henderson. 1994. *Honor.* Chicago.

Storrs, Ronald. 1937. *Orientations.* London.

Stowasser, Barbara F. 1993. "Women's Issues in Modernist Islamic Thought." In *Arab Women: Old Boundaries, New Frontiers.* Edited by Judith E. Tucker. Bloomington, Ind.

Stowasser, Barbara F. 1994. *Women in the Qur'an, Traditions, and Interpretation.* Oxford.

Stowasser, Barbara F. 1997. "The Ḥijāb: How a Curtain Became an Institution and a Cultural Symbol." In *Humanism, Culture and Language in the Near East: Essays in Honor of Georg Krotkoff.* Edited by Asma Afsaruddin and A.H. Mathias Zahniser. Winona Lake, Ind.

Stowasser, Barbara F. 1998. "Gender Issues and Contemporary Quran Interpretation." In *Islam, Gender, and Social Change.* Edited by Yvonne Yazbeck Haddad and John L. Esposito. Oxford.

Suleymanova, Elmira. 1995. "Report on the Beijing Preparatory Meeting in Asia." Position paper presented at the Azerbaijani women NGOs meeting, March 4. Baku.

Suny, Ronald. 1990. "Transcaucasia: Cultural Cohesion and Ethnic Revival in a Multinational Society." In *The Nationalities Factor in Soviet Politics and Society.* Edited by Lubomyr Hajda and Mark Beissinger. Boulder, Colo.

Swietochowski, Tadeusz. 1985. *Russian Azerbaijan, 1905–20: The Shaping of National Identity in a Muslim Community.* Cambridge.

Tapper, Nancy. 1979. "Mysteries of the Harem? An Anthropological

Perspective on Recent Studies of Women of the Muslim Middle East." *Women's Studies Quarterly International* 2:481–87.

Taraki, Lisa. 1989. "The Islamic Resistance Movement in the Palestinian Uprising." *Middle East Report* 156:30–32.

Tavakoli-Targhi, Mohamad. 1994. "Women of the West Imagined: The *Farangi* and the Emergence of the Woman Question in Iran." In *Identity Politics and Women: Cultural Reassertions and Feminisms in International Perspective.* Edited by Valentine Moghadam. Boulder, Colo.

Tekeli, Sirin. 1986. "The Emergence of the Feminist Movement in Turkey." In *The New Women's Movements: Feminism and Political Power in Europe and the USA.* Edited by Drude Dahlerup. London.

Tekeli, Sirin. 1990. "Women in the Changing Political Associations of the 1980s." In *Turkish State, Turkish Society.* Edited by Andrew Finkel and Nukhet Sirman. London.

Tekeli, Sirin. 1995. *Women in Modern Turkish Society.* London.

Tessler, Mark, and Jolene Jesse. 1996. "Gender and Support for Islamist Movements: Evidence from Egypt, Kuwait, and Palestine." *Muslim World* 86:200–15.

Tett, Gillian. 1994. "Guardians of Faith: Women in Soviet Tajikistan." In *Muslim Women's Choices.* Edited by Camillia el-Solh and Judy Mabro. Providence.

Thapar, Suruchi. 1993. "Women as Activists, Women as Symbols: A Study of the Indian National Movement." *Feminist Review* 44:81–96.

Tohidi, Nayereh. 1991. *Azerbaydjan Respublikaci Devlat Statistika Komitesi.* Baku.

Tohidi, Nayereh. 1994. *Situatsionniy Analiz Polozheniia Zhenshchin v Azerbaidzhane.* Baku.

Tohidi, Nayereh. 1996. "Soviet in Public, Azeri in Private." *Women's Studies International Forum* 19:111–23.

Tohidi, Nayereh. 1997. "The Intersection of Gender, Ethnicity and Islam in Soviet and Post-Soviet Azerbaijan." *Nationalities Papers* 25(1):147–67.

Tohidi, Nayereh. 1998. "'Guardians of the Nation': Women, Islam and Soviet Modernization in Azerbaijan." In *Women in Muslim Socie-*

ties: Diversity within Unity. Edited by Herbert Bodman and Nayereh Tohidi. Boulder, Colo.

Toprak, Binnaz. 1981. *Islam and Political Development in Turkey.* Leiden.

Toprak, Binnaz. 1993. "Women and Fundamentalism in Turkey." In *Identity Politics and Women: Cultural Reassertions and Feminisms in International Perspective.* Edited by Valentine Moghadam. Boulder, Colo.

Tucker, Judith. 1983. "Problems in the Historiography of Women in the Middle East: The Case of Nineteenth Century Egypt." In *International Journal of Middle East Studies* 15:321–36.

Tucker, Judith. 1985. *Women in Nineteenth-Century Egypt.* Cambridge.

Tucker, Judith. 1998. *In the House of the Law: Gender and Islamic Law in Ottoman Syria and Palestine.* Berkeley.

Usher, Graham. 1995. *Crisis in Palestine.* Washington, D.C.

Wadud-Muhsin, Amina. 1992. *Qur'an and Woman.* Kuala Lumpur.

Walther, Wiebke. 1993. *Women in Islam.* Princeton.

Wikan, Unni. 1984. "Shame and Honour: A Contestable Pair." *Man* 19:635–52.

Williams, Raymond. 1977. *Marxism and Literature.* Oxford.

Women's Studies Center, Birzeit University. 1995a. "The Future of the Palestinian Women's Movement: Continued Struggle, New Agendas." *News from Within* 11:3–10.

Women's Studies Center, Birzeit University. 1995b. "The Palestinian Women's Movement: What Future?" *News from Within* 11:18–21.

Yamani, Mai. 1996. "Some Observations on Women in Saudi Arabia." In *Feminism and Islam: Legal and Literary Perspectives.* Edited by Mai Yamani. New York.

Yule, Henry, and A. C. Burnell. 1886. *Hobson-Jobson Dictionary.* Repr. 1989. Calcutta.

Yusuf, Zohra. 1992. "A Rising Graph?" *Herald,* January.

Yuval-Davis, Nira, and Floya Anthias, eds. 1989. *Woman, Nation, State.* New York.

Zain al-Din, Nazira. 1928. *Al-Sufur wa-'l-Hijab.* Beirut.

Zain al-Din, Nazira. 1929. *Al-Fata wa-'l-Shuyukh.* Beirut.

Zubaida, Sami. 1997. "Religion, the State, and Democracy: Contrasting Conceptions of Society in Egypt." In *Political Islam: Essays from Middle East Report*. Edited by Joel Beinin and Joe Stork. Berkeley.

Zuhur, Sherifa. 1992. *Revealing Reveiling: Islamist Gender Ideology in Contemporary Egypt*. Albany.

Index

HARVARD MIDDLE EASTERN MONOGRAPHS

1. *Syria: Development and Monetary Policy,* by Edmund Y. Asfour. 1959.

2. *The History of Modern Iran: An Interpretation,* by Joseph M. Upton. 1960.

3. *Contributions to Arabic Linguistics,* Charles A. Ferguson, Editor. 1960.

4. *Pan-Arabism and Labor,* by Willard A. Beling. 1960.

5. *The Industrialization of Iraq,* by Kathleen M. Langley. 1961.

6. *Buarij: Portrait of a Lebanese Muslim Village,* by Anne H. Fuller. 1961.

7. *Ottoman Egypt in the Eighteenth Century,* Stanford J. Shaw, Editor and Translator. 1962.

8. *Child Rearing in the Lebanon,* by Edwin Terry Prothro. 1961.

9. *North Africa's French Legacy: 1954–1962,* by David C. Gordon. 1962.

10. *Communal Dialects in Baghdad,* by Haim Blanc. 1964.

11. *Ottoman Egypt in the Age of the French Revolution,* Translated with Introduction and Notes by Stanford J. Shaw. 1964.

12. *The Economy of Morocco: 1912–1962,* by Charles F. Stewart. 1964.

13. *The Economy of the Israeli Kibbutz,* by Eliyahu Kanovsky. 1966.

14. *The Syrian Social Nationalist Pary: An Ideological Analysis,* by Labib Zuwiyya Yamak. 1966.

15. *The Practical Visions of Ya'qub Sanu',* by Irene L. Gendizier. 1966.

16. *The Surest Path: The Political Treatise of a Nineteenth-Century Muslim Statesman,* by Leon Carl Brown. 1967.

17. *High-Level Manpower in Economic Development: The Turkish Case,* by Richard D. Robinson. 1967.

18. *Rebirth of a Nation: The Origins and Rise of Moroccan Nationalism, 1912–1944,* by John P. Halsted. 1967.

19. *Women of Algeria: An Essay on Change,* by David C. Gordon. 1968.

20. *The Youth of Haouch El Harimi, A Lebanese Village,* by Judith R. Williams. 1968.

21. *The Problem of Diglossia in Arabic: A Comparative Study of Classical and Iraqi Arabic,* by Salih J. Al-Toma. 1969.

22. *The Seljuk Vezirate: A Study of Civil Administration,* by Carla L. Klausner. 1973.

23. and 24. *City in the Desert,* by Oleg Grabar, Renata Holod, James Knustad, and William Trousdale. 1978.

25. *Women's Autobiographies in Contemporary Iran,* Afsaneh Najmabadi, Editor. 1990.

26. *The Science of Mystic Lights,* by John Walbridge. 1992.

27. *Political Aspects of Islamic Philosophy: Essays in Honor of Muhsin S. Mahdi,* by Charles E. Butterworth. 1992.

28. *The Muslims of Bosnia-Herzegovina: Their Historic Development from the Middle Ages to the Dissolution of Yugoslavia,* Mark Pinson, Editor. 1994.

29. *Book of Gifts and Rarities: Kitāb al-Hadāyā wa al-Tuḥaf.* Ghāda al Hijjāwī al-Qaddūmī, Translator and Annotator. 1997.

30. *The Armenians of Iran: The Paradoxical Role of a Minority in a Dominant Culture: Articles and Documents.* Cosroe Chaqueri, Editor. 1998.

31. *In the Shadow of the Sultan: Culture, Power, and Politics in Morocco,* edited by Rahma Bourqia and Susan Gilson Miller. 1999.

32. *Hermeneutics and Honor: Negotiating Female "Public" Space in Islamic/ate Societies,* edited by Asma Afsaruddin. 1999.